Beginning the World

Also by Karen Armstrong:
Through the Narrow Gate

Beginning the World

Karen Armstrong

St. Martin's Press
New York

ACKNOWLEDGEMENTS
I should like to thank my Head Mistress, who was my very
good patron while I was writing this book and also thank my
colleagues and pupils for their encouragement and support.

BEGINNING THE WORLD. Copyright © 1983 by Karen
Armstrong. All rights reserved. Printed in the United
States of America. No part of this book may be used or
reproduced in any manner whatsoever without written
permission except in the case of brief quotations embodied
in critical articles or reviews. For information, address
St. Martin's Press, 175 Fifth Avenue, New York, N.Y.
10010.

Library of Congress Cataloging in Publication Data

Armstrong, Karen.
  Beginning the world.

  1. Armstrong, Karen.   2. Ex-nuns—Biography.
I. Title.
BX4668.3.A75A32   1983   271'.9 [B]   83-9641
ISBN 0-312-07181-7

First published in 1983 in Great Britain by Macmillan
London Limited.

First U.S. Edition

10 9 8 7 6 5 4 3 2 1

For my Mother and Lindsey

My guardian, the picture of a good man, sat down by my place, keeping his hand on Richard's.

'My dear Rick,' said he, 'the clouds have cleared away, and it is bright now. We can see now. We were all bewildered, Rick, more or less. What matters! And how are you, my dear boy?'

'I am very weak, sir, but I hope I shall be stronger. I have to begin the world.'

'Aye, truly; well said!' cried my guardian.

'I will not begin it in the old way now,' said Richard with a sad smile. 'I have learned a lesson now, sir. It was a hard one; but you shall be assured, indeed, that I have learned it.'

BLEAK HOUSE
Charles Dickens

Beginning the World

CHAPTER ONE

In the World but not of it, 1969

I WAS LATE.

Nervously I pushed open the heavy glass door of my college dining hall and felt the immense noise strike me in the face. Four hundred students and thirty dons on High Table had already started dinner and were chatting in a roar of conversation that cruelly assaulted my cloistered ear drums. Feeling conspicuous, I pulled down my mini-skirt self-consciously, reminded myself of the Oxford custom of bowing slightly to the Principal in mute apology for being late for the formal meal, and then started walking across the room, trying to look nonchalant. Keep on walking casually, I told myself firmly. Head *up*, don't forget! Shoulders *back*. And try swinging your arms. Nearly opposite the Principal now – oh, yes – don't forget to apologize.

It was then that it happened. To my horror I found myself kneeling on the ground and felt winded with confusion as I realized what I had done.

I had kissed the floor.

Abruptly the cheerful hum of conversation and clatter of cutlery ceased and, scarlet-faced in the momentary silence, I looked up to face a host of curious, amused and uncomprehending eyes. Unconvincingly I blew my nose as I scrabbled to my feet, trying to look as though I'd knelt down to pick up my handkerchief. The babble of voices broke out again, explosions of laughter erupted in various parts of the hall and the meal was resumed.

It was then that I fully realized the enormous task before me. For seven years I was a nun, vowed to poverty, chastity and obedience in an austere teaching order which lived by the Rule laid down by St Ignatius Loyola, the founder of the Jesuits. I entered the order aged only seventeen on a warm September day in 1962 and began an intensive period of training which was to

I

transform me from a schoolgirl into a nun, a conditioning that was designed to last a lifetime.

But in 1967 the Order sent me to Oxford to gain a degree in English Language and Literature with a view to teaching in one of their schools. At Oxford I was taught once again to criticize and to think. The critical faculty which I had learned to quell came to life again while I was studying in college, but when I returned each evening to my convent, I found that I could not switch it off to become again the obedient, self-effacing nun. For a year I struggled with this new, emergent self, for I desperately wanted to stay in my Order. It still seemed to me the best life that anyone could have to be professionally intent on seeking and loving God. Finally, however, the two selves snapped apart. I suffered a breakdown and eventually had to admit that I could not continue. Sadly I wrote to the Sacred Congregation for Religious in Rome and two weeks ago the dispensation from my Vows had come through. I was no longer a nun.

Or was I? Breathless with embarrassment I searched the dining hall for an empty seat. What a fool everybody must think me. Just now my body had automatically knelt in its customary gesture of contrition and apology; it could not remember that I was no longer a nun. There had been many other moments like this, but none so spectacular. I still tried to lift the heavy skirt of my habit when I went up a flight of stairs. My hands constantly fumbled for the long ceremonial sleeves to hide in. I missed the voluminous protection of my habit like a newly amputated limb. But up till now I'd been able to hide this.

'Karen!' An ear-splitting yell pierced the column of conversation, and looking in its direction I saw Rose, waving energetically from the other side of the room and indicating an empty space between her and Brigid. Thankfully I started threading my way through the tables trying to avoid the curious stares that some of the students were giving me, but as I went many of them tugged at my cardigan calling out 'Quite a dramatic entrance, Karen!' Their cheerful laughter transformed my journey to Rose's table into a kind of royal progress and I felt stunned by their warmth. Far from disapproving, they seemed positively to have enjoyed my mistake!

Rose beamed up at me, her fresh, intelligent face alive with curiosity. 'What on earth were you doing?' she demanded. I looked round the table, tentatively testing their reactions. Rose was sitting next to Brigid, a dark, pretty Scottish girl, and next to her was Jane, a modern languages student, whom at first I'd found rather alarming. She had a mass of aggressively dyed red hair, a confident manner and an outrageous selection of clothes. Long dangly ear-rings weighed down her lobes and her purple, silky dress might well have been borrowed from her grand-mother's wardrobe. She was, I knew, a lapsed Catholic, and at first I'd found this rather shocking. As I'd got to know her better, during the last fortnight, I found her outspoken honesty attractive. After all, who was I to talk? It was she who spoke first.

'We all feel great reverence for our honoured Principal.' She waved a serving spoon towards High Table where, I noticed with a spurt of fresh embarrassment, several of the dons were gazing at me with raised, amused eyebrows and obviously discussing the event. 'But to kiss the ground as you entered her presence is surely a little excessive, isn't it?'

I giggled nervously, sank into my seat and tried to hide from the glare of unwanted publicity by shutting the eyes of my mind from the rest of the room and looking with self-conscious fascination at the dish of roast beef.

'No, but seriously,' Rose pursued, pushing the water jug across to me, 'what were you doing? You looked so funny! It wasn't a joke, was it? You weren't trying to be facetious?'

'Good heavens, no!' I looked up, startled at the very idea of such levity. 'No, Rose. It was a mistake.'

'What kind of mistake?' Jane asked curiously. 'You mean you just said "Whoops! Kissed the floor by accident! Silly me!" What do you mean?'

I hesitated slightly, knowing that I had to explain and yet curiously loath to.

'Well, in the convent we always kissed the floor when we were late for meals.'

'What!' I had caught the attention of the entire table now. Nine pairs of eyes regarded me in scandalized incredulity; I ducked away from them, taking refuge in a scrupulous examination of the roast potatoes before I selected one to put on my plate.

'Do you mean that sort of thing still goes on in convents?'

Brigid asked. 'I should have thought it went out with the Middle Ages. I can't imagine any of the nuns who taught me at school doing that kind of thing!'

'I can,' said Jane darkly, reaching over to pass the vegetable dish down the table to Rose.

'Yes, but your nuns did sound rather old-fashioned, Jane,' Brigid protested.

'They were sex-starved cretins, masochistic morons and sadistic perverts,' Jane replied calmly. 'Pass the meat, please.'

They all laughed. 'No, but *my* nuns were beginning to learn how to drive cars, and that kind of thing,' Brigid persisted. 'They were really up to date and rather sophisticated. Was your order old fashioned, like Jane's, Karen?'

'No, not at all. I think *all* nuns kiss the floor, it's a common monastic habit.'

Brigid and Rose stared back in horror. 'I just can't believe that that sort of thing still goes on,' Rose said. 'It seems so pointless and melodramatic. You're really disillusioning me. Nuns always seem so practical and sensible – '

'Rubbish!'

'All right, Jane! But they've always seemed sensible to me! I just can't imagine them going in for all that kind of nonsense.' Rose shook her head energetically.

I looked at them helplessly. If they found that tiny little detail of the religious life unacceptable what on earth would they say if I told them about corporal mortification, about flagellation, accusing myself publicly of my faults in the weekly Chapter, of kissing the feet of the whole community or saying five Pater Nosters with my arms in the form of a Cross when I was doing a Refectory Penance? All things that over the years I came to take for granted; they no longer raised even a flicker of surprise when I thought about them. What I accepted as normal most people in the world would consider at best distasteful. While for me the smallest details of their lives with their freedoms and quest for enjoyment were strange. I looked round the table at the circle of friendly but puzzled eyes and wondered whether I should ever be able to share their point of view.

'Well, all I can say is that you must be immensely relieved to have got out!' Rose selected an apple from the fruit bowl, polished it absent-mindedly on her sleeve and bit into it. I tried to copy her casual gesture but felt so odd that I gave up the project, quartered it neatly, snipped out the cores and resumed my nun-like posture, hands folded primly in my lap, feeling at once more comfortable. 'It sounds a dreadful existence to me,' she went on.

'Oh, it will all be changing soon.' I avoided the issue, sidestepping the grief that I felt about to pounce on me unawares. 'The Vatican Council has told religious orders to bring themselves up to date. It will all be different in future.'

'Karen, you haven't answered Rose properly.' Jane was watching me shrewdly. 'You are relieved to be out in the world, aren't you? No regrets?'

They were all watching me again, their faces smiling and expectant. Of course I could see it all from their point of view so clearly. The idea that I could possibly regret leaving a life that to them seemed barbaric and masochistic would be inconceivable. I was now 'free' to fall in love, to travel, to enjoy all manner of sensuous and spiritual delights that had hitherto seemed closed to me. Yet the convent was where every bit of me belonged. As I listened to the immense noise of the dining hall, I felt assaulted by a medley of sound: chairs were being scraped back, plates were clattering, girls were shouting to one another across the hall. I didn't belong here. I should be sitting in the convent refectory, listening to the toneless voice of the reader, where all was quietness, restraint and control. After supper the nuns would process down the long shadowy cloister reciting Psalm 129 and then kneel in the Chapel, lapped round by the stillness, waiting on God. How could I explain all that to Jane? To reveal my pain was an obscenity. It would be like tearing my clothes off and standing naked on the table, baring myself to their scrutiny. A nun could never share her sadness with any other living creature. 'We are to be strong women, Sister,' Mother Walter, my novice mistress, told me once, 'dependent on nobody, close only to God.'

'You don't regret it, do you, Karen?' Jane pressed.

I smiled blandly up at her. 'Oh, no. Of course not!'

Cheered, the others stood up and smiled. The meal was over, the subject closed.

*

There is a Gospel story which tells of a rich young man who wanted to follow Jesus. But when Christ told him that he had to give away all his possessions to the poor and follow Him in complete poverty and freedom from earthly things, the Gospel says the young man went away sad, 'for he had many possessions'.

I felt very much like that young man when I first left my Order. I too had offered myself to follow Christ in a special closeness, and when I'd seen what it would cost me I too went away sad. I was sad at that time; there was a lump of heaviness that I carried round with me always, a feeling that I'd had a chance to do something wonderful and had pusillanimously thrown it away. I'd often wondered how the young man felt about his riches afterwards. Would they seem trivial and unworthy now that he'd glimpsed something even more precious?

Quite understandably most people thought my troubles were over, now that I'd left the Order. But, as well as the sadness, I felt a sick panic, continually throbbing just below the surface. I was afraid that I wouldn't be able to cope with the demands of this strange new world, and that I viewed it now with such disenchantment that I'd never be able to adapt. If that happened I would be lost irrevocably, just as I'd always felt the rich young man was. Looking back on those first years after leaving the Order I realize how easily that could have happened. And what a lucky escape I had.

It didn't help that Jesus watched the young man go and said, 'How hard it is for those who have riches to enter the Kingdom of God; it is easier for a camel to enter the eye of a needle.' Of course at the time there was no danger of my being bogged down with earthly riches in the form of money. I had an ILEA student grant, which was hardly excessive. No, the riches I was afraid of were all the things the world held valuable. Indeed I'd left the Order to find some of them: love, friendship, the delights of the intellect and of the heart. And every day I encountered new 'riches' which might irretrievably separate me from God. I wanted them, yet at the same time I didn't want them at all. On the other side of the convent wall they seemed suddenly very paltry.

At first I couldn't find a solution to this dilemma. Gradually, day by day, I would learn to look at the riches of the world with a less jaundiced eye. Sometimes it would happen even against my will.

'Come in, Karen.' Mrs Jameson, my tutor, looked out of her room and summoned me in for my tutorial. With my essay carefully folded into my file, I followed her into the elegant sitting room.

'Sister's just going,' she said pointedly, smiling fixedly at Sister Mary Sylvia, who beamed softly back. Slowly Sister gathered her things together, smiled shyly at me and with religiously downcast eyes sidled noiselessly from the room.

'Oh my God!' groaned Mrs Jameson, flinging herself wearily into the brocade chair by the window. She clutched her forehead histrionically, smiled despairingly at me and raised an eyebrow in mock dismay. 'Hopeless! hopeless,' she muttered. 'Do you know Sister Mary Sylvia, Karen?'

I nodded. I certainly did. Sister had joined the College this academic year. She was short, plump, middle-aged and clad in a grey traditional habit. Although we were in the second year of our course, Sister had joined our class because she was doing the BA in only two years, having acquired a degree from a foreign university some years before. She naturally fell to my charge, everybody assuming that I understood the problems of nuns. And Sister Mary Sylvia had many problems. Like me she was completely out of her element, as well as being in a foreign country, and I was always being called in to pick up the pieces. At the request of our Anglo-Saxon tutor I had spent several afternoons that term trying to show Sister how to write an essay – advice which, with her usual beaming smile and knowing chuckle, she completely rejected. 'That is not the way to write a literary essay,' she said reprovingly, shaking her head. To continue in the face of such complacency was difficult but I persisted. After all, how would I fare in the world without support and advice? I must do as I would be done by. Then the College Librarian had cornered me one day last week and begged me to show Sister Mary Sylvia how to use the Library. The simple College system of filling in a lending slip and filing it appropriately seemed beyond her; nor could she remember where any of the sections were. 'I've tried and tried,' the Librarian was

7

almost wringing her hands in despair, 'but nothing seems to go in. I wonder, Karen, if *you* could help. You may know of some way . . .' She tailed off, looking at me hopelessly.

I agreed to try and spent hours with Sister, filling in slips, tramping with her the length and breadth of the library. To no avail. 'Thank you, Karen. That was most interesting,' she beamed, but a few days later she was as lost as ever. She seemed unable to remember that the Philology seminar took place every Thursday afternoon at three o'clock in the small lecture theatre. Every week the tutor would look around and sigh 'No Sister Mary Sylvia, I see. Karen, *could* you . . .?' and off I would go on a mission of recovery to find Sister in the most unlikely places. Once she was sitting alone, smiling happily, in the middle of the Dining Hall, surrounded by College servants who were busily waxing the floor and laying the tables for dinner.

'But, Sister, you couldn't possibly have thought we were having the class here!' I protested, hating myself for being impatient but driven to it by sheer exasperation.

Sister Mary Sylvia simply smiled back, and I felt alarmed. Something was badly wrong.

And now Mrs Jameson seemed at the end of her tether. She sighed and settled herself comfortably in her chair, looking rather like her own elegant Siamese cat. Tucking her legs neatly underneath her, she shook her head. 'No, I'm very worried. Very worried indeed.' She lit a cigarette and inhaled deeply.

'Mrs Jameson,' I asked, venturing a question which had increasingly puzzled me. 'How did she get in to the College? Did she pass the entrance exam?'

'No, no, no!' Mrs Jameson said emphatically. 'No, we have the British Council to thank for this. Apparently,' she went on caustically, 'she got a First Class degree abroad and wanted to come here to do the BLitt. Well, I read a couple of essays of hers that she sent over. Nothing outstanding, not up to Research standard. But she could do the BA. Fulminations from the British Council! How can you make this outstanding person do a mere BA? Compromise. We agreed that Sister could do the BA in two years and then, if she did well enough, do research. But,' and here Mrs Jameson lowered her voice dramatically, 'I don't think she could possibly have written those essays she sent over. Not possibly! Oh, she may have been all right once, when

8

she got her first degree. But that's some time ago.'

'She doesn't seem able to cope on the simplest level,' I said.

'Quite! Well, I've spent the last hour trying to persuade her to take an extra year over the BA. If she does there's an outside chance that she might pass and she can write "MA Oxon." after her name, which should satisfy her convent, I thought. But she said "No. That is not good enough. I am expected to get a First".'

'A First!' I shrieked. A First Class degree seemed to us all the pinnacle of academic achievement. Sister Mary Sylvia's essays were barely up to O-level standard.

'Quite.' Mrs Jameson stretched herself and leaned back wearily. 'I said "*Who* is expecting you to get a First?" No answer, of course.' She stopped and looked at me abruptly. 'Who do *you* think expects her to get a First?'

I didn't need to think for a moment. 'Her superiors,' I said promptly.

'Quite.' Mrs Jameson snatched off her spectacles and eyed me fixedly. 'Quite.'

'In the Religious life there's no such word as can't.' I quoted the oft-repeated maxim.

'Quite.' Mrs Jameson leapt up, strode over to the window and stood looking out at the students hurrying past to park their bicycles. 'And it seems to *me* that she's getting worse. She'll crack up, you know. Really badly. Because things can only get worse for her next year. As Finals approach. It's quite criminal!' she sighed impatiently. 'At Christmas I even wrote to her superiors explaining the situation. No use at all! A charming little letter came back saying that Sister Mary Sylvia would do what they expected and that prayer works many marvels.'

'Is there anything I can do?' I asked. 'I don't think there is, but I'm quite happy to keep on trying.'

Mrs Jameson shook her head. 'It's all any of us can do. No, it seems hopeless. Hopeless.'

She suddenly wheeled round to face me. 'On the other hand,' she said deliberately, 'you, Madam, can certainly get a First. If you work at it.'

I stared at her incredulously. For a moment a future in the world seemed a real possibility. Even an attractive one. 'Do you really think I can?' I asked.

She shrugged. 'Yes, of course. If you go on as you are doing.'

My mind was racing. If I managed to get a First then perhaps I could be an academic. Imagine being able to read and study all my life and get paid for it. It seemed too good to be true.

At the end of the tutorial we discussed my next essay, which was to be on *Twelfth Night*. 'But you must see the Stratford production first,' she said. 'I saw it last week. It's a most intelligent production.'

'I'm going next Tuesday.'

'Good!' she nodded briskly. 'Well, don't write your essay until you've seen it. It'll alter a lot of your ideas, I expect.'

'But my tutorial's on Wednesday morning first thing,' I suddenly realized. 'We won't be back here much before midnight on Tuesday.'

Mrs Jameson raised her eyebrows and smiled. Teasing but not entirely teasing. 'I re-read a Dickens novel in bed every night.' She looked at me inscrutably.

Suddenly I felt back on familiar territory.

'Can you get it done?' she asked with apparent casualness. 'You'll have the early hours of the morning to write it.'

I smiled slowly and nodded. 'Yes, I think so,' I said, feeling once again the security of a goal and exhilaration in the quest for a different perfection.

Oxford, of course, was another cloister. It walled me away from a frightening world which I knew existed outside but which I wanted no part in. Oxford was easy. At first. I loved my work and in the small, enclosed world of the College I gradually found my feet. Within weeks I was asked to stand for the Junior Common Room committee and to my astonishment was elected Secretary. It seemed I could cope. But all the time I was aware that burying myself in my books was shelving the problem of the real world. Until I could come to terms with life outside the University libraries and the quest for intellectual excellence which ignored the emotions and passions, I would still be living as a nun. Alone in the midst of a crowded world. But involvement frightened me. And the pleasures of the world were not pleasurable to me in the least.

Yet I didn't want to remain alone; involvement with the world could only be a matter of time.

*

The first time I went to a party after leaving the Order I felt this conflict strongly.

'What sort of things happen at parties?' I asked Rose nervously.

'Oh!' she laughed. 'Nothing much. Dance, drink. You know. . .' She broke off when she saw my face. 'Or, rather, I suppose you don't! It's nothing to worry about, Karen. Really.'

I smiled back, trying to mask my dismay. As, so far, I neither danced nor drank I could not imagine what I should do all evening. I was dreading the whole affair. Would people feel sorry for me because I couldn't dance? Or because I had no one to dance with? Or – horror of horrors – would some well-meaning soul feel it his kindly duty to ask me to dance?

The noise of the party knocked me sideways. Pounding, crashing cacophony rent the air, smashing through my trembling eardrums to throb violently in my head. I felt winded and violated by the din.

'Come on, Karen!' Jane noticed my instinctive physical recoil and grabbed my arm. The amplified sound of voices screaming against a jangle of guitars and clashing cymbals seemed to have become a new element to struggle through, the more so as the room was plunged in darkness with flickering coloured lights making it seem like an underground cavern. I allowed Jane to pull me into a corner and, following her example, sat gingerly on the floor. In the lurid light, I could see that we were sitting with a small group of people whose faces, I realized now, rather belatedly, were vaguely familiar. Quickly I responded to their smiles and waves of welcome. Why on earth did they use lights that made our faces look like two-day-old corpses? Jane's face looked stone grey against the burgundy blueness of her hair, her brightly painted lips looked black. She was clinging to the arm of the young man who had brought her to the party. Mark looked almost too handsome before we came into the room. His dark, curly hair was precisely the right length, his skin exactly the right shade of tan, his clothes managing to be elegant without being foppish. In this light he looked like the dying Chatterton and his smile was ghoulish.

Quickly I turned away and studied the dancers. Mesmerized I watched them leaping, twisting, gyrating together in pairs. Or even, I noticed with astonishment, singly. They shot into the air, hands waving, legs flailing out at odd angles, twirled on the spot, jiggled their elbows as though they were running a race. Their bottoms heaved and wiggled in time to the music.

There was something oddly familiar about the dancing all the same. I mustn't be shocked, I kept telling myself. Yet I felt threatened. The lack of restraint, the abandoned sensuality of those twisting bodies and glazed expressions hit me in the solar plexus. I still felt it immodest when I ran upstairs or rushed to catch a bus. This frank writhing flouted every religious standard I'd held during the last seven years. And yet I was no longer a nun; this is my world now, I thought aghast. All the same, I found myself thinking, mustn't it be marvellous to be able to dance like that? For a brief second I glimpsed the release that such physical freedom must give.

'Karen!' Jane was shrieking in my ear to try and make herself heard above the music.

'What?' I bellowed back.

'You – look – bewildered!'

Suddenly I remembered what the dancing reminded me of. 'It's like one of those tribal mating dances you see in films about darkest Africa.'

Mark roared with laughter. 'You're absolutely right! Isn't she, Jane?'

'You know,' I went on, 'each partner displaying his body to the other for approval.'

'Of course!' Mark said. He took Jane's hand and squeezed it. 'In a way it is. It's just the preliminary!'

The group of people round us laughed. I was just about to ask 'Preliminary to what?' when I suddenly realized what he meant and breathed a sigh of relief that I hadn't made a complete fool of myself. Of course. The dancing was a preliminary to sex! I looked back at the panting, sweaty couples, pulsating to the music, and took a deep breath. All these people and none of them married. In my Catholic circles pre-marital sex had been the unspeakable bogey of my adolescence. Here it was publicly flaunted and accepted. I felt profoundly shaken and, glancing furtively around the room, I suddenly saw these new acquaintances in another light. Sex, which had hitherto been as remote from my life as Antarctica, surrounded me on all sides claustrophobically.

'Come and dance?' Mark leaned over towards me and grinned, extending his hand in invitation. I shrank back and tried to pass it off with a shaky laugh.

'No!' I smiled at him pleadingly. 'I can't, Mark. Thanks so much, but I don't know how. You go and dance with Jane.' The music changed now to a slower tune and the couples ceased their writhing and fell exhausted on one another's necks, their limbs entwined.

'Of course you can,' Mark protested. He patted my knee. I felt my skin crawl and prickle under my dress. 'You just go with the music. Do your own thing. Look, there's nothing to it!'

I watched a man run his fingers up and down a girl's bare back and saw her burrowing her face deeper into the folds of his neck. I felt sick.

'No, really. I'd rather not. Thanks.'

'Leave her alone.' Jane, who had been watching me carefully, smiled at me reassuringly. 'Go and get us a drink, Markie. Red or white wine, Karen?'

Wine! I had scarcely ever tasted alcohol before. But drinking was definitely easier than dancing, and all that it implied.

'Red, please.' I tried to look nonchalant, as though I ordered glasses of wine every day. The rest of the room seemed welded together by the music. The dancers gyrated and even the people sitting screaming at one another on the floor near me seemed attached to it. A hand here, a foot there beat time, paying unconscious homage to the music. Occasionally someone would break off and mouth the words of the song to himself or smile at someone else as though the music were a mutual talisman. Only I seemed outside the current, out of tune with the spirit of the room.

'What are the words?' I asked Jane. I'd been trying to make them out for some time.

'Words?' A lean, red-haired man sitting next to Jane looked at me in surprise.

'The words of the song,' I explained. 'They don't make sense. It sounds like "Lucy . . . in the sky . . ."'

'Lucy in the Sky with Diamonds.'

'With *diamonds*?'

'You must have heard it before.' Jane looked incredulous.

'No. Should I have?'

'Well,' Jane and the young man looked at one another at a loss for words. 'Well . . . it's the Beatles.'

'The *what*?' Beetles, diamonds, yet another worldly enigma. 'What are the Beetles?'

I now had the astounded attention of the whole group. Jane collapsed against the young man's shoulder and he put his arm round her and pulled her up close. My head reeled. I thought that Jane belonged to Mark but now she seemed quite happy in the arms of another man as soon as Mark's back was turned.

'How gorgeous! Oh, Karen, you are marvellous.' Jane was rocking with laughter. 'How extraordinary! Markie!' I looked up nervously as Mark approached with a large bottle of wine and three glasses. Was there going to be a jealous scene? Mark simply looked enquiringly at us all and didn't seem at all abashed to see the red-haired man's arm round Jane. 'Mark! Karen's never heard of the Beatles!'

I took a sip of the sour wine which burned the back of my throat and tried not to splutter. But as it reached my stomach I felt a warm and friendly glow. I took another sip.

Jane, the young man, whose name seemed to be Robin, and Mark were all explaining antiphonally that the Beatles, whoever they might be, were probably one of the major single factors in the social revolution that had happened, apparently, during the Sixties, that they were spokesmen of our era. I finished my first glass of wine, insulating myself from the noise, the sex and the mysteries of my new world. With resigned and alcoholic detachment I watched Jane kiss Mark on the lips while he patted her on the behind, saw Robin pull Jane on to the dance floor and watched Mark watching them clinging passionately together in time to the music without a flicker of jealousy or annoyance. 'Listen!' Mark commanded, filling up my glass again. I leaned forward trying to pick up the magic of music that had no resonance with anything in my past or with anything in me, but, for Mark's sake, I tried to look reverent and comprehending.

'You are amazing!' Mark was laughing gently into my face, his features creased in affectionate amusement. I gave up the effort to enjoy the Beatles – why on earth had they called themselves after some rather unpleasant insects? – and smiled back at him.

Then he leant forward, gently traced a finger down my nose and kissed me lightly on the lips.

For a moment the world stood still. Frozen in horror, I watched Mark smile, pat my cheek and turn back to the music, fortunately quite oblivious of the havoc he had caused in me. The roughness of his male skin, the hint of bristles, the distinct scent of after shave all revolted me. I had brushed with the alien masculine world and retreated instantly back into my interior cloister. Yet even as I recoiled I felt the loneliness of my state in that friendly room.

Not long after the party I succumbed to a flu bug that had been pouncing sporadically throughout the college. Headache, sore throat, high temperature, aching limbs, the lot. For a day I struggled on, refusing to admit that it was no good, then found that I was staring at a page of Middle English without reading a word, and crawled into bed.

I woke in the early evening to a tap on my door.

'Come in,' I called.

Charlotte, a girl reading English in my year, poked her head round the door.

'Karen? Oh Lord, you *are* ill! I wondered if you were.'

'How did you come to wonder?' I struggled into a sitting position and smiled at her blearily. Charlotte stood, a rather comical figure, in the doorway. She had a long mass of brown, untidy hair on top of which was a blue felt hat with a chiffon yellow rose tucked jauntily into the band. Her face with wide, Celtic cheekbones and strange greyish eyes looked worried and she hovered on the threshold, obviously unsure whether I really wanted her to come in.

'It *is* nice to see you, Charlotte,' I said quickly, realizing how nice it was. Charlotte and I had smiled at one another across crowded seminar rooms but never really got to know one another and now I was pleased to have the chance.

'Are you sure?' Charlotte looked doubtful, tiptoed gently across the cork tiles and sat down gingerly on the orange bedspread. 'It's awful being ill in this place. You feel like a sitting duck for all sorts of unwelcome visitors.'

'How did you know I was ill?' I asked curiously.

'Well, you weren't at the Ballads lecture this afternoon. And then someone here said they hadn't seen you in lunch and someone else said they'd seen you looking pretty groggy this morning, so . . .'

I stared back at her astonished and touched. The thought that all those people had noted my absence and speculated about it made me, in my flu-bound state, feel ridiculously moved. I smiled weakly back at Charlotte.

'Anyway,' Charlotte dived into a capacious raffia bag, 'I brought a few goodies along, just in case. Look! Half a dozen eggs – I'll scramble them for you. You must eat something and that'll be soothing. Some bread, butter, fruit – have you got a dish for these grapes, Karen? – and some orange juice. Always drink a lot when you've got a temperature!' she finished with mock severity.

I stared back at her, astounded, trying to jabber some inadequate thanks. Charlotte waved them away and proceeded to transform the little study bedroom. A bunch of anemones was put into the pretty vase the students had given me, a glass bowl of fruit and a jug of orange juice brightened the white low coffee table by the bed. The bedside light was rearranged so that the room had a cosy, muted glow and the brilliant orange of the curtains and bedspread no longer dazzled but seemed rich and dull areas of warmth and lustre. I leaned back on the newly puffed pillows and stared round bemused. All this luxury. Dimly one part of my mind felt a little guilty. There was nothing really the matter with me, it was only 24 hour flu – in fact I was feeling better already. Yet I could not help revelling in the transformed room. It was all such a treat. I'd lost any idea of objects being pleasurable in themselves. I looked at the anemones – purple, crimson and scarlet against the starkly whitewashed wall; the dark glass curves of the vase complemented the graceful way they drooped or disported themselves and the dim light threw their shadows on the white ceiling. Such a simple idea and it could give such pleasure. I looked down at the fruit in the bowl beside me; suddenly I could see why Cézanne had wanted to paint fruit: the gleaming greens and reds of the polished apples, the purple luxuriance of the grapes; they looked – I smiled at the appropriateness of the cliché – nice enough to eat. And yet it would be such a shame to alter their pattern by removing a piece. Until now pieces of fruit were simply objects that, when I'd worked in the kitchen, I counted out mechanically into plastic bowls. As I surveyed my room with new eyes at the possibilities it revealed, I could see that perhaps a simple print might be nice over the desk, a plant on the big window seat and a cushion.

Charlotte hurried back into the room with a dish of scrambled eggs which she'd cooked in the communal kitchen.

'You've made the room gorgeous, Charlotte. Thank you!'

Charlotte looked around. 'It's okay. I don't like these modern rooms much, myself. Next year, why don't you look round at some of the rooms in the old, Victorian houses on the site? They're much larger and have so much more character.'

She poured me out a cup of tea, and then, to my amazement, dropped a piece of lemon on top.

'Tea's probably better for you at the moment than coffee,' she explained, while I nibbled on a piece of dry, wafer-thin toast.

'Charlotte! What *is* it?' I breathed as I tasted the delicate, smoky liquid, subtly flavoured with lemon.

'Earl Grey.'

'Is it *tea*?' Convent tea had been strongly brewed in huge metal pots, the milk already added. When there was some left over after a meal, we reheated it for the next meal, in the name of holy poverty, so as not to waste it. The reheated tea came out of the spout bright purple. This – I took another sip – was a completely different experience.

Charlotte looked surprised – an expression I was beginning to recognize whenever I revealed some worldly ignorance. 'Yes, haven't you ever had it before?' I shook my head. 'Good Lord! Well, you must get yourself some. It must be marvellous discovering all this for the first time!'

'Charlotte, how much do I owe you for all this?' I picked up my purse. Charlotte waved it away, firmly, her face crimson with distress.

'No, Karen. No, *please* don't! Tell you what – when you're up and about again, let's go to the flicks or something and you can treat me. By the way, what are you reading while you're in bed?'

I nodded towards the late Henry James novel on my bedside table.

'Oh my God!' Charlotte hooted with laughter. 'No, for goodness' sake give yourself a rest! Not James while you've got a temperature! Here.' She dived into her raffia bag again, and pulled out a pile of women's magazines. 'Read something mindless for once.'

'Thanks, Charlotte. Thanks very much.' I eyed them doubtfully.

'They won't bite you!' Charlotte laughed at my expression. 'No, read them! I insist. If you have to justify it to yourself tell yourself it's research. Really, you'll learn an awful lot about what's involved in being a woman of the world from these. It won't be a waste of time. Cheer up!' Impulsively she squeezed my hand and instantly I froze as I always did when someone touched me.

'I'm fine, Charlotte,' I heard myself saying briskly – too briskly. I smiled blandly and brightly to ward off any further expression of concern. 'I'm sure you're right. And for a start,' I removed my hand deftly from hers and patted the pile of magazines, 'I'll thoroughly enjoy reading these.'

Sadly I watched her take me at my word. 'Great!' she said glancing at her watch. 'Heavens! Is that the time? I must rush off if I'm going to get any dinner myself! Look, take care. Have a good sleep and I'll pop in and see you after breakfast tomorrow.'

'Thanks so much,' I beamed back at her. 'You really have made all the difference, you know. I feel much better already.'

She left and I heard her feet clattering down the stairs and further and further away across the quad until they faded away altogether.

Poor Charlotte! How could she possibly have known that I would take her so literally when she urged those magazines on me as 'research'? As soon as she had gone, I hauled the pile onto my lap and started grimly to read my way through the lot. Red-nosed and shiny-faced with fever, sniffling into a tissue, I gazed in bleary horror at the picture of womanhood in the late '60s that the magazines depicted, earnestly studying it as my new blueprint for the future.

Today, I noted solemnly, a woman had to dress in the latest fashion, her face was a work of art composed of blushers, mascaras, eyeliners, highlighters and lipsticks. I'd hardly heard of any of those things. How on earth did anyone have the time? Especially with all the other things a woman was supposed to do. She was expected, I gathered incredulously, to hold down a stimulating job, rush home and change into some trendy leisure gear, cook the most superb dinner for her man of the moment. As I stared, glassy-eyed, at the elaborate photographs of Crown Roast and Charlotte Russe, my heart sank. However was I going to cope? It was a very far cry from the cooking I'd done so far. I thought back to the meals I'd cooked in the convent; the waterlogged vegetables, the custard made with powdered milk, the rehashed lunches which I'd reproduced for supper coated liberally with cheese sauce – we'd called that 'Resurrection'.

Sighing despairingly I turned back to the magazine and blenched. Gone were the days, obviously, when a young bride went virginal and ignorant to her husband's bed; nowadays, provided she was 'taking precautions', she was virtually cheered into a bed of sin.

On and on I read, with the same intensity as I studied Shakespeare or Theology. Charlotte had given me the magazines to cheer me up; they were supposed to be fun. My problem was that I didn't know how to have fun and the message I was getting from the magazines was making my hair stand on end. If I could have foreseen the immense pleasure I'd get in the future from cooking, for example, I'd have been astonished. If I could have known that one day I'd find clothes and make-up fun I'd have been horrified. To me, sitting up in bed that evening wearing my thick nun's calico nightdress, they seemed the basest triviality. I who had an immortal soul to save, who had once thought herself called by God to the highest vocation on earth, to concern myself with such ephemeral trumpery!

It wasn't that we never had any fun in the convent. We had lots of it – long eight-mile walks on feast days, picnics in the summer; once, when the children had gone home for the holidays we even played netball – good, clean fun. The trouble with the fun presented in those magazines was that it was neither good nor clean. To me it was trivial, self-centred, sensual and – in the case of sex – positively disgusting. The knowledge that one day I'd come to enjoy this 'trivia' would have been inconceivable. Me find pleasure in my body! It is just as well that prescience is denied most human beings. The shock that night would have been too great. Oh, Karen, what a falling off was there.

I fared little better when I turned to the quiz: 'What kind of woman are you?' Again my whole approach was wrong. Instead of reading the answers tongue in cheek, I seriously expected that quiz to tell me exactly what kind of a woman I was. Heaven knows, I needed to know!

The first question read: *'You have had a quarrel with your boyfriend. . .'* Well, I was out of that for a start. Not only did I not have a boyfriend, I could not even remember the last time I had a quarrel with somebody. Nuns never answered back; they always backed down as a matter of course. I turned to the next question: *'Your boss has unjustly told you off for something you haven't done and you are determined to tell him what you think.'* Was I? Our superiors were always reprimanding us for things we hadn't done; it was a part of our training in the Third Degree of Humility. In the early days it was hard not to blurt out 'But, Mother, I didn't . . .' Yet after a while it didn't seem to matter much any more. *'You have just bought an outrageous outfit. . .'* I thought of the safe little collection of clothes hanging up in my wardrobe. I still felt hopelessly ill at ease in them all. My body was like a sack of potatoes, furtive and graceless in its new, shocking exposure. My hair hung in two curtains over my eyes, to replace the veil, I suppose. The nearest thing I had to anything 'outrageous' was a scarlet pinafore dress I'd bought from the Scotch Wool Shop. Scarcely *haute couture,* and beside the extraordinary garments in this magazine it looked the epitome of convention.

I put the quiz away without being any the wiser about my particular brand of womanhood. I was completely off the chart.

What I was doing, of course, was seeking a role model. I'd had one for years in Jesus Christ, and also in the Saints, whose lives I'd read voraciously, and in my Superiors. 'Doing my own thing' – a phrase I'd come across for the first time when Mark used it – was a completely alien notion. There was no way I could have found myself a model of behaviour as I flipped disconsolately through the magazines. I thought back to my conversation with Mrs Jameson. I was an academic woman – that was the answer. None of this applied to me. I let the magazines slither off the bed and with relief heard them plop softly onto the floor.

Instead of cultivating my body, I'd concentrate on my brain. Instead of a trivial hedonism, I had a lifetime of lofty cerebral activity ahead of me. Good, clean intellect. None of the dons bothered with that kind of nonsense – I glanced at the glossy pile beside the bed with a new contempt. Neither would I. Exhausted, I fell asleep.

Yet I didn't realize that the seeds had already been sown. They would one day burgeon and bring forth – not a model girl, Heaven knows! – but a woman who later learned that triviality could often be life-enhancing, cookery creative and sex not disgusting but an expression of appreciation and tenderness. That the seeds of sensual enjoyment had been sown must have been obvious in the quick, greedy glance I threw at the room refurbished by Charlotte before I put out the light; the anemones, the fruit, the subtle lighting. The buds of some of the flowers had already unfurled and, jewel-like, they flaunted themselves extravagantly.

CHAPTER TWO

Home

I PUT OFF going to see my family; the whole idea was too frightening. And now, with deadly irony, I'd come home in time for this. . . .

We stood, a windswept and bedraggled clump of people, around the open grave. The sky was grey and overcast and a light spring rain was blowing long, thin needles into our faces. It was a huge cemetery on the outskirts of Birmingham. Graves stretched away from us on all sides in neat, tidy rows; crosses, angels, slabs almost as far as the eye could see. We were in the Catholic section; a walled-in orthodoxy segregated us from the heretical and the godless corpses that surrounded us. At a discreet distance the hearse and the funeral cars were parked on the tarmac road that bisected the cemetery. Cars belonging to the family were ranked behind it, their reds, blues and silvers incongruous in this place of the dead.

Beside me my sister Lindsey, who was now, incredibly, 21 and a drama student, huddled miserably into her maxi coat. Her long, black boots were caked with mud and she stared at them mutinously. She was quite out of her element; her elaborate hair style was blown askew by the wind and the mascara that caked her eyes was running in black rivulets down her cheeks as the tears brimmed over in hot, short spurts. On the other side of the grave stood my father, looking bored and solemn at the same time, his large powerful shoulders thrust back proudly as he stood to attention. Beside him, my mother stood as tense as a race horse, looking down into the grave where her mother, my grandmother, was to be buried.

I'd always loved my grandmother. Zany, charming, alcoholic, she was definitely the black sheep of the family. Her secret drinking made her a compulsive liar – 'Madge thinks it's a mortal sin to tell the truth,' one of her brothers said. She'd had a wicked and promiscuous past when my mother was growing up. But, for all that, I knew that we were alike. Granny had always wanted to be a nun and this probably influenced my own decision to enter a convent, to save myself from a similar life of sin and unhappiness. After all, if God *had* intended her to be a nun and she had turned down her vocation then it was no wonder her life was a mess, I reasoned. If you foil God's original plan for you, then of course the rest of your life will be out of true. And a few days before I came home for the first time since leaving the Order she died of tuberculosis and drink. It was almost as though I'd lived out her own vocation for her vicariously; now that she was dead there was no longer any need for me to continue my own religious life.

I pulled my mind back to the funeral service. Father Fitzgerald, our parish priest, was gabbling through the prayers in a sing-song, mechanical manner that I remembered only too well. Beside him my grandfather, the chief mourner, stared bleakly with a simple expression of sorrow at the coffin, his large trilby hat pulled well down over his eyes, his feet apart like a polar bear.

'May the Angels lead you into Paradise,' Father Fitzgerald's voice brightened. Now we were near the end. A little boy clad in a black surplice held an umbrella over his head ineffectually, for the rain was dripping steadily from it on to Father's left shoulder. Periodically he gave the umbrella a bad-tempered jerk. 'At Thy coming,' he sniffed loudly – through cold, not through emotion – 'may the martyrs receive thee and lead thee to the holy city, Jerus*alem*.' The last syllable was heavily intoned as a signal to the acolyte that he had reached the end of a page. Father groped under his cassock, produced a grey handkerchief and blew his nose stertorously – sound effects for the celestial trumpets? He stared gloomily at the new page, cleared his throat and continued, 'May the choir of *angels* receive thee, and may you enjoy eternal rest . . . .'

Suddenly I recognized the prayer, which the bungled delivery had for a moment disguised. I remembered the funerals at Tripton. We walked, bearing candles in a long procession of Professed, Novices and Postulants, from the convent church, down the cloister and into the little cemetery. The *In Paradisum* chanted on one note had, at various points, broken into polyphony that was half a lament and half a cry of triumph. Over and over again we sang the strange chant while overhead the passing bell tolled until finally we all stood around the new grave. This seemed a hideous parody; I could almost see the silent line of nuns bidding their sister a last farewell, taking holy water from the stoup, sprinkling it into the open grave and departing singly and silently into the convent to resume the work of the day. . . .

Father Fitzgerald leant over my grandfather, whispering loudly, 'Perhaps you'd like to pay your last respects to your dear wife.' He pressed something into his hand.

Bewildered, my grandfather looked down at the long, pink bladder. He looked uncertainly at my mother, down at the grave and then, questioningly, back at the priest.

Father beamed and nodded encouragement. 'Squeeze!' he ordered, waving us all briskly into line. We stared, mesmerized. Grandpa squeezed, and, in a clear, obscene arch, a jet of holy water spurted onto the coffin.

It was an undignified end to a witty and brave life, but I consoled myself with the thought of how much my grandmother would have enjoyed it. As I walked to the car I pictured her, spectacles as usual grimy and held together with sellotape, trotting in the wake of the dignified procession described in the *In Paradisum*, her eyes flickering uneasily from archangel to martyr, on her way to celestial bliss. I smiled. Yet again we were in uncanny sympathy; my old life was dead, like hers, and I was only too conscious that I fitted into my new existence no better than she did.

My parents had never wanted me to become a nun. They were Catholics, but not particularly fervent about religion, and were horrified when I announced my intention. Mother Katharine, my headmistress, urged them not to stand in the way of my vocation. How could they dare, she asked, stand in the way of God's Will? Awed and out of their depth, they finally gave their consent and during the next seven years they were allowed to visit me only once every six months. Inevitably we drifted apart but they were delighted when I wrote to tell them I was leaving. They had got their daughter back and everything would be just as it was before.

Of course that was impossible. I had become a different person during those seven years. I knew that my parents had no idea of the kind of experiences I'd had in my Order. They didn't even know that I'd had a nervous breakdown only a few months ago. And it was impossible for me to tell them. If I found it hard to let Charlotte hold my hand, if I instinctively kept my fellow-students at arm's length, I was compelled by the same logic to hold my parents even further away. My Vow of Chastity didn't only forbid sex. It meant also that I had to abandon other forms of human love; even friendship. During my novitiate we were never allowed, in free recreation periods, to talk to another sister 'in a two' in case we formed what was called a 'particular friendship', something that was at that time considered a great evil in the religious life. I'd often asked God to help me stop being fond of a fellow nun, lest my love of her detract from my love of Him. Towards the end of my religious life I'd rebelled against this attitude to friendship and now I longed for friends myself but had no idea how to go about getting them.

And I was embarrassed by love. I was embarrassed by all emotion but love in particular. I wanted it but my hackles instinctively rose as at something unclean when I came into contact with it. My parents loved me very much but after years of religious reserve I had to learn all over again not only how to give love but how to accept it. Gradually I started letting people get through to me. Slowly I started getting acclimatized to a warmer emotional atmosphere, and when I'd learned to let other people love me, I was able to find my parents again.

But in those first years all I seemed able to do was cause them pain.

'What's it like to be home again, Karen?' my father asked, during lunch after the funeral.

'Lovely.' I could hear the hearty coolness in my voice and tried to make up for my inner nervousness with a smile.

'How does the flat look? Does it seem different?' asked my mother eagerly, passing me a plate of quiche.

'Well, it seems smaller somehow,' I said carefully, trying to share my impressions with them as honestly as I could. The flat was actually airy and spacious, but years of living in institutions, in vast buildings with huge rooms, made it seem frighteningly claustrophobic. The newly painted green walls – they had been magnolia when I had gone away – seemed to close in and press us all together. It made me feel confined and jumpy. I saw my parents look crestfallen and hastened to reassure them. 'I love the green walls, though. What an inspiration that was! They're exactly the same colour as the carpet!'

My father beamed. 'We mixed it ourselves. It was a hell of a job. But worth it.'

'Oh, definitely,' I agreed fervently.

'Your room's almost exactly the same as it was when you left,' my mother went on happily. 'Did you notice?'

I did indeed. It was appalling. Everywhere – from my school books, the crucifix over my bed, the desk where I'd studied for my A-levels – my seventeen-year-old self sprang out at me. I remembered the last time I had been in the room, leaving to go to the convent; how happy and expectant I had been. Life seemed to be opening out into an inspired vista, a quest for God and for holiness. And now, everything was over. I had not proved worthy of my vocation and coming back like this I felt more defeated than I had at any time during the last two months.

Now I smiled blandly at my mother. 'It was lovely seeing it again,' I said politely.

I could see both my parents were expecting something more. They were watching me intently for show of some emotion befitting the occasion. When I'd arrived at the station I did not rush up and fling my arms round them, as I watched Lindsey do a few minutes later. I turned my cheek coolly up for them to kiss in the same way as I had done to my superiors for years, to receive the embrace of the Order: a brush of the wimple on each cheek and then a pushing away. When I watched Lindsey kissing them so affectionately I longed to be able to do the same. But I couldn't.

'Well,' my father said, a trifle sharply, 'it's lovely to have you back, darling.' I felt my stomach turn over at the endearment. No one had called me anything more affectionate than 'dear' – and that word was usually used sarcastically by Superiors – for seven years and I felt unnerved and violated.

'It's lovely to be back,' I replied. Too quickly. Too glibly. Keep away, I was trying to tell him. Don't come too near. I can't bear it.

'I must say,' Lindsey, who was listening to the conversation with unusual quietness, broke in cheerfully, 'I'm glad you're out of that hell hole! I used to loathe coming to see you, Karen. Those awful gloomy parlours, smelling of books and incense, those stiff and starchy teas with all the nuns standing round watching every mouthful we ate, as though we were freaks in a side show!'

'I used to hate it that you weren't allowed to eat with us,' my mother said, testily. 'So inhuman! That was the spirit of the whole place, wasn't it? Especially Tripton. And so tense!'

'Those Church services!' Lindsey groaned. 'I used to faint every time we went to Benediction and I've *never* in my life fainted anywhere else. Sister Patrick, that nice lay sister at Tripton, used to think it was terribly funny. But it was all so perfect, Karen. You Novices used to come in in a long procession and genuflect all together without a signal. It was uncanny! And the candles were lit, just so, and there was never a single wrong note! It was all too bloody perfect. Wasn't it?'

I listened with increasing irritation. It was all true. I could see my family looking at me eagerly, longing for me – at last! – to say how awful it had really been, to endorse their discomfort during the last seven years. Yet I couldn't. I couldn't bear to hear them criticize the religious life when they'd seen none of the beauty and vision of it, either. Instead I smiled, rather frostily, and murmured 'Mmm, in a way,' becoming instantly one of the chilly and inhuman nuns they'd been attacking.

'And do you remember,' my mother went on, incited to further complaints by my air of priggish disapproval, 'the time we dropped into the convent because we were actually passing the door and Mother Walter wouldn't let us see you? She was furious, absolutely furious!' So, years after the event, was my mother.

'Well,' I tried to sound conciliating but the nun in me was still too strong to let the point go, 'it was the Rule.' For me that one word said so much. The Rule was each nun's blueprint for perfection, her way of following Christ.

'Rules, rules,' said my father impatiently, 'that's all they ever thought about.'

I felt my parents' emotions tugging at me. Just remembering that incident made Mother clatter more loudly with her cutlery, slice her pastry viciously. The hurt and anger trembled round her compressed mouth. I could see her point so clearly, but felt frozen as the air twanged with emotion, used as I was to the chilly restraint of convent life.

'And you – you were completely cowed by the system,' my mother continued. It wasn't an accusation. Quite. 'You were so terrified of stepping out of line.'

'It wasn't that exactly,' I tried to explain, following her out into the kitchen with a pile of dishes. 'It's just that conformity was part of our Vow of Obedience, so –'

Crash. Clatter. The cutlery was hurled into the sink. The very air was jagged with tension. I felt assaulted by it on all sides like a new, dangerous element, pushed by it back into my habit of reserve.

I smiled at my mother, silencing her and driving us all apart from one another.

'That *was* a lovely meal!' I said primly.

In many ways it was nice to be back. With Lindsey I went out shopping for summer clothes and she helped me to be braver in my choice. By no means was I as adventurous as she, though. While I was trying on a cotton frock, Lindsey strutted about in a silky pyjama trouser suit with a breathtakingly plunging neck-line and wide billowing pants that showed off her hips to perfection.

With my parents I went to a concert, to the theatre and the cinema, and rediscovered many old joys. But always, ultimately, I knew I was holding out on them.

'At least the worst part is over!' my mother declared confidently, as we strode, *en famille*, across the Lickey hills one Sunday afternoon. 'It must have been hell making up your mind to leave. Nothing will ever be as bad as that again.'

'And it's so lovely to have you here!' My father reached out, put his arm round me, and drew me towards him.

I felt my body grow rigid with horror. Involuntarily I pulled away and we looked at one another, aghast at what had happened. His eyes were bright with pain.

As we made our way back to the car later, I made myself put my hand through his arm. He looked down at me, delighted and, deliberately, I smiled back. The clumsier feel of his body, the rough material of his coat, his heavier breathing as we puffed up the hill, were all alien and male. To walk as closely to any other human being as this seemed profoundly unnatural. Against my will, I felt my hand stiffening on his arm, the feeling that had prompted the gesture freezing. Eventually I had to let it go.

'We have to change at Banbury,' Lindsey announced as the train pulled out of New Street station.

The holiday was over for both of us. I was going back to Oxford to begin the summer term and Lindsey was returning to her drama school in London. She had decided to take the slow train to Paddington so that we could travel together as far as Oxford.

'It'll be fun to be together.' She leaned back and smiled generously at me. 'It's great having you back. It's like having a brand new sister! Oxford must be marvellous. Are you enjoying it?'

I nodded emphatically. I felt drained by my visit home and the thought of my room in College was alluring.

'I love the study,' I told Lindsey.

'But what about your social life?' Lindsey interrupted. 'Men, for example. Oxford's full of them. You could be having an amazing time.'

'What about yours?' I avoided the issue. 'Have you got a lot of . . .' I tailed off, uncertain of the term. 'Boyfriends' sounded horribly twee and, looking at my beautiful and sophisticated sister, quite inappropriate.

'Men?' Lindsey nodded. 'Oh, yes! I mean, there's never any shortage of them, is there?' she said nonchalantly. 'I mean, the world's full of them.'

Today she was wearing a white frilly blouse and skin-tight crimson velvet trousers. Her long, elegant legs were curled up under her, her thick dark hair hanging loosely round her shoulders. She was obviously no virgin. My little sister. I stared at her for a moment, awed; she had crossed the sexual Rubicon and left me behind, had gone on ahead to a mysterious world where I could never follow.

'Is there anyone special?' I asked.

'There has been.' Lindsey sighed and looked out of the window. 'I'm always in love, but I always seem to get dumped in the end. Oh, there are always men to take you out, aren't there? People to have fun with, people to sleep with. But I really do want someone to love me back, really love me, not just fancy me.'

'Do you want to get married?' Somehow I couldn't associate this glamorous creature with domesticity.

'Of course!' Lindsey looked incredulous. 'Don't you? I don't want to be alone all my life.'

'No.' I smiled back uncertainly. I didn't want to be alone. But marriage meant men, it meant sex, and I didn't seem to want those either. 'But Lindsey, you're so young – you'll change! There are girls at College who've had one boyfriend all the time they've been there. They study together all day, she darns his socks and irons his shirts, cooks him a meal every evening. And I keep thinking of my own mistake at their age.'

'Oh, sure! That *is* stupid.' Lindsey dismissed this with a wave of her hand. 'They've had no other experience. And I wasn't thinking of getting married tomorrow,' she smiled wickedly, 'or even next year. But one day – yes. I'm going to find someone who loves me and doesn't just use me. I don't know where he is or how I'm going to find him. But I will. I know I will.'

At Banbury we had to change platforms and, lugging suitcases, we started to hobble down the platform. Before we had gone a few yards, a man, young, prosperous-looking and intelligent, materialized at Lindsey's elbow.

'Would you like a hand with your bag?'

'Oh, fantastic!' Lindsey dropped her case like a hot brick and smiled directly into his eyes. They were on a level, I noticed, as I, even shorter than usual because of my burden, squinted up at them; larger, godlike beings who owned the world. 'I was just wondering how I was going to make it to the London train.' Lindsey's voice was warm with gratitude and – yes – invitation. 'I'm not taking you out of your way?' The two of them started off together, Lindsey walking lightly and freely now, the man barely seeming to notice the case in his obvious interest in her.

'Are you okay, Karen?' Lindsey asked, concerned, looking over her shoulder as I struggled along, two steps behind.

'Fine!' I panted. 'Absolutely fine!' I gave my arms a rest and threw my tangled hair out of my eyes. The young man looked, suddenly checked and peered down at me, and then looked back at Lindsey, clearly wondering how she could be connected with this dowdy frump.

'This is my sister,' Lindsey introduced me. 'We're travelling together.' I smiled at him apologetically.

'Great!' said the young man with forced enthusiasm.

'Only as far as Oxford,' I reassured him. The case was banging painfully against my ankle and forcing me into the stature of the Hunchback of Notre Dame. Sweat was breaking out on my forehead in the warm spring sunlight and, I knew, my face was getting red and shiny.

'Oxford?' the young man cheered up instantly. 'Ah, I'm going on to London. What about you?' He turned hopefully to Lindsey.

'London,' she promised, as we reached our train. Her bag was swung gracefully on to the rack and, cool and unruffled, she arranged herself decoratively on the seat. I struggled after them, sweaty, dishevelled and out of breath, lugging my recalcitrant bag in my wake. Still, in the midst of my discomfort and embarrassment at playing gooseberry, I could see it was funny. With cries of polite concern, the young man, whose name, it transpired, was Tony, took my case from me, while I flopped, exhausted, on to the seat opposite Lindsey, who grimaced at me ruefully.

As the train hurried along towards Oxford I watched my sister talk. Or, rather, it was not really a conversation she was having; she was simply listening to a monologue of Tony's past life, his achievements, his hopes for the future in merchant banking. Her eyes were riveted in fascination on his face. She laughed at his rather tame jokes as though he were Peter Sellers, she expressed incredulity, astonishment, sincere and intelligent agreement. And Tony loved it. As each mile progressed I watched him feel treasured, a richer, fuller individual, a conquering hero. But why, I wondered, doesn't he ask Lindsey anything about herself? Oh, he did, in a way, from time to time, but then swung the conversation back to himself again. And Lindsey encouraged this, as self-effacing as a nun. She was a different person. She was playing an elaborate game. And winning hands down.

'Here we are!' I said, relieved, as the train drew into Oxford station. I hailed the cluster of spires and domes with the exhilaration of a traveller who'd been absent from his home town for years.

Tony leapt to his feet with a radiant smile of relief, threw my case eagerly out on to the platform and pumped my hand. 'It's been lovely to meet you,' he said, too heartily. I could see myself reflected twice over, tiny images in his pupils, the bookish, dreary older sister.

Lindsey leant from the train and our cheeks brushed awkwardly. Her eyes met mine and she winked vulgarly and grinned. A whistle blew and the train pulled her off to her world of conquests. I waved with no regrets at all. I was back in Oxford where I belonged more than anywhere else in the world.

Yet, some weeks later, I really did feel I was going home in a deeper sense. Back to the convent.

When I saw the familiar handwriting and the Tripton post mark I was surprised, then worried. It was from Sister Rebecca, probably the nearest thing I had to a friend in the Order. Together as students at Oxford we had shared my last traumatic year as a nun. Now she was writing from the Provincial House at Tripton. I tore the envelope open anxiously.

Sister Rebecca's letter astonished me. She was asking me, in the most restrained way, if I could come and see her. The alarming thing was that she was being allowed to request a visit. We had been trained to eschew rigorously all visits from friends and I, a renegade nun who had abandoned her vocation, could hardly be considered a suitable companion for her. And yet, she told me, Reverend Mother said I would be most welcome. Rebecca herself would meet me at the nearest station.

Anxiously I scanned the faces of the people waiting at the barrier. No sign of Rebecca yet. Perhaps she'd been delayed. As I handed in my ticket, however, my eye was suddenly caught by a nun who was sitting underneath the old-fashioned wall clock opposite. There was something terribly familiar in the way she inclined her head solemnly over her lap and stared unseeingly at the floor. She was dressed in one of those modern habits that made her look rather like a dowdy nurse: a short navy blue mackintosh, a small veil of matching material, which showed a little of her hair in front, flesh-coloured stockings and black rubber shoes. I knew that the Order had modernized the habit, but this nun couldn't be Rebecca. I looked around the entrance hall again, but felt my eyes drawn back to that painfully thin figure, gazing anxiously down at the tiled floor. Then she looked up; her face lit up with delighted recognition and for a moment my heart stopped.

Sister Rebecca was a beautiful young nun with the face of a Botticelli madonna. This nun looked as though she had just come out of Belsen. Her face had shrunk so that the eyes were huge and protuberant, and beneath her cheekbones there were cavernous hollows. Her neck seemed too thin to support even this small head. Her legs, I noticed, as she stood up, had no calves and the knee bone stuck out grotesquely. She was five foot ten and could not have weighed five stone.

Hastily I forced my own features into an answering smile. 'I didn't recognize you for a second in your new habit,' I explained as we met, still trying to disguise my horror.

We exchanged the nun-like kiss, pressing each other's cheeks with our hands on one another's shoulders. Then we stood back and looked at each other. I kept myself smiling.

'Karen!' Her voice was still the same at least, low and soft. 'It's so good of you to come.'

'It's lovely to see you.'

Together we crossed the station yard and got into the convent car.

'How long will it take us to get there?' I asked.

'About forty minutes, if the traffic is OK. Are you nervous?'

'I don't know yet,' I said. 'What's it going to be like? Are they going to be nice to me? Or are they going to point me out to the novices and tell them to say "there but for the grace of God go I"?'

We laughed. 'No. They'll be full of the new charity and understanding that go with Vatican Two,' she said. 'You'll find lots of changes.'

'What sort of changes?' I asked, watching the little town go by.

'Oh. No Rule of Silence and different clothes are what you'll see outside the enclosure. Inside it's all very different. No Refectory Penances, Chapter of Faults, Physical Penance, less formal prayer, more baths . . .'

'Stop!' My mind reeled. 'What are you putting in instead of all this?'

Rebecca groaned. 'Endless discussions and committees about Vatican Two.'

33

There was a silence as the car sped along the country lanes. Already I could begin to recognize the countryside that had been so familiar to me at Tripton.

'Karen,' Rebecca's voice was more hesitant. 'Thank you for not saying anything.'

I looked at her questioningly, taking in yet again her appalling transformation. 'About your weight?' I asked.

She nodded. It was, I realized, a year since we'd met. At Oxford she was losing weight. We both were. But not like this.

'When did it happen?'

'Very quickly,' she sighed. 'It suddenly started dropping off me while I was in London, doing the Dip.Ed. I've finished that. And they've sent me down to Tripton. To teach in the school.' Her voice was flat.

'Will you like teaching?' I asked.

'No. I'll hate it.' I didn't try to remonstrate. I could see that it was true. Her general air of thoughtful understatement would be disastrous in the classroom.

'But what's the matter with you?' My voice still trembled with shock.

'It's just been diagnosed. *Anorexia Nervosa.*' I knew what that was now. One or two girls had it at college.

'Aren't you eating?' I asked. 'You must be. Or have they done away with the Rules about eating too?' I adopted a sing-song tone as I recited them: 'Two helpings of at least one course at every meal, one and a half pieces of bread for breakfast, one piece of bread each for tea and elevenses. You must be eating!'

'Yes, I'm eating all right,' she smiled at me. 'No, apparently this is an extreme form of the illness. I'm eating but not absorbing the food.'

'So you have no control over it at all, then?' If that was so how was she going to get better? I was suddenly frightened – *was* she going to get better?

Rebecca shook her head. She coughed slightly, a tiny cough that seemed to rack her whole emaciated frame.

'But what are they doing about it?' I asked desperately.

'Nothing.'

The silence rang between us. I glanced at her sidelong, saw the muscles outlined in her neck, the terrible hollows under the

34

chin, the huge Adam's apple. No. They wouldn't do anything; I knew that.

'All a matter of will power, I suppose,' I said bitterly.

'Something like that.'

'But you need a doctor!' I exploded furiously. 'You can't go and teach looking like that.'

'Oh, yes, I can.' There was an edge to her voice which was the closest thing to anger I had ever heard in her. 'I'm going to be a sixth-form mistress. And, in a few years, I shall be the next Headmistress at Tripton.'

'*What!*' I stared at her incredulously. 'But you'll be hopeless! — sorry!' She looked at me and laughed.

'Dear Karen. I knew you'd understand.'

'Well, you know what I mean. They must know what you feel about teaching.' I looked back at her again. 'It'll kill you. You've *got* to go to a doctor. A proper one. In London or somewhere. You won't get the expert help you need in a place as tiny as Tripton.'

'No. I know.'

'But, Sister.' I fought to keep my voice under control. 'Have you talked to them? It does say in the Rule that if, after prayer, you know it is your duty to represent something to your superior, you can do it.'

'Reverend Mother is very understanding.'

I had never had much to do with Mother Peter, the big-boned, tall nun with the remote, crackly voice. But as the car turned into the long drive at Tripton, past the long avenue of cedar trees towards the fourteenth-century convent, I remembered her smile; shy but spontaneous and warm. She would help Rebecca. If she could.

'Have you talked to her about it?' I asked.

'Yes.' Rebecca turned to face me. Her smile was so calm that it seemed an obscenity. 'She told Reverend Mother Provincial that I needed a doctor. In London.'

'And . . . ?' But really I didn't need the answer.

'Reverend Mother Provincial said she had no one to replace me here at the moment.'

I sighed impatiently but even as I did so I felt part of myself responding to Mother Provincial's words. I knew what lay behind them. It wasn't that she was more interested in the smooth running of the convent. As Superior it was her duty to help her nuns to conquer themselves. My impatience was a response based entirely on the natural not on the supernatural order.

Yet, despite this inauspicious beginning, as soon as I got inside the convent something in me responded and relaxed. I'd come home. As I smelt the familiar wax polish and saw the gleaming rust and gold floor tiles stretching ahead of me across the large courtyard near the front door, I took a deep breath.

'What's it like to be back?' Rebecca asked gently, watchful of my mood.

'I don't know . . . yet.' I looked at the large, life-sized crucifix on the opposite wall, heard the clanging of the gong in the distance. Automatically I paused to listen and count the strokes. Three clangs. A pause. Then another two clangs. A special bell to summon one of the nuns. Not 'my' bell, though. Then I remembered that I didn't have a 'bell' any more. That I didn't belong. At the far end of the courtyard was the heavy enclosure door. If I went through that I knew exactly what I should see: the long cloister reaching far into the distance, the deep window embrasures and, on the right, the large doors to the Refectory. Except that I couldn't enter the enclosure any more.

'Do I have to see Reverend Mother or anything?' I asked Rebecca nervously. Suddenly I felt shy, unreasonably sad at being excluded and I wondered whether it had been a good idea to come. But toying with this kind of nostalgia could only be a dangerous dream, distracting me from my real task.

Time and time again during the next twenty-four hours I would be caught up in a moment that was so completely familiar to me that for a split second I forgot I was no longer a nun. Coming back to Tripton had revived reflexes that I'd forgotten I'd got. Walking with Rebecca down the country lane I'd walked down every day for three years, listening at night to the clock tower bell chiming every quarter, automatically laying down my pen or my coffee cup at the first sound of the bell that summoned the community to prayer. I felt drawn back into the old atmosphere and routine. The confusions of the world outside faded and I felt at peace.

Yet there were other differences besides the major change in my own status. As Rebecca and I walked across the lawn from

36

the guest house I was suddenly rooted to the spot. A nun, clad like Rebecca in the short, utilitarian habit like a nurse's uniform, ran across the path that led towards the Postulants' garden. I caught a fleeting glimpse of her face. Mother Serena, who was Reverend Mother Provincial's personal secretary. What had upset me?

'Mother!' Mother Serena shouted loudly and again I felt myself stiffen automatically. 'Mother!'

From round the corner another nun appeared suddenly in answer to the summons. 'Yes,' she yelled back.

'Reverend Mother wants you. Quickly!' And the two nuns trotted back into the convent.

The little incident had taken less than a minute. What was it that was wrong? Of course. In my day, so short a time ago, nuns never ran, they never shouted. There was absolutely no reason why they shouldn't, of course, I reminded myself. There was nothing sinful about running or shouting. But still something jarred.

That little scene made me gradually aware of other changes, more subtle than the simple discarding of the traditional habit. The old, hushed silence of the convent was gone. Nuns stood in groups chattering loudly during the recreation periods. There was in the air, particularly among the younger nuns, a defiant casualness. Voices rang loudly up and down flights of stairs as the nuns called to one another in the course of their work. Laughter rang forth in loud spurts. Doors were shut noisily and footsteps clattered on staircases. Even in church the attitudes of silent listening seemed to have disappeared. In the old habit you had to kneel perfectly still. If you didn't your veil fell around your shoulders in a large tent and your legs got twisted and tangled in the heavy skirts. Now that the modern dress gave nuns greater freedom of movement, many of them fidgeted restlessly as though the imposed stillness had become more of a strain. And if a nun ceased to pray and be silent inside herself, where was she? Perhaps she ended up like me, no longer able to meet the huge demands her vocation made upon her.

And yet, for all the new restlessness, as I knelt in the Tripton chapel for Mass in the morning I caught once more a sense of God present – just out of reach, perhaps, but still present. For the first time since I had left the Order, the Mass seemed to make sense. Instead of a mindless gabbling competing with the crying of babies and a lack of concentration that was almost palpable in the congregation, there was once again that straining of attention.

But then, as the Community processed up to receive communion, I caught sight of Rebecca. Her profile was terrifying and I knew that unless something was done – and done quickly – she would die. What were they thinking of? Rebecca told me that they talked much more frequently at meals, that instead of the hard, straightback chairs in the community room there were comfy armchairs. Life was meant to be more human now behind the enclosure door. And yet the fundamental attitudes were unchanged. Rebecca could sit in her armchair in the community room (and thank God for that; she was so thin that any harder kind of seating was intolerably painful for her, she told me but she was being allowed to walk undisturbed towards a senseless death.

No, I told myself, watching the serene faces coming back from the communion rails, I mustn't let myself fall into the trap of romanticizing the religious life. Could God really be present, as a few moments ago I had thought He was, to preside over this appalling neglect? But there was one thing that was hopeful in the situation. Her superiors had allowed me to come and see her. I had a duty here; I had to try and make them see what was happening to Rebecca.

'Hello, Karen.' I looked up from my breakfast in the parlour. How odd it was to be waited on in this way, as I had waited so frequently on visitors, bringing in coffee, toast, eggs when just a few yards away the community were eating bread and marge.

Mother Frances was standing beside me. Hastily I got up and she kissed me, cheeks pressing against mine, no sullying contact with the lips even now that the modern head-dresses made proper kissing a possibility.

'Hello, Mother,' I smiled nervously back. Mother Frances had been my Mistress of Scholastics and it was she who had handed to me the dispensation from my Vows last January. Out of the concealing folds of the habit she looked much larger, the broad shoulders making her rather small head appear less in proportion than before. She had recently been made one of the Provincial Councillors and, although she was only in her late forties, she was one of the highest-ranking supervisors in the Order.

'Sit down,' she gestured towards the table, 'and get on with your breakfast.'

'I've finished, thank you, Reverend Mother.' It was odd. Even though Mother Frances was no longer my superior I instantly fell back into the role of young nun in her presence, unable to swallow another mouthful while she was waiting to speak to me.

'Well,' she laughed, 'you look very different since we last met! How are you?'

'Fine,' I replied automatically. Then suddenly I found myself breaking out of the conventional fiction. 'No, actually, Reverend Mother, I'm not fine at all. It's terribly, terribly difficult.'

Mother Frances looked uncomfortable. 'Oh, well.' She smiled briskly, flushing slightly and avoiding my eyes, appearing fascinated by the crumbs on the gleaming table top. Whimsically she started tracing a swirly pattern in them. 'It's early days yet. There's bound to be a difficult period of adjustment, but I'm sure it's only a matter of time.' There was a finality in her tone that pushed me back inside myself. 'Feelings don't count.' How often I'd been told this. I was ashamed of my emotional revelation and felt myself somehow sullied and unclean.

'Well.' Mother's voice lifted a tone or two to indicate a change of subject. 'And how do you find Sister Rebecca?' Her eyes narrowed slightly as she looked back up at me, her head cocked slightly to one side.

I took a deep breath. My earlier resolution about this seemed to be ebbing away in face of her cool gaze.

'Dreadful, Reverend Mother,' I said with as much firmness as I could muster. 'Are you going to arrange for her to see a doctor?'

'She's seen a doctor, as you know.' Again there was a note of reproof. 'There is a chance, though, that it *might* all be due to an over-active thyroid. We'll just have to hope for the best.'

'An over-active thyroid? Can it make you as thin as that?'

'Apparently it can. Let's hope it *is* that. If she *is* suffering from that nervous illness caused by not eating enough . . .'

'You mean *anorexia nervosa*,' I insisted.

'Yes,' Mother Frances laughed grimly. 'Well, if it *is* that, that would be dreadful. Quite unacceptable.'

'Unacceptable?' I stared at her, bewildered by this choice of word. 'But, surely, Reverend Mother, if it is *anorexia* whether you accept it or not is neither here nor there. It's just a fact, something that's happened whatever you all think about it. And, Reverend Mother, she'll die if she goes on like this.'

Mother Frances laughed drily, her eyes amused. She got up to go and looked quizzically at me, her hands resting on the table.

'I don't think anyone ever dies of *nerves*, Sister – Karen, I mean,' and the finality and ridicule she put into the sentence silenced me. I could almost feel my argument congealing in my head and crumbling away.

'Nerves!' Mother Frances laughed her short barking laugh as she looked at me with amused exasperation and got up to go. She kissed me and sighed, this time conjuring up my own 'nervous' breakdown and the tears, fainting, vomiting and bleeding that had punctuated my religious career.

'You and Sister Rebecca,' Mother Frances shook her head again as she left the room. 'You are a pair!'

Yet as Sister Rebecca drove me back to the station later that day my worry and indignation returned. However despicable 'nerves' might be, there seemed little you could do to get rid of them. And, as I glanced sidelong at Rebecca, I knew they could be lethal.

'What are you going to do?' I asked bleakly.

'I haven't much choice.' Rebecca sounded infuriatingly calm. I longed to shake her into some new urgency. 'We'll just have to hope and pray that Mother Provincial changes her mind. I think Mother Peter is going to try again.'

'But you can't just leave it to chance!' I almost shouted. I watched her wince slightly and noted, with shock, that a few weeks ago I could not have shouted like that. 'You've got to do something!'

'What?' Rebecca smiled gently. 'Come on. You know it isn't possible to do anything at all. Think of Obedience. Remember the Novice St Ignatius writes about whose superior commanded him to go out and bring him a lioness. An action done under obedience is never a failure, however mad it may seem. The novice *did* go and the lioness came quite peacefully and willingly. God does give us special strengths and grace when we act under obedience. I'll be all right. He'll take care of me.'

'You know what the Jesuits say happened to that novice's superior, though, don't you?' I muttered darkly. 'They say the lioness then ate him for giving an unwise command!'

We laughed, uneasily, together.

'But that's *their* business, not mine,' Rebecca smiled brightly. 'I've just got to do what they say.'

'I suppose you just think that I'm giving you the worldly, natural viewpoint,' I sighed. 'I'm in the world now, of course, and not looking at things from the supernatural point of view any more. I should be urging you to come to London with me *now* to see a doctor. But that's stupid. You can't do that.'

'"Each one should give himself up into the hands of his superiors,"' Rebecca quoted St Ignatius' Rule of Obedience, her eyes boring steadily into mine, '"as a dead body allows itself to be treated in any manner whatever."'

'I know, I know.' I felt weary and defeated. And torn, as though by questioning this – something I'd never have done a year ago – I had lost something precious. I smiled wryly at Rebecca. 'Sure you don't want to come with me?' I asked as we reached the platform barrier.

She smiled back at me and shook her head. Huddled in her thin mackintosh she was shivering violently, freezing cold on a mild, even warm summer day. Of course she would stay where she was, even if it killed her. A nun was meant to die to herself. Rebecca was just taking the idea to its logical conclusion.

We stared bleakly at one another for a moment and I felt shaken by my own impotence and the ambivalence of my feelings.

'Take care of yourself,' I said quickly, and by mutual consent we turned away from each other's pain. It was only when I was half way down the platform that I realized how inappropriate my parting remark was.

CHAPTER THREE

Success, 1970

'OH, NO,' I thought as the terror struck. 'Not again. Not here.'

I gripped the desk in front of me and struggled to rise to my feet. On all sides the light flickered evilly and a sweet, sickly smell rose in my nostrils, choking me and blotting out the familiar world. The lecturer's face blurred and became unrecognizable, his voice splintered into meaningless sounds. Fear crashed through me, rising higher and higher to ever new pitches of intensity as I struggled through to the gangway until it rose to a crescendo. I stood there for a moment, swamped in confusion, panic racing through me, my limbs trembling convulsively, while the light flickered, and nausea squeezed my stomach. Then the terror seemed to yawn emptily and swallow me up; it was over. There was a merciful darkness, a sense of falling down, down a long narrow shaft . . .

For years, ever since my second year in the convent, I had had what seemed to be fainting spells which my superiors diagnosed as hysteria and weakness of will. I accepted this diagnosis without question, not only because my superiors were in the place of God and so this must be His judgement, but because these attacks where I fell to the ground, unconscious, were accompanied by so much emotion: there was terror beforehand and afterwards a sense of desolation that lasted for hours, usually accompanied by uncontrollable weeping. When I finally had my breakdown, these attacks had seemed to herald this; had they been trying to tell me that I was not suitable for the religious life? My body, I thought, rose in revolt at these times and, literally, threw me off balance to show me that I was forcing myself along the wrong path.

But if this was the case, why did the attacks continue after I had left the religious life? For continue they did. Until now, at Oxford, I'd been lucky; they had not happened in public but in the privacy of my own room and once in the corridor of the old college house in which I now lived during my last year as an undergraduate. I hugged this shameful secret to myself. Nerves, nerves! When would I ever outgrow them? Other people had stress in their lives without falling on to the ground in a dead faint and coming round weeping and wailing. Terrified of one of these attacks occurring in public, I sometimes even refused an invitation just in case I 'fainted' while I was out.

I came to to the sound of quiet sobbing somewhere in the distance. It seemed to come from a long way away but was drawing closer all the time. The smell had gone now and only dust filled my nostrils and my cheek seemed to be resting on something hard, while a band of pain pressed down on my forehead. As I opened my eyes I saw brown shiny swirls snaking away from me, which slowly, slowly as my brain started to work again resolved themselves into the grain of a polished wood floor. After more confused seconds I remembered where I was and what had happened. The sobbing was coming from me. With a groan I rolled over, face downwards on the floor, to shut out the world for just a few more merciful minutes.

'I think she's coming round now.' I shook my aching head to force the meaning of the words home. Who could it be? It was a man's voice. Oh, no! The nausea I was suddenly conscious of gripped my stomach harder. It must be the man I'd come to listen to. What was the word for that? Oh, yes, a lecturer. His name . . . was . . . Dr Crosby. Shame kicked me in the pit of my stomach. I had interrupted the lecture. I braced myself to meet the cold anger and contempt that always greeted my return to consciousness in the convent. However kind he was Dr Crosby must be feeling fed up.

'Look, I think we'd better call it a day, don't you?' Dr Crosby said to the audience and there was a murmur of agreement. I tried to protest, but as I struggled up to speak, I felt his hand firmly press me down again and mists of confusion and bewilderment swept round me. I closed my eyes. . . .

Fortunately there was no one I knew at the lecture. It was a small one and in the French department. I'd only gone because Rebecca had got me interested in the *Chanson* when she was doing her degree. Dimly I could hear the tramping of feet around me. 'We'd nearly finished anyway,' Dr Crosby was saying. 'It's not worth going on now. See you all next week!'

'Karen . . . Karen? Are you okay?' I froze.

'You know her, do you?' Dr Crosby sounded relieved.

'Yes. Karen? It's Jane.'

There was nothing for it. No escape route was possible. I rolled over and smiled weakly at Jane, whose usually cheerful face looked pale and worried. 'Poor old you!' she smiled back reassuringly. 'You did give us all a shock. I must say, Karen, you do provide us all with some dramatic moments!'

'How are you feeling?' Dr Crosby was squatting beside me on the floor, his large face crumpled and enquiring.

'Fine!' I raised myself on one elbow. 'Look, I'm terribly sorry. I don't know how to apologize enough for ruining your lecture. It's so stupid of me. I – '

'For goodness sake!' Dr Crosby looked mystified. 'It's not your fault. You didn't do it on purpose. We're just sad for you! You still don't look too good to me. You've got quite a high colour and it was a long faint. Better see a doctor, don't you think?' he appealed to Jane.

'Definitely,' Jane was still smiling too. 'Poor Karen!'

I fell back again winded with shock this time. Not my fault! Poor old you!

'Look, what about a taxi?' Dr Crosby suggested.

'Excellent!' Jane smiled at him gratefully.

'Taxi!' I gasped in horror. Taxis for me were unbelievable luxuries. Spending money – especially spending money on myself – presented huge problems to me. I would sit in my room for hours, swathed in a bulky collection of sweaters and coats, rather than put a shilling in the meter.

'Really!' I pleaded. 'I'm fine now. I can walk, honestly. Or even get a bus. But not a taxi.'

'Don't be a fool, Karen!' Jane said affectionately. 'Yes, please, Dr Crosby. A taxi would be lovely.'

'I'll phone,' he replied, and I listened to his footsteps clattering further and further away, making the boards under my head vibrate and rumble.

On the way home I kept glancing nervously at Jane, looking for signs of disgust and impatience. She might just have been putting on a good show in front of Dr Crosby. But not at all. She

44

chattered cheerfully in the decadent taxi, escorted me to my room and insisted that I rest while she made me a cup of coffee.

'I really do feel better now,' I assured her truthfully, nervously counting the coins she was feeding into the meter.

'Have you ever fainted before?' Jane lay down comfortably on the rug and smiled up at me, her eyes curious and concerned, not angry. 'You made an awful noise when you fell. A dreadful, hollow groan. I always longed to faint at school. I tried everything – put blotting paper in my shoes, held my breath. Not a chance! I always thought it would be a sign of such delicacy and refinement – you know? Only sensitive girls seemed to faint. Whereas I was supremely healthy and horribly down-to-earth. Not a hope!'

In spite of myself, I found I was smiling. 'I used to think that too when I was at school. People used to fall with such a satisfying plop.'

'But have you ever done it before?' Jane persisted.

I nodded. I couldn't deceive her after all this kindness. Jane looked thoughtful. 'I must say that it didn't look like an ordinary faint to me.'

I looked up sharply. 'What do you mean?'

'Well, you were out for such a long time. When I've seen people faint before they practically come to as soon as they hit the floor. But you were out cold for ages – at least five minutes. And, you weren't all floppy and graceful – sorry to wound your vanity! – you were quite rigid. You were even shaking slightly all over. And very red in the face! None of that deathlike pallor.'

I sighed. 'I suppose that's because when other people faint it's because they haven't had enough oxygen or something and they come to as soon as the blood reaches the head again. But my fainting's not like that.'

'Why?' Jane sat up and looked puzzled. 'What is it?'

'Nerves,' I said gloomily. 'In the convent they said it was hysteria and weakness of will.'

'Oh, screw that!' Jane said energetically. I looked up and she blushed. 'Sorry about the language!'

'No, no! It's not the language,' I assured her quickly. 'I just didn't understand what you meant.'

'Well, all that nonsense about weakness of will! It's such a nun-like thing to say. The nuns I was at school with were hot on

45

it too.' Jane went on. 'Nerves? Hysteria? I suppose that could account for it.' She screwed her nose up doubtfully. 'You were crying as though your heart was breaking when you started to come round. And I suppose all that convulsive shaking could be tension. Your eyes were open too for quite a time and Dr Crosby couldn't get you to focus them – you were obviously still "out" in some way. It *could* be nerves, I suppose. No wonder, really. You've had an awful time one way and another.'

I smiled uncertainly, still hardly able to credit her attitude.

'Do you feel guilty about leaving your Order?' she asked suddenly, pouring fresh coffee for us both.

'Yes,' I replied simply and was then shocked by myself. What was I doing, burdening her with my problems? Yet the next moment I felt a sudden relief as though something inside me was released and set free.

'I'm not surprised.' Jane stirred her coffee vigorously. 'The Catholic Church is an absolute guilt-monger. I should know! Rationally you do see that there's no need to be guilty at all, don't you, Karen? Not that that makes the slightest bit of difference. But it *is* nonsense, isn't it?'

'Yes, I suppose so,' I said. The warmth of the fire on this chilly November morning was seeping through me luxuriously. Jane's calm acceptance of my 'nerves', the disgusting exhibition of my faint and now of my irrational guilt warmed me too. 'You see, although I've had a dispensation from my Vows, I still feel that I'm a terrible failure. The Order accepted me and that's an infallible sign of a religious vocation. The only sign of a vocation that the Church accepts.'

'And so that means that God *did* call you to be a nun and so naturally you've done an appalling thing in throwing it up! Don't tell me, I can imagine it all!' Jane replied and flung herself back so that she was staring at the ceiling. 'The Church really has it all wrapped up, hasn't it? Nothing simple like: Karen made a mistake. Oh, no! A big number about God and infallible signs. And of course, as a convent girl myself, I know that a vocation is the highest honour God can confer on anyone. So in throwing that away you've flung God's special gift back in His face! Isn't that right?'

'Yes!' I stared at her, astonished at her swift and complete understanding. 'Absolutely right.'

46

'It takes one Catholic to understand another!' Jane sat up and grinned back disarmingly. 'I know the system only too well.'

We sat quietly together, listening to the peaceful popping of the gas fire, while I savoured the immense luxury of human sympathy. At this moment the burden of guilt I hugged to myself seemed lighter.

'How do you live with it?' Jane asked sharply. 'How do you live with guilt? I don't know how to live with mine. Yet both of us go round smiling and cheerful. Today was the first sign I've ever had that you weren't blissfully happy.'

'Are you guilty?' I asked in astonishment.

'Guilty as hell!' She flung out her arms dramatically and made a wry face. 'Hell being the operative word! A lapsed Catholic. How could I not be? I'm living in mortal sin.'

'Mark?' I asked tentatively.

'Mark indeed!' Jane smiled. 'Behold a fallen woman!'

'And you can't go to Communion and you can't go to confession unless you promise never to sin again.' I understood her dilemma perfectly. 'Do you miss it?'

'Of course I do. All that liturgy! It's so beautiful. When Mark and I were in Paris last summer and went to Mass in Notre-Dame, I wept because it was all lost. Even Mark was impressed. "You gave all that up?" he asked. "You're heroic!" But it's no good kidding myself that I believe any of it any more. I don't, if I'm honest. But the habit of guilt remains, doesn't it? The Catholic Church has a really good line on guilt.'

'Oh, I do feel better!' She jumped up after a short silence. 'Thanks so much for listening.'

I found myself smiling back happily. 'Thank you.'

'It's a pleasure! I feel I know you better and that's good.' She was looking round. 'This is a nice room, Karen. So much nicer than that modern box you were in last year. But what you need now is a record player. I've noticed how keen you are on music.'

I smiled dismissively as at an impossibility.

'What did you do with that Prize money?' she asked firmly. 'The Violet Vaughan Morgan Prize that you won last Christmas? It was a hundred pounds, wasn't it?'

'Oh, that.' I'd almost forgotten about it. Terrified at possessing all that money I'd thrown it in the bank on deposit so as not to have to think about it any more.

'It's in the bank.'

'Well, for goodness' sake, Karen! Spend £25 and get yourself a memento of that bloody prize. It's not a waste of money! It's an investment in peace of mind. I couldn't survive without music. Anyway, you owe it to yourself! Your musical education is woefully neglected. You've got a duty to make it up.'

She was right. For a second the prospect of music whenever I wanted it took my breath away. All that peace for just a few pounds and the turn of a switch. It might even help my 'nerves'.

'All right, Jane,' I said. 'Tomorrow.'

'No more concessions!' trilled Miss Franklin. She settled her heavy body back in the winged chair and regarded us myopically through her thick spectacles. 'No more concessions!' Her prim mouth took on a self-satisfied smirk.

'Miss Franklin, the Junior Common Room won't accept this,' Maureen protested. 'It's quite unjustifiable.'

'No more concessions!'

It's like a gramophone record, I thought impatiently, stuck in a groove. Miss Franklin, the new Dean of Discipline, was obviously delighted with the way she was standing up to the undergraduates.

Maureen and I exchanged glances. Balanced side by side on the uncomfortable horsehair sofa, our long scholars' gowns trailing on the floor, we made an odd pair. Maureen, president of the Junior Common Room, was a radical. Sharp, clever, the winner of one of this year's Kennedy Scholarships for study in the United States, she loathed oppressive authority on principle. Her childish, freckled face was made suitably ferocious by formidable eye make-up, and her long hair hung past her waist. Beside her I felt the epitome of convention, but during our time in office together, I'd warmed quickly to her honesty and outspoken fearlessness.

We were getting nowhere. Mrs Jameson had completed her long term as Dean and resigned with relief last summer to devote herself entirely to her teaching. She'd enforced the College rules with sense and humour; if you were caught with a man in your room after midnight, when all visitors were supposed to be off the premises, she smiled drily, collected the half-crown fine and told you to be 'more careful' in future. Or so

I had been told. Naturally I had never been in that position. If you were caught climbing over the College wall after the gates were locked at midnight, the sixpenny fine was collected and you were advised to look where you leapt next time – preferably not into the arms of the Porter while he was doing his night rounds. It was a constant bone of contention between the Junior and Senior Common Rooms. An experimental scheme had been adopted whereby the College gate would be locked later at night. Mrs Franklin, on taking office, had stopped this scheme, enforced the rules rigidly, putting up the fines and stepping up the punishments. Copulating in College property had to cease. She belonged to that cabal in Governing Body that Mrs Jameson called 'the Virgin Vote'. After a few short weeks the students had rebelled and Maureen and I, as secretary of the JCR, had been sent by the Common Room to discuss the matter amicably. Our minuscule glasses of sherry were the only signs of amicability so far.

'But Miss Franklin,' I tried again. 'You can't call these concessions. You're taking away rights that have already been granted, they're not concessions.' There was, I realized, an irony in the fact that I, certainly the most virginal undergraduate, should be on this mission at all.

Miss Franklin gave that pleased little smirk again. 'There has been far too much slackness in recent years. You are here to work, not increase your sexual expertise.'

I could feel Maureen swell with rage beside me and open her mouth to reply. I kicked her gently. To stop her losing her temper.

A large, fat cat waddled into the room and stood mewing up at Miss Franklin.

'We shall be reporting back to the JCR,' Maureen said coldly. 'I can only say that we shall now have to take more militant action.'

Miss Franklin's face had changed. Heaving the cat into her lap she buried her face in the tabby fur. A rattling purr broke on the room. Miss Franklin kissed its head. 'Rajah will tell you that won't do any good,' she crooned at the cat. 'Will it, Rajah? Who's a beautiful boy?'

'We're talking to you, Miss Franklin, not to the cat.' Maureen jumped and stared at me open-mouthed and then choked into her sherry. She kicked me pointedly and stared straight ahead, grinning. I was amazed at myself. I'd actually answered back. And answered back an authority figure, to boot. It was the cat that was responsible. I recalled the nuns who, as their human affections atrophied over the years, fell in love with the current cats. You couldn't love your sisters in Christ, but there was nothing in the Rule to stop you loving the cat.

Miss Franklin flushed; a beetroot stain crept up her neck and slowly suffused her cheeks.

'I think we have said all we have to say to one another.'

'My God!' Maureen exploded as soon as we got outside. 'That woman! She's unbelievable! What about you, then?' She grinned. '"We're talking to you, Miss Franklin, not to the cat!" What happened to the amicability?'

'Sorry, Maureen,' I said ruefully. 'Something came over me.'

'Still,' Maureen glowed with satisfaction, 'the talking's over now. Now's the time for action.'

I sighed. I'd encountered authorities like Miss Franklin in the Convent. They were impermeable. Maureen's youthful optimism made me feel sad. Demonstrations and banners might be fun, but Miss Franklin would love it. Flanked by the Virgin Vote she would be in the limelight, holding out for high academic standards against the forces of Eros. I felt a ghost walk over my grave. No, I didn't want sex, couldn't countenance the idea. But at least, I resolved, I could campaign for free love for others.

'We'll call a JCR meeting for the lunch hour,' Maureen said cheerfully. There was a spring of anticipation in her walk. 'Can you put a few good posters up in the Dining Room?'

'Maureen,' I said slowly, 'do you see what I see?'

'Fucking Hell! Sorry, Karen.' I made an impatient gesture. The days had long gone since I had been forced to look up *fucian* in my Anglo-Saxon dictionary to find out what this popular expletive meant.

'What about that, then?'

Beside the College wall, underneath the climbing-in spot, workmen were erecting a huge hedge of barbed wire. Supposing someone hadn't seen this today – it was quite possible if you lived on the other side of the site – and jumped into it late tonight? Miss Franklin had overreached herself. Climbing over the College wall was a traditional and accepted custom at Oxford and Cambridge. The issues were crystal clear.

'Right!' I said grimly.

'We'll organize a sit-in immediately.'

'A sit-in's no good, Maureen,' I said. 'I've got a better idea.'

Clad in black trousers and sweater and wearing thick gloves we snipped grimly. JCR funds had been voted to acquire sets of wire-cutters for the select band of volunteers and it was now 2.00 a.m. Slowly, inch by inch, the hedge was demolished. We had been at it for an hour already; it would take at least another hour before the mass of treacherous wire lay in a heap of ten-inch fragments in the middle of the lawn. Harmless. Miss Franklin would see it as she went across to the Hall for breakfast in the morning. There would be no hour of glory. She would lose face not only with the Virgin Vote but with her more liberal colleagues.

'Karen,' Maureen whispered. 'The gate's opening!' We froze against the wall, switched off our torches and apprehensively watched the wooden door open, the floodlights of a car beam on to the lawn and one of the dons' cars slide silently into the grounds. We recognized the Saab.

Mrs Jameson got out and locked the gate behind her. Then she stood, her white fur coat gleaming softly in the moonlight, and stared at us for a long moment.

'Well done!' she called.

It was my first rebellion and I felt absurdly pleased with myself, but at the same time I found myself worrying about the issues I'd been fighting for. Was I going to end up cooing at a cat, a dog or canary, or was I going to have a normal love life? I had no idea. I felt vaguely jealous of other girls and stared at them with a kind of awe as they cuddled up to their lovers, wondering how on earth they could bring themselves to do it. I could not imagine how anything so rankly physical could have any relation to the finer parts of me – my mind and soul.

I had to learn to relate to my own body before I could begin to respond to anybody else's. It was not an easy thing to do. The era of the mini-skirt was the worst possible time for anyone to leave a convent. Once it had emerged from its enveloping yards of black serge I suddenly discovered I had a body, with a waist, breasts and legs. I hated it. Nobody could really see my face because I hid it with two long flaps of hair in front – a pathetic effort, I suppose, to replace my veil. I was ugly because I was so unhappy, and unhappiness can be very repellent. My spiritual unhappiness pervaded my body and stamped it with a character of misery which could only drive other people further away. As I remember all this, it now seems astonishing that I managed to emerge from this *impasse*.

Then, of course, there was the whole problem of men. Some women, I know, leave religious orders and marry very quickly, very successfully. They obviously have a healthier attitude to sex and to men than I had at that time. One of my motives for entering a convent in the first place might well have been sexual escape. I don't know why this should have been so. My sister and I were brought up exactly the same and Lindsey certainly never had this problem. Maybe I was just very impressionable and the whole anti-sex attitude of Catholicism did its work efficiently on me: any kind of sex, unless it's performed safely between married sheets, with a definite possibility of conception (though, as a great concession, Mother Church allows the uncertainties of the Rhythm method and all the anti-aphrodisiac routine with thermometers), is a mortal sin punishable by Hell fire. I was terrified by Hell as a child – there were some very effective Retreat sermons on the subject – and sex just seemed too risky. What the adults around me, all Catholics, thought they were saying was 'Sex is wonderful; sex is holy; it is an image of Christ's relationship with the Church.' But underneath that was quite a different emotional message which pervaded everything they said, just as it runs in clear counterpoint to every positive Church teaching on human love; the message was: don't do it. When I had my first period I remember saying aloud, 'Now a man can really harm me,' in a sort of solemn wonder. I responded with a lugubrious dread to my first moments of womanhood.

So on leaving my religious order I was not one of those nuns who leap over the wall straight into the arms of a man. There just hadn't been any men in my life at all to this point and I was 25 years old. I found them, not surprisingly, extremely puzzling, and I was not tuned in to the whole mechanism of courtship and flirtation which underlies male-female conversation all too often. 'Karen, tell me the meaning of life!' a man moaned one evening at a party, flinging himself onto the sofa beside me, his head practically on my shoulder. 'The meaning of life?' I queried cerebrally, sitting up alertly. 'How interesting!' And I proceeded to tell him. Poor man! He limped away pretty smartly to take his attentions elsewhere. It seems incredible that I ever managed to get through to men.

And to make things even harder, I had, as an ex-nun, an added problem which not only made me see men as strange and incurably silly beings but also made it next to impossible for them to relate to me naturally at all. . . .

Nervously I pushed open the door of the pub and looked inside. No sign of Lindsey. I'd agreed to meet her for a drink after a day spent reading in the British Museum.

Another first time. Standing uneasily by the door I realized I'd never been in a pub before.

The Edward VII near Paddington looked rather sordid and dreary on the outside but I found myself feeling pleased as I looked round at the rows of glasses winking in the early evening light, at the cunningly contrived corners and settles where groups of people laughed or else bent forward in pairs talking earnestly. There was a friendly smell of beer and smoke and the dim, brown light in the room seemed to shut out the noise and restlessness of the outside world into a cocoon of relaxation and enjoyment.

It couldn't have been more than a year ago since Father Simpson had startled us so much in the convent at Skipton. He was Confessor to the nuns there and often stayed the night in the convent in the small apartment overlooking the Chapel. That night I was given the job of preparing his room and, after supper, appeared there with a jug of hot water which I stood on the marble washstand and swathed carefully with towels to keep it warm. As I was turning down the bed Father Simpson came into the room behind me, sat down in the armchair and took out his books.

'Oh, Father,' I said, as instructed, 'would you like a drink brought in last thing tonight, after Examen?'

His craggy, heavily jowelled face regarded me steadily and I could see him taking me in; a young nun whom he hadn't seen before.

'What is there, Sister?'

I ran through the list of things I was told to offer. 'Well, there's cocoa, Horlicks, Bournevita . . .'

'Good God, no.' He looked steadily at me. 'I'll have a whisky and soda please, Sister.'

I gaped at him. Surely he knew that we didn't have alcohol in the house. The closest any of us came to drink was the communion wine; we used to keep the dregs carefully and put them in our Christmas puddings.

'Whisky and soda, Father?' I faltered.

'What are you going to do about that, my girl?' I could see him chuckling wryly. 'Yes, Sister, I'll have a whisky and soda, thank you,' and firmly he turned back to his book.

I fled down to the Superior and threw the community into a state of consternation and dismay. Eventually two older nuns, whose virtue and religious stability were long tried and proven, were dispatched to the local off-licence. I was considered far too young in religion to brave such worldly perils.

And now, just over a year later, here I was sitting in a pub! I leaned back, trying to look nonchalant taking in the round shiny tables with the red and white beer mats, the opaque mirrors on the wall which glimmered down dully into the brown and pink room and, fascinated, watched the barman pulling a pint, carefully levelling off the foam.

Suddenly I heard a voice that was familiar and jerked myself out of my reverie.

'Karen!' Lindsey waved energetically across the room. 'Terrific to see you! Oh, no!' She grimaced comically at the crowd of men with her. 'I put on a skirt specially for her and she turns up in trousers!'

The group laughed obediently and turned towards me. What an anti-climax that must be, I thought ironically, but was surprised to see their faces alight with interest.

'Wow! A nun in trousers!' breathed a dark, gypsy-looking man with a neat, trimmed beard and a floral shirt.

'Come and sit down!'

'Have a drink! What, what, what can I get you?'

Bewildered, I sat down at the table opposite Lindsey, and

smiled doubtfully at her. 'How are you?' I asked.

'Fine!'

'Do they look alike?' someone asked.

'Not really! But then Lindsey wasn't a nun for seven years!'

There was a burst of shared laughter as though the notion – as indeed it was – was absurd and I found myself laughing too as I accepted a glass of red wine.

'These yobs are all from the drama school.' Lindsey waved towards them in a sweeping gesture. 'They'll be going soon, but they wanted to come and meet you!'

'Certainly,' a man, whose name seemed to be Jim, replied, 'it's not every day you meet an ex-nun. Everything you've ever wanted to know about nuns but have never had the courage to ask!'

Everybody laughed again. I was puzzled. What on earth could interest them about the religious life – the long hours of prayer, the endless cleaning, sweeping and polishing, silent periods of study and reading, the recreations of genteel, polite conversation?

'Come on, Karen.' Peter, my neighbour, a cheerful-looking youth in a tweed sports jacket and incongruously brilliant peacock cravat, smiled at me and offered me a cigarette. 'Tell us all!'

'What do you mean?' I don't blush easily but to my embarrassment I could feel a dark flush mounting up my neck and flaming in my cheeks. There was something in the air that disturbed me. Not just the teasing and the questions – they were harmless enough and friendly. Phil, in the tight jeans, smiled at me and leant across the table. I suddenly noticed an intent and eager intimacy in his eyes. I smiled uncomfortably back. It was no use thinking that he was smitten instantly by my overwhelming charms; perhaps he felt sorry for me.

'Do you mind talking about life in the convent?' he asked.

'No. Not within limits, I suppose. It depends what you want to know. I honestly can't think you'd be very interested.'

Everybody laughed. 'We are! We are!' Peter crowed. 'My favourite fantasy!'

'Fantasy?' I looked at him, puzzled, causing louder gales of mirth.

'Mmm . . .' He leant back, his fair eyelashes fluttering as he closed his eyes and smiled with exaggerated lewdness, 'those thick black skirts, heavy underskirts, flannel petticoats . . .'

'Black lisle stockings.' Someone else took up the litany.

'Suspenders.'

'And white, white flesh, hidden for ever from the world!'

Peter put his arm round the back of my chair and grinned. Immediately, I leaned forward, away from him, feeling nausea. 'You don't mind, do you?' he asked. 'We don't mean to be offensive.'

I looked back at Lindsey and raised my eyebrows and shoulders in a silent question.

'Nuns are a turn-on,' she yawned with mock boredom, 'to many crass males of the species.'

I recognized the phrase – Jane's coaching in current slang had been an efficient one – but I was astonished. 'You can't mean it!'

'Oh, wow, yes!' Phil, I noticed, was still gazing at me with that intent and – yes – predatory stare. 'Fabulous! It's the conceal-ment, I suppose, the mystery, the inaccessibility, for God's sake!'

'Imagine,' Jim took up the cry, 'a houseful of virgins, young, beautiful creatures in starchy wimples, chains round their waists, crucifix over the bed. All longing for it.'

They were laughing at themselves now, guying the idea, but the initial *frisson* that had made me blush was still there, a disturbing counterpoint running silently beneath the laughter.

'Did you wear a wimple?' I could see that, instead of undress-ing me with his eyes, Phil was dressing me up. He leant across and took my hand, stroking it with his thumb, 'and a rosary, and crackly, calico knickers!' Sickened, I pulled my hand away.

'And what about the other nuns?' Peter asked, as he leaned towards me and spoke beerily into my face. 'Were they beauti-ful, mysterious and – sexy?' he giggled and waggled his eye-brows.

I suddenly cast a mental eye round the Tripton community. The glasses, the huge waists, the lumpy figures under the capes, Reverend Mother Provincial's beaky nose, Mother Frances' rolling seaman's gait and their brisk matter-of-factness. A houseful of beautiful virgins! All longing for it! I looked round the table of young men, and gave way to a great gust of mirth.

'They were splendid, brave women,' I finally managed to splutter, 'but not what *you* mean by virgins!' Again I started to giggle at the absurdity.

'Aw! Don't disillusion us,' someone pleaded, 'you'll ruin my sex life if you go on like that. Leave us a little room for fantasy.'

I wiped my eyes and looked at them weakly. 'But how extraordinary that you should find nuns a turn-on! Why is it?' I turned to Lindsey. 'I mean, do *you* have fantasies about monks, for instance?'

Everybody laughed. 'No, I *don't!*' Lindsey cried. 'I should imagine it'd be a hideous experience. It's men, Karen, you'll get used to them in time!'

Looking round the table at the flushed, bearded faces, the heads hiding so many extraordinary ideas, I wondered. Did I want to? I shook my head inwardly. Better, far better to keep to the cloistered groves of academe.

'Karen, thank you so much for coming over so quickly. A cup of tea?' Mrs Jameson waved the pot invitingly.

I nodded my thanks and sat down, curious to know why I'd been summoned to visit her on a Sunday afternoon.

'How's the work going?' Mrs Jameson asked, handing me a delicate, bone-handled cup. 'You're not revising too hard, I hope?'

'Oh, no, no,' I replied vaguely. Finals were now only a fortnight away. I looked inquiringly at Mrs Jameson.

'It's Sister Mary Sylvia,' Mrs Jameson sighed.

'How is she?'

'Much the same.'

I had gone on trying to help Sister Mary Sylvia. I'd had her for tea in my room and gone over translations with her, got her books out of the library. But it was useless. She'd finally broken down and was in a mental hospital. Pushed – like Rebecca – further than she could go.

'Will she be able to do the exams?' I asked Mrs Jameson. 'Surely it would be better if she took an *aegrotat*.'

'It's the same old story.' Mrs Jameson looked tired. 'I've talked to her, I've written to her superiors and do you know, Karen, do you know, they are *still, still* talking about her getting a First and doing research next year! I just can't believe it.'

'I can,' I said bleakly. 'I can imagine it all right.'

Mrs Jameson paused. 'Yes,' she said quietly, 'yes, I suppose you can. Well, look, my dear, the reason I've called you over this afternoon was to ask you if you were thinking of going to visit Sister Mary Sylvia in hospital.'

'Well, yes, I was, I – '

'Because if you were,' Mrs Jameson overrode me, 'don't. I've had this letter from her today – I'll just read you the relevant bits.' She pulled on a pair of spectacles and read in a low monotone, 'Ever since I have met Karen Armstrong my life has been a misery. You, Mrs Jameson, have been my one true friend in Oxford while Karen has gone round committing crimes and atrocities to lay them at my door and ruin my career.' She snatched her spectacles off and looked at me silently, smiling slightly.

'Crimes and atrocities,' I breathed.

'Mad, of course. Quite, quite mad.' She looked at my horrified expression. 'Oh, I don't think for a moment there's anything in it! Good heavens, no! I just didn't want you to waste time trekking out to the Warneford and be met with an ugly scene at the other end! That's all.'

'But why me?' I asked. 'Is it because I've been accepted to do research and she hasn't?' If I only managed to get a good enough degree to win a government grant, I would be staying on at Oxford for at least another three years, writing a doctoral thesis on Tennyson. The prospect filled me with a giddy and dazed bliss. I'd even found myself some free lodgings with an academic family, the Stanleys, in return for help with their small son. Everything seemed to be working out at last. If – if – I managed to get a really good degree.

Mrs Jameson nodded. 'I expect so. And also, somewhere, there may be envy of the fact that you've escaped from your convent. Something she'll never be able to do, poor woman.'

'At least,' she said, as I got up to go, 'at least, whatever your life brings in the future, you have managed to escape. Whatever happens, I'm convinced you're better out of your convent.'

I smiled back at her, suddenly confident. 'Yes. You're right. Absolutely right.'

*

It was a hot, sticky day in July. The room in the Examination Schools seemed to echo emptily as the five of us trooped in and sat in a miserable little huddle against the wall. We stared in terror at the Board of Examiners who were sitting around three sides of a large table in the bay window, sixteen dons in full academic dress. They were looking at us with a mixture of boredom and disdain. Opposite them was one lonely chair and the ten question papers of the final exams we had sat last month.

It was a good sign to have a Viva; in the English faculty only those who were borderline cases between classes were summoned to the oral examination as well as all candidates who were being considered for a First Class Degree. No Viva, no First. Worriedly I reconsidered all the weak spots in my paper. Vivas, I knew, could go on for hours. I could feel my brain stalling and seizing up in panic. It was no good, I'd never pull it off.

Miserably I tried to compose my features and listen to the Chairman who was reading out the times for our Vivas, waiting for my own name to be called.

'Miss Ainsworth, could you come along at 9.30?' I looked up at the huge clock on the wall; it was only five to nine now. Perhaps they had to have some last-minute discussions. 'Mr Andrews at 11.00.' My heart sank. Poor Miss Ainsworth, who was sitting next to me, had gone a pale shade of green. One and a half hours. 'Mr Allcott at 2.00 this afternoon, please, and Mr Aitken at 3.30.' I looked up wildly while the Chairman's voice continued calmly. 'And Miss Armstrong,' he nodded briefly with the same courteous little smile that he'd given the others. 'Will you stay here now, please?'

I watched the others troop out of the room and stood up slowly, adjusting my gown.

'Come over here.' He pointed to the chair and I started the interminable journey across the carpet, my eyes, fixed, nun-like, on the ground.

It took a while before I recognized the sudden explosion of sound that stopped me dead in my tracks. It was clapping. I looked up to see the whole of the Board on their feet applauding; the men had doffed their mortar boards. Had they gone mad? I stared in bewilderment at the broad smiles that many of them were giving me. Then, slowly, I understood, remembering what I'd been told of this old tradition.

The clapping petered out. 'Miss Armstrong,' the Chairman said, looking slightly embarrassed, 'we wish to congratulate you on your papers, which were all excellent.'

Slowly I could feel a smile breaking over my face, a warm glow of delight spreading through my body. I had done it. Somehow I had managed to get a congratulatory First. For all my difficulties in dealing with the world, this proved that ultimately I would be able to cope. I would survive. The road stretched ahead of me, clearly and surely.

CHAPTER FOUR

Shalott, 1971

'AND HERE'S YOUR room.'

Judith Stanley pushed open a door at the very end of a dark corridor and I stepped inside, rather apprehensively. The Stanleys' house came as a bit of a shock. The hall was painted scarlet, the living room a violent purple and the kitchen had been a brilliant orange. 'Had once been' applied to most of the rooms, which had clearly not seen a lick of paint for years. Dust lay along the surfaces in peaceful, undisturbed drifts. Everywhere there was clutter. As I walked into the hall I tripped over a coat which lay spreadeagled just inside the front door. (There were some perfectly good hooks just opposite, I noticed, but they seemed to be supporting a grime-laden collection of tennis racquets and garden implements which were wedged confusedly together against the wall.) On every shelf books, papers, coffee mugs with fossilized dregs of Nescafé lurking at the bottom, jostled cheerfully and unashamedly together. Something had seemed to happen to the banister, as a thick rope was slung along the wall instead, and at the top of the stairs we both stepped over a large pile of washing which uninhibitedly blocked our path. I found myself smiling as I remembered the immaculate, starkly ordered rooms of the convent where everything had its place and was rigidly kept in line. But something in me responded to the unconventional colours and the mess. There was a cheerful, clashing disregard for appearances. I'd always been an untidy person before I became a nun and tidiness was a difficult virtue for me to acquire. Perhaps I felt happier in this kind of disorder.

Nervously I looked round my new room and breathed a sigh of relief. The walls were a faded pale green and on the floor the worn carpet had long ago lost any colour or definition of pattern it may once have possessed. There were two pretty, leaded windows surrounded by flowering creeper and green leaves which gave the room a cottagey air. A wash basin, a divan, two sagging armchairs and a desk. All I needed.

'Is it all right?'

Judith Stanley sounded nervous and anxious. This surprised me. At college I'd often seen her striding around in militantly flamboyant clothes, refusing to compromise with either age or elegance. Her long, black hair was straight, and her tanned skin, lined and innocent of make-up, made her look rather like a Red Indian. She never taught me – her subject was statistics – but her students reported her low threshold of boredom, her intolerance of stupidity and her dismissive manner, which made her a formidable tutor. She was, I knew, Left Wing and Radical. It was with a certain trepidation that I had answered the advertisement she pinned to the college board: a free room, centrally situated in Oxford, in return for some rather difficult child minding.

'Thank you, Mrs Stanley, it's very nice.' She relaxed. 'Of course,' she said, 'you'll need a book-case. I've got one, actually, in my other sons' old room. We could go and get it now if you liked.'

I followed her back down the passage. As we passed the pile of washing she gave it an absent-minded kick. A pair of underpants, thus dislodged, fluttered down the stairwell.

'Here we are. Ghastly, isn't it?' she sighed, noting my jaw drop as I looked round the room which was completely papered in sheets of newspaper, now stiff and yellow with age.

'Well, it could be a lovely room,' I said truthfully. It was bigger than mine, had sloping ceilings and the same pretty creeper-framed windows.

'Yes, I know.' Mrs Stanley looked round it, defeated. 'The boys insisted on doing it. One day I'll have to strip it but, you see, it's layers thick.' She scrabbled dismally at the stiff, board-like newspaper. 'It'll take weeks! And they took out the light fitting too, so there's only that tiny lamp.'

'Did you let them do it?' I was amazed. I couldn't imagine ever being permitted to do such a thing.

Mrs Stanley laughed, a rueful sharp bark. 'I wouldn't have been able to stop them.'

'And are they at home now?' I asked. I looked up at the ceiling. 'Fuck Off!' was painted across it in thick, red letters.

'Oh, no. They're all grown-up, finished at University and living in communes being hippies and bricklayers.' Mrs Stanley's face looked stripped suddenly of its stern mask and she looked vulnerable and sad. 'They don't come home often. Here,' she turned abruptly towards a tall white-painted bookshelf. 'This will do and there's another small one downstairs I can let you have. When you've unpacked, come down for a drink and you can see it then.'

'What shall we do with the books in this book-case, Mrs Stanley?'

'Oh, for heaven's sake, call me Judith.' The words were impatient but the intention, I knew, was friendly. She looked hopelessly round the room which was stuffed with old guitars, heaps of books, broken-down gramophones and, I suddenly spotted in the gloom, a bicycle. 'We'll have to pile them up on this bed,' she sighed.

'We must talk about Simon.' Judith handed me some sherry in a tiny silver goblet and went and sat opposite me on the white sofa. There was a strange mixture of elegance and disorder in the sitting room that I liked. It had originally been two rooms but the dividing wall had been knocked down and the other room was now Judith's study, its walls entirely covered with bookshelves crammed to overflowing. The sitting room had large, small-paned french windows that looked out on to an immaculately kept garden that now glimmered green and silent in the evening light.

'Yes, Simon.' I looked back at Judith attentively. Simon was her ten-year-old mentally handicapped son, the reason for my being here. 'What exactly is the matter with him?'

'Well, he's autistic. Do you know what that is?'

I nodded. 'Yes. He's withdrawn, can't communicate with the outside world. Silent all the time.' He sounded a bit like me, yet I felt apprehensive. I'd never had anything to do with the mentally handicapped and wondered how on earth I was going to cope.

Judith laughed. 'Well, Simon's not silent. Far from it! He never stops talking. He loves words.' Her face had softened while she spoke of him and her rather gruff voice took on a range of different inflections expressing anxiety, sadness and a desperate eagerness to present her son in an attractive light. She was defensive too, I noticed, and was speaking more slowly and carefully. 'He has an extraordinary vocabulary. But he talks in realms of fantasy most of the time so he *is* withdrawn in his own world.'

'Has he always been like this?' I asked. Judith stretched out her thin bare legs and studied her feet which were clad in clumsy men's sandals.

'It was a birth injury,' she said. 'I had him very late – he's much younger than my other children, of course. I was forty-six. It was a risk.' I realized how often she must have gone over and over this, blaming herself, feeling endlessly guilty. 'But he was born with the cord round his neck, so for a few seconds he didn't get any oxygen and that destroyed part of his brain.'

'How does he show his injury?' I asked. 'Is he difficult to look after?'

'No,' Judith said quickly, 'not if you treat him properly. You have to latch into his fantasy of the moment and go along with it. He does have terrible tantrums – he'll lie on the ground and scream and then it's impossible to do anything with him.' She smiled ruefully at me. 'I seem to have a particularly bad effect on him that way. Really those temper tantrums are due to fear. You see, he can never get used to things, so a lot of frightening events – like loud noises or thunder and lightning – always retain the force of the unknown and the inexplicable.'

'How awful!' What had I taken on? 'But how do you manage – with your job and everything? He must need full-time attention.'

'Well, he goes to a special school. It's not really right for him, it's for ESN children, and we've got a Nanny. It's her afternoon off. She's a treasure,' Judith said sternly. 'It's vital that you get on with Nanny. She's been with us twenty-seven years. Ever since my daughter was born.'

'Good Lord!' I said weakly. I conjured up a picture of a stiff and starched Nanny in uniform who, judging by Judith's firm tone, was not easy to get on with.

'Lots of people,' and here Judith's tone became angry and impatient, 'said we should have Simon put in a home. But that's ludicrous! We manage very well here. With Nanny and now you. Nanny lives in and has Saturday afternoon and evening off – you and I share him then – and Wednesday evenings, when you'll have him. We can't just send him away. That seems terribly irresponsible to me. And in his own way he's happy here. He adores Nanny and he loves grown-ups – other children worry him.'

'Is that because they're frightened of him?' I asked.

'Yes, I suppose it is. And they're little and scurry about. Simon's very tall for his age. But he meets lots of interesting people here and he loves a lot of our friends. Then we've got a house in Cornwall where we spend the Easter and Summer Vacs and that's marvellous for him. It's a very big house on a cliff and he feels less hemmed in. You must come with us down there. We have lots of nice people to stay.'

'Thank you,' I said weakly.

'You see,' Judith was still arguing with an invisible foe, 'in many ways it's better for him here than in a home. He's stimulated by adult conversation – he'd never have developed his vocabulary as he has in a home where most of his friends would have been sub-normal. And he can read. The doctors told me I mustn't push that, that he'd never be capable of reading. I think that they thought we were obsessed with it because we're academics. But it happened by accident, really. He used to sit next to me at breakfast while I read the newspaper, so to keep him quiet I used to make him pick out all the "o"s, then the "a"s and so on and suddenly he started reading by himself.'

'Will he read to himself?' I asked, brightening at the prospect of some kind of civilized activity.

'No, he hasn't the concentration for that.' My heart sank. 'He likes being read to, but Nanny does that, usually. You must find your own thing to do with him. He tends to put people in compartments and he'll never allow you to usurp some-body else's activity. I play backgammon with him on Saturday evenings – or try to,' she grimaced. 'He usually gets in a temper with me. And he helps me in the garden and we go for a walk.'

'I see. What are my "duties" exactly?'

'Well, you'll have him after supper on Wednesdays in your room until he goes to bed at about 9.00. Then for about an hour after lunch on Saturdays until I get home from college. You and I work in shifts on Saturdays. I'll have him at about 2.30 and keep him for the afternoon and give him his supper. Then you have him after supper in your room. Like Wednesdays. Oh, yes, and there's something else I haven't told you. Simon's an epileptic.'

Oh, no! Hideous pictures of shuddering, incontinent bodies, mouths foaming, high-pitched screaming throats and diabolical violence flashed through my mind. Then I looked up at Judith's face. Yet again I was struck by its vulnerability. She gave the impression of being so brittle and cerebral in college and yet she loved Simon and obviously suffered with him blow by blow. It would have been so much easier to have just shoved him in a home.

'I *am* sorry,' I said.

She smiled wanly at me. 'Yes, that happened last year. He had his first fit in the kitchen one Saturday afternoon. He has tablets now, of course, but he still has the occasional fit – usually when he's overtired or has done anything particularly exhausting or exciting.' She took breath ready to give me the next lot of instructions and then jumped to her feet. 'Have some more sherry. Sorry to tell you all this at once but it really *isn't* as bad as it sounds. You're not worried, are you?'

'No, of course not,' I lied, and watched Judith refill our glasses, striding across the room gracefully yet stealthily, like a rangy cat, in her leather mini-skirt and ancient suede jerkin. She must, I realized, be fifty-six, but she didn't look anywhere near that age.

'So.' Judith filled my glass and sat down again, legs crossed, looking in the fading light more like an Aztec now than a Red Indian, with the contours of her face shadowed sharply. 'Because of the fits somebody has to sit with him while he goes to sleep. That seems to be the chief danger-spot and he really can't cope with them alone. I have to sleep with him – '

'Do you?' I looked at her aghast, realizing afresh how this problem had smashed right across her life.

'Yes. You see, he's terrified of the dark. And my husband is such a light sleeper that he'd never get any sleep at all and Nanny simply isn't strong enough. She's getting on and needs her sleep. We have the big room at the top of the house. On Wednesdays and Saturdays you'll sit with him until I come up to bed and then I wonder if you'd be willing to relieve Nanny on other nights if I'm late, out at a dinner or something? Only if you're free, of course. You can read,' she added hastily. 'He'll go to sleep with my bedside light on and you can sit on my bed till I come up.'

'Fine,' I answered, hearing my false heartiness fall hollowly into the room.

'Well,' Judith consulted her large men's wrist watch, 'he'll be back soon. My husband's taken him out in the car, so that you could settle in in peace. I do worry about that. He's a terrible driver, my husband. He never has his mind on the road.'

There was the rattle of a key in the front door. My heart missed a beat and I leant back in the battered leather armchair trying to look casual and interested.

'He'll be very shy at first – might even throw a tantrum,' Judith warned me in an urgent whisper. 'The thing to do is to take no notice. He'll come round eventually when he gets used to you.'

I nodded and swallowed hard.

'Mummy!' A loud yell came from the front hall together with a clatter of footsteps. 'Mummy! Mummy!' The voice was sharp and imperative.

'In here, Simon.'

There was an explosion of footsteps behind me as Simon burst into the room.

I was quite unprepared for him. During my conversation with Judith I had been bracing myself for a drooling idiot, blank, dull eyes, lifeless hair, gangling limbs. When I turned round in my chair to look at Simon the forced smile I had nervously plastered on my face turned involuntarily into a real smile of pleasure. He was beautiful. He stood tall and slim – almost as tall as I, his skin delicately sunburnt, his face long and elegantly structured with piercing blue eyes, framed by golden curls. When he saw me he stopped dead in his tracks.

'Who is that?' He spoke quietly, separating each word and speaking each one very distinctly. He pointed at me and stared. It was not a friendly stare.

'It's Karen, Simon. She's come to live here and help to look after you. Won't that be nice?' Judith's last question was spoken nervously with an anxiety that belied the sentiment. Simon continued to stare at me with hostility.

'Hello, Simon.' I could hear the same anxiety in my own voice and cursed my stupidity.

Simon suddenly ducked his head away and walked to the far end of the room. His gait was the only thing that gave any hint of a handicap, I noticed. He shuffled clumsily and his arms hung by his sides like unco-ordinated parts of his body.

'Go away!' he roared suddenly and flung himself face downwards on the floor. Judith made a reassuring face at me and went on talking, crossing the room and kneeling beside him.

'Karen's such a nice girl, Simon. Why don't you come and say hello? She'll be sleeping in the room next to your playroom and perhaps later you can help her finish her unpacking.' God forbid, I quailed at the prospect. From Dr Stanley's study next door the strains of a Mozart piano concerto stole into the room.

'Be quiet!' Simon yelled again, 'or I shall become very angry indeed!'

Judith gave up and came and sat wearily back on the sofa. 'Edwin!' she called. 'You must meet my husband,' she added to me.

'What?' A muffled rejoinder from the next room competed with the Mozart which then stopped abruptly.

'Come here and meet Karen!'

There was another confusion of footsteps in the hall. The door of the sitting room was flung back after much fumbling and rattling of the door handle and Dr Stanley appeared. He came towards me, his clever, Jewish face smiling absently as though he had just been snatched from another world; a mane of uncombed and windswept hair flew around his head, and his clothes were untidy and did not quite fit him. As he walked I suddenly realized that Simon's shambling deportment and swinging arms were not part of his handicap; they were his father's.

'How do you do?' We shook hands. 'It's very nice to have you with us.' He was, I realized, intensely shy.

'This is Karen Armstrong,' Judith said. 'Karen, Edwin Stanley.'

'The Royal Arms!' The words were spoken loudly and deliberately from the jumble of limbs on the floor. We all turned eagerly in Simon's direction. He continued to lie on the floor, face downwards. 'The Royal Arms,' he announced again.

We all looked at one another. Dr Stanley shrugged his shoulders elaborately as he flung himself into an armchair near the bookcase, seeming to land in it safely by chance rather than by design. 'A pub, I suppose,' he muttered. 'I don't think we've taken him to one called the Royal Arms. He probably saw the sign during our drive this afternoon. Simon, tell Mummy and – er – Karen where we went this afternoon.'

'The Royal Arms.' Simon was transfigured. He scrambled into a sitting position and beamed happily at us all, his eyes alight. We stared back smiling but mystified.

'No, we didn't go to the Royal Arms, Simon.' Dr Stanley's voice was husky and patient. 'We went to – ? Can you remember?'

'No.' Simon flapped his arms around, dismissing his father's question as an irrelevance, still beaming. He got up, shuffled back towards us and pointed at me, his head on one side, making a careful assessment. 'The Royal Arms!'

'Oh!' I suddenly understood. 'My name. *Arm*strong.'

'Yes!' Simon was entranced with his own joke.

'Oh!' His parents' faces, which had been straining in an effort to comprehend, relaxed in relief and delight.

'That's a good joke, Simon,' Judith said.

Simon came up close to me, having finished his scrutiny to his own satisfaction. He smiled angelically into my face. 'It's the Royal – ?' He left the sentence unfinished.

'*Arms*!' I capped and we laughed at each other. We had made connection.

'Simon, what about helping Karen and me to carry the little book-case up to her room,' Judith said to capitalize on this unlooked-for harmony.

'Yes!' Simon danced into Judith's study and proceeded to fling the books with joyous abandon round the room, despite his mother's pleas for him to go gently and quietly. I tried to retrieve the books and pile them neatly on the floor. Fortunately there were not too many of them.

'Mummy! What's this?' Simon was suddenly arrested in his activity. He bent low over the book-case, peering into the crevice between the book-case and the wall. 'Karen,' like his father again he did not pronounce his "r"s, 'come and have a look at this.'

To humour him Judith and I went over, only to have our smug

and superior expressions wiped from our faces in genuine astonishment.

'How ludicrous!' Judith breathed entranced. 'It's fantastic! Edwin, come and have a look at this.'

A small rose tree had somehow forced its way up from the foundations, broken through the floorboards and grown, thin and spindly, behind the bookcase to a height of eighteen inches. We all stared at one another and burst into astounded laughter. It seemed to epitomize the extraordinary nature of my new home.

'It's a tree!' Simon danced round, 'growing in the living room!'

'Nature reasserts itself in the midst of human chaos,' Dr Stanley murmured in self-parody but in genuine pleasure at the phenomenon. He looked at me interrogatively. 'There's a poem – what is it? "Laughing Ceres re-assumes the land."'

'Pope,' I answered. '*The Epistle to Burlington.* "Deep harvests bury all his pride has planned". Nature getting its own back on the horrible country house.'

'"And laughing Ceres re-assumes the land."' The rose tree and all else forgotten, Dr Stanley went back to the living room to hunt for a copy of Pope.

'You'll have to keep that rose tree here,' I said to Judith as we staggered out of the room under the weight of the bookcase. Dr Stanley nodded serenely at us from the sofa, his spectacles askew, clutching the Complete Works of Pope in an awkward grasp. 'Marvellous poem,' he said, watching our efforts absently.

And so my new life began.

In one sense academic research was the worst thing I could have chosen to do. In fact I have more than a sneaking suspicion that graduate research – in Arts subjects at any rate – is potentially one of the most unhealthy and dispiriting occupations open to man. At Oxford, anyway. For one thing Oxford became a ghost town overnight, emptied of all my friends who had had the courage to uproot themselves from the safe groves of academe and seek their fortunes in the great world outside. There were fortunately two exceptions: Jane, who like me had graduated with a First, was also doing research, on Baudelaire, and Charlotte, who had installed herself in a bedsitter up the Iffley Road, was beginning her career as a writer, working in the local Tax

Office as a clerk to pay the rent. But apart from them – and apart from the huge blessing of the Stanleys (one of the greatest bonuses Fate ever dropped in my lap) – I was alone. This, of course, was the last thing I needed.

Writing a thesis is not at all like working for a BA degree, where you are constantly guided and your assignments are all short-term. You are faced with five years of solitary study sailing up a creek of arcane and possibly useless knowledge. If anybody else *does* know anything about it you've picked a bad subject, for an Oxford DPhil must be entirely original. So in October 1970 I started sailing even further away from the rest of the world. Looking back on it now I am appalled. Surely I could have seen that I had enough problems relating to the world without this. It is so obvious that I was substituting for my religious cloister another cloister that was just as exclusive, just as rigid in its demands, just as limiting in its aims.

Perhaps at some level I did realize. It was the cloistral aspect of research that was precisely so appealing; it was so like the world I knew – cerebral, unconcerned with the emotions, pure and passionless. I felt safe. Freedom from any cloister at all was not only terrifying; I had no conception of a life that had no confining walls. I literally could not see that there was a life after Oxford.

If I'd gone to London, thrown myself full-tilt into the raw world there and then, I would have had to knock down the walls that still shut me off from the rest of the world. It could have been the making of me. Or the breaking. Because of course in another sense Oxford was all I could cope with at that time. Whereas now I cannot imagine a life spent away from London, this huge, casual city, in 1970 it could have finished me off altogether. Would I have been able to form for myself a village full of friends, who might live scattered all over the vast metropolis but nevertheless form a charmed circle round me, protecting me from London's huge impersonality? Now I have such a circle of close friends; seeing them is an excitement and a joy all the greater because I had to wait so long to get them, and because in London the obstacles to friendship are so great that they add a fillip to any relationship. I love the hurly burly of London life now, but I doubt if I could have managed it twelve years ago.

As my Oxford life darkened round me during those research

years I clung limpet-like to the fact that academic work was something I could do. And do well. It never occurred to me that there were other things I might be able to do better, or at least with massive enjoyment. I was so delighted to have found something I could manage in this world that I blocked out 90 per cent of it in favour of the safety and familiarity of the world of scholarship.

And so my new life began. For the first few weeks I managed to impose my own shape on the day. In fact it seemed fun. I had a gas ring in my room but I was allowed to use the Stanleys' kitchen whenever I wished. It was never a question of my being excluded from a close family life – cooking my solitary meals while listening to the family and Nanny eating in the Dining Room. Far from it: we were a houseful of separate people, eating, sleeping and living separately but co-operatively. Nanny and Simon ate together, but Dr Stanley, Judith and I queued up for the use of the cooker or skirted round one another politely while we cooked three separate meals. Usually Dr Stanley and Judith lunched and dined at their own respective colleges, sometimes one would be at home in the evening, rarely were we in all three together. After breakfast when Simon left for school the house emptied. There were just Nanny and I in the house. And Nanny *was* a treasure: an apple-cheeked, white-haired, archetypal nanny without a grain of starch, devoted to the family, doing her best to fight against her arthritis and age and the rising chaos in the house.

The day would begin with the sounds of confusion downstairs. Edwin Stanley rushed about the hall with cups of coffee which he put down and forgot about, Judith studied the newspaper, looking gaunt and weary in a brown camel-hair dressing gown and black National Health reading glasses, her uncombed hair pushed sternly behind her ears. And Simon chattered ceaselessly, reading out scraps in the newspaper. We were all performing an intricate minuet round the toaster with Nanny as the only peaceful focal point.

'Moon rises!' Simon invariably shouted, rushing down the passage into the kitchen. 'Karen, Moon rises! 6.45!'

'What *is* he talking about?' I asked Nanny that first morning.

'It's in the paper. The time the Moon rises each evening. It's the first thing he looks for every day.' Nanny shook her head, smiling over the saucepan of porridge. 'It's one of his little games. You'll soon get used to us, Karen.'

And so I did. I got used to waking up to Simon's imperative announcement every morning that the moon would rise, to a house where rose bushes grew in the living room and where the walls were covered with newspaper. When I came in and Simon was in the house I got used to the unfailing ritual of his greeting.

'The Royal —!' he shouted from Nanny's room where the two of them watched the television.

'Arms!' I shouted back as a matter of course, checking in. I too was absorbed into the rhythms of the house which gradually came to be the only place in the world which was strange enough to absorb my own strangeness.

I looked down at the scales. Seven stone twelve. Good. I felt a relief and a sense of achievement. I'd lost two pounds already this week. And it was only Wednesday. I might, if I really tried, manage to lose my target of five pounds by Sunday morning but — there was no doubt about it — the weight was dropping off more slowly now. The first half stone had been easy. Once I hit eight stone, though, I stuck for nearly a week. I had to cut down my intake of food still more.

It started quite slowly. I'd taken to missing lunch. Somehow it began to feel obscene to sit alone in an empty house, stuffing myself with food. I'd never eaten alone before. For nearly nine years all my meals were taken in large rooms or dining halls crowded with people. Sometimes, downstairs, I could hear Nanny getting her own mid-day meal and knew that she was cooking up a few scraps left over from yesterday, listening to the radio for company. I'd never catered for myself before and the price of even the simplest meal for one person shocked me. In fact I had plenty of money. My post-graduate grant was ample for my wants because, unlike most students, I paid nothing for my lodging. But that autumn I spent money extravagantly. The midi skirt had arrived. Joyfully I rushed out and bought myself some calf-length skirts and dresses and threw away my mini skirts, resolving that never again, no matter what fashion dictated, would I wear anything of that sort.

Yet a renewed interest in my appearance made me scrutinize

my body more carefully. For the first time I noticed how big – in fact how enormous – my hips and stomach were in relation to the rest of me. No doubt if I'd lost a little weight before, even the mini would have suited me better. My thighs were far too large, indeed my legs looked like tree trunks. I'd really have to see about losing some weight. I was eight stone twelve. Perhaps, just for a start, I'd bring myself down to eight and a half stone.

Missing lunch seemed the obvious solution. I needed to economize after spending all that money on clothes and it would mean that I could work all day without interruption. The hunger pains I suffered during the afternoon became a matter of pride. I was getting far too soft with myself lately. And when, each morning, I studied the scales in the bathroom, I had a sense of virtue rewarded. There was an achievement here, something that could be measured accurately day by day and, as I sank deeper into the bottomless quagmire of my research, it became more and more important to be able to look at some areas in my life where I was being successful and to weigh up my success.

Because what had my life amounted to, really? I'd failed as a nun and chosen myself rather than God. Now that I had my First I wondered why I had been so anxious to acquire it. If I'd managed to get one, a First couldn't be such a massive achievement after all. I'd forgotten that all worldly success was ephemeral. Nothing lasted and nothing except God could completely satisfy us. What was it St Augustine had said? 'Thou hast made us for Thyself, O God, and our hearts are restless until they rest in Thee.' My decision to be a nun was an acknowledgement of that truth and my pursuit of worldly glory was a ridiculous deviation from everything I really believed.

When I got down to eight and a half stone I still looked pretty much the same. There seemed no improvement whatever. I was overweight because I indulged my body and that reflected my soul which was puffed up with pride and vanity. As well as cutting out lunch I now cut out all bread and butter and nibbled dry crispbread and drank black coffee for breakfast. For supper I allowed myself two boiled eggs. I noticed how much money I was saving. Good. It was disgusting, really, how much money I'd been throwing away irresponsibly to cram myself with food I didn't need. Everybody seemed to eat too much. Wherever I looked in the streets I seemed to see men with massive beer bellies or women with protuberant breasts and enormous barrel bottoms. How effete we were in the West. No wonder the Communist countries thought we were decadent. Every other shop seemed to sell food; the windows were jammed with buns from which cream and jam exploded, with the raw flesh and pallid carcases of dead animals, with mountains of butter and pyramids of bread. I found a new diet which didn't deal in calories. The high figures involved there began to horrify me; the idea of eating anything with two hundred calories became frightening. This new diet dealt in starch units from one to ten. If I cut out butter, bread, sugar and ate plain yoghourt, cottage cheese and a particular brand of crispbread as well as my eggs I need only eat five starch units a day – only a third of those prescribed as a minimum if you wanted to lose weight.

The weight dropped off satisfactorily. My hip bones suddenly appeared, so did my ribs. My flesh was vanishing, ounce by ounce, pound by pound. The selfishness and greed for glory which bloated my spirit and made it lose God should disappear with it. It was right that I should disappear too. After rejecting God and divorcing myself from Him I could only wither away like one of the branches that has been lopped off the central, fruitful vine.

'Karen!' Cautiously I parted the curtains of my room and looked out. There, down on the lawn was Jane, hands on her hips, standing in the middle of the Stanleys' front lawn. I smiled, pleased to see her. 'Can I come up?' she shouted. I nodded and indicated the back door which was always left open.

'Karen, where have you *been!*' Jane burst into my room and grasped me firmly by the shoulders. I gasped involuntarily and tried not to stiffen as I still did when anyone touched me. She shook me slightly and let me go. 'You've been terribly elusive recently. Why ever don't you drop round and see me! I only live two hundred yards away, for Christ's sake!'

I smiled at her. This evening she was all in black: a skin-tight sweater and black velvet trousers showed the ample curves of her body generously. Why did plumpness somehow look right on Jane and not on other people? I wondered. Not on me, certainly. Perhaps it was because unlike me Jane was fitted for the delights of the world and the pleasures of the flesh.

'I've been busy, Jane,' I protested. 'Honestly. You know I look after Simon three nights a week. And, be fair! You're nearly always out!'

'But not every night, and not during the day!' Jane retorted. 'No, don't try to slip out of it. You've been becoming a hermit, haven't you?'

'Not really,' I protested, though it was true, I realized. My own room was a haven to me. Night after night I sat listening to music. At the moment I was hooked on Beethoven's last quartets, and the witty yet tragic music brought me to a peace which I found less and less these days when I tried to pray. God seemed to have become very distant. Music was the closest thing I had to peace of mind.

'Well, I'm not standing for it.' Jane strode over to my wardrobe, pulled out my jacket and threw it over my shoulders. I laughed, feeling relaxed and swept along by her. 'Come on! You're coming for a drink. Mark's down from London.'

'Don't you want to be together?' I asked, wondering why indeed I'd kept away from Jane so long. When I was with her she made life seem so much simpler. 'I don't want to intrude,' I said as we hurried down the staircase, jumping over Simon's scooter which lay dangerously in the hall at the foot of the stairs. With couples I endlessly had a feeling that I was an awkward third party, and the world seemed increasingly full of couples. Rose and Brigid married. Charlotte so occupied with her man, Jane in London most weekends with Mark, who now had a job there. My contemporaries seemed engaged in a mating game that I had no part in.

'We *are* together, Karen!' Jane looked at me amused. 'I think you must imagine that lovers spend their time locked in each other's arms whispering endearments all the time! Don't you? Or ceaselessly rolling around in sexual ecstasy!'

I giggled. It did sound ridiculous when Jane put it like that but actually I supposed I had vaguely thought something like that. The private lives of lovers seemed an unimaginable state of affairs, something from which I quickly averted my mind. I had no notion how lovers would behave.

Jane had a room in a hostel for graduate students. It was a nice modern room, large and airy. Mark was sprawled in an armchair and on the bed was Robin, whom I'd seen with Jane on the evening of my first party in the world. He had straight red hair and a thin face, like a rather decadent-looking angel. Mark greeted me easily and handed me a glass of wine which I drank quickly. Tonight I wanted to get away from myself; the wine was blunting the edges of my loneliness. Mark filled my glass again, I listened hard to the conversation the others were having.

'You see,' Jane was pouring wine, talking earnestly to Robin, 'suppose Mark gets a job in – in – Strathclyde or Aberdeen, well.' She turned quickly round at a groan from Mark, who staggered with the wine back to his own seat in mock horror at the prospect. 'You might get a job there and be glad of it! You're not going to get a University lectureship as easily as you would have done a few years ago. Things are beginning to tighten up.'

'And you are, I suppose?' Mark answered back pleasantly enough, but with a dangerous glint in his eye.

'Yes, of course she is!' Robin interposed. He was leaning back on a pile of cushions, watching Jane and Mark curiously, his eyes roaming with amusement from one to the other. 'She's much cleverer than you are, Mark, *and* you know it. And if you get married that will be a problem.'

'Are you really going to get married?' I stared at Jane, astonished. Rose and Brigid, yes, I could see them settling down; they were both dying to have babies. But Jane always seemed to be too independent, and to want too many other things.

'Probably.' She smiled at me and then turned round to grin sarcastically at Mark. 'Can't live without him, really. Besides, he's too handsome. Can't let him slip through my fingers.'

Mark beamed at me. 'Karen needs some more wine.' He gestured at the bottle. 'Robin, fill her up, can't you? You're really putting it away tonight, I'm glad to see. What would your Reverend Mother say if she could see you now?'

I giggled. A golden alcoholic glow was taking over.

'Were you at a Convent school, then?' Robin asked as he leaned across with the bottle. 'So was Jane, I gather. I can't say it's left much of a mark on her.'

'No. But I was a nun, you see, for seven years.' I leaned back in my chair and contemplated the fact, which suddenly seemed rather detached from me and was floating away like a champagne bubble.

'A nun!' Robin's thin effete face lost its cool for a moment.

'Were you really? So that was why you'd never heard of the Beatles! I *see*! A nun – really?'

'Really and truly!' I said carefully, raising my glass in mock salute.

'Karen!' Mark was delighted. 'You're very laid back tonight. I've never seen you so relaxed.'

'Mmm. I must get drunk more often.' I was only half joking. For once I was forgetting the weight of guilt and my body felt my own.

'You look better,' Jane replied judiciously. 'Perhaps Karen needs to drown her sorrows.'

'Don't we all,' said Robin lazily, refilling Jane's glass. He looked back at me. 'You a nun. Wow. You've made my evening.'

'I must say, it's nice to see Robin's composure shattered ever so slightly,' Mark said, holding out his own glass.

'Yes, but Jane,' I leant across to her. I was tired of the ex-nun topic for one evening. 'What will you and Mark *do* if you get jobs in different places? You won't give up your career, will you? I just don't see you doing the housework.'

'God forbid!' Jane protested and rumpled Mark's hair affectionately. 'You're lucky, Karen! At least you haven't got that problem yet!'

'You're not getting married, then?' Robin asked me. 'You will! All women do in the end!'

'Of course she will!' Mark was sitting next to Jane on the divan now and had put his arm round her. Jane leant against him, her head fitting perfectly into the hollow of his neck. 'You want to be married, don't you, Karen?' She smiled dreamily up at me, flushed and happy.

'I don't know,' I replied slowly, aware of Robin's intent gaze.

'Or are men the problem?' Robin persisted. His pale green eyes, cold as pebbles, were fixed on me dully.

'No, of course not!' I said briskly, pulling myself away from the intensity of his stare, retreating back into my inviolate shell yet feeling its fragility. Shells could so easily be smashed and then what would happen to this cowering, quivering self of mine that shrank from the world as often as it put out tentacles to meet it?

As I got up to go, rising rather unsteadily to my feet an hour later, Jane and Mark looked so complete together on the divan. Again I felt cold and lonely.

'I'll be seeing you again soon,' Robin said.

It sounded like a threat.

A potato masher pounded hard into my brain, squeezing it into long worms of sensation which coiled untidily over one another. Automatically I clapped my hands round my skull to keep the slithering mess intact. Terror had become a new dimension in my bed-sitting room. It clung to the walls, twined itself round the curtains and crawled up the legs of chairs and tables. Somewhere a warm liquid was bursting to the surface and running in steady rivulets but my thought processes were so scrambled that I could no longer name this phenomenon as tears, nor did I know that the cavities they were springing from were called eyes. The world was entirely strange to me; nothing was recognizable and all I was aware of was a terrible fear and a panic that turned my insides liquid and froze me so that I was shivering violently. I was slipping off the edge of the world, inch by inch, pushed further and further towards a long tunnel from which I knew I should never emerge . . .

Then I saw them. I had known for some time that there was something else with me. Something I did not want to see. In the corner was a pile of toads. They were a brilliant emerald green; they had long golden legs and forked tongues that flicked towards me. Jewel-like eyes surveyed me coldly as, slimily, they crawled over one another, coupled and embraced, giving off a sweet-sickly stench that made me gag.

On one level I knew that those toads were not there. Rationally I was aware that if I tried to put out my hand to touch them, my hand would meet thin air. And yet I could not connect this knowledge in any way with the fact of what I could see. Mesmerized with horror I watched the toads crawl round the floor. Round and round the room. Coming nearer and nearer to me. And when they reached me I knew that I should die.

These strange and terrifying attacks occurred more and more frequently. Shopping one day in Cornmarket, I watched in horror the women behind the till in Marks & Spencer swell to monstrous size. Their faces became deformed and their small peculiarities of bone structure became weirdly exaggerated until they no longer resembled human beings. I put my wire basket down on the shop floor and stumbled in a blind panic out of the shop. What was I doing here? Where was I? What had I got in my basket? A deformed woman was shouting at me, her face contorted in strange shapes which I watched with appalled fascination, making no sense of the words. She was pointing to my handbag. I stared at her blankly, panting slightly in terror, nausea creeping through my body. Somebody had pulled my purse out of my bag for me and opened it. Inside were strange round objects, that glinted at me incomprehensibly. People shouted and I ran, ran away as fast as I could, coming to myself ages later in the Radcliffe Square, outside Brasenose.

I stared bewildered at the tranquil scene before me. On my left the Bodleian rose, court after court stretching peacefully away from me. It was November and today a light, cold rain was falling. With a start of surprise I realized that I was shivering and wet through; my hair was hanging lank and sodden round my face. Gradually I felt the panic die away, felt a click in my head and the world fell back into place.

I hurried home to the Stanleys, seeking the safety of my room. But this safety I knew was a delusion. This strange insanity could fall like a bolt from a clear sky wherever I was. It was so odd. I felt perfectly well, even happy most of the time. In other respects my mind was working normally and I enjoyed grappling with the new problems of my thesis. And usually I fell back into that normality again, away from the spectres, the terrors of my mad new world of horror.

But what – and suddenly I felt cold with fear – if one day my mind stayed in this madness? And if madness were to be my lot, even if it never got any worse than this, would it not be better to be dead?

Simon sat at my desk, his head clasped between his hands, rocking it backwards and forwards. His dressing gown had come undone and it spread outwards, touching the ground, and his pyjamaed legs twined themselves in fear round the legs of my chair.

'What's the matter, Simon?' I pleaded. 'Come on, look at me and tell me what's wrong.'

He obstinately turned his face away, as he always did when anyone asked him a direct question that was not part of his fantasy world. His chin was pressed down hard on his chest and he muttered carefully and distinctly in a growling undertone.

'Karen wants to know what's wrong. But Simon refused to answer her. Absolutely refused. The question was impossible.'

I looked at him helplessly, marvelling at the degree of articulateness that surrounded the central blank of his brain. If it had not been for that birth accident he would have been brilliant. I knew what the trouble was tonight. Nanny, when she had brought him into my room, had whispered:

'He thinks there's going to be a storm. It was those black clouds we had earlier. I've *told* him there won't be. But . . .' She sighed and shook her head.

Simon still refused to look at me. Was it really an imminent storm that frightened him or was the storm only a shorthand for nameless terrors that without warning plunged him into mental paralysis? Judith had told me that these strange attacks of his were probably related to his epilepsy; that they were a state called *jamais vu* when a temporary electrical seizure empties the world of its consoling familiarity.

'Look.' I took his hand, but he instantly snatched it away and clapped it over his ear. 'There isn't going to *be* a thunderstorm. If you like we'll listen to the weather forecast.' I knew it was hopeless. At these times ordinary sensible reasons meant nothing to Simon.

'I've got a record with a lovely thunderstorm on it,' I said. 'You can hear the thunder and the lightning quite clearly, but it's all been made into lovely music by a man called Beethoven.' Simon lifted his head and stared at the wall over my right shoulder but I could tell he was listening. 'And then,' I went on, 'suddenly it's all over and you can hear the thunder going further and further away over the hills just as it does when there's a real thunderstorm. And everything is so peaceful; the music becomes so happy and joyful.'

Simon swivelled round in the chair and studied my washbasin.

'Would you like to listen to it?' Why not? I suddenly thought. He transforms everything into a ritual to make the terrors of his disordered life as bearable as possible. Perhaps that was the meaning of all ritual. Even religious ritual. The music might formalize the storm for him.

'The Royal – ?' Simon'said softly and interrogatively.

'Arms,' I said automatically and we giggled together. 'Would you like to listen to it?'

Simon got up, walked very deliberately over to the cane chair in the corner and gathered his dressing gown around him. 'Put it on,' he said sternly.

'I *beg* your pardon,' I said, feigning shock and anger.

'You're not angry!' Simon's face was alight with glee. My insistence on good manners and good behaviour was another of our ritualized games. In this house where informality was the order of the day it was a novelty, not a tedious and ubiquitous grown-up requirement.

'I most certainly shall be,' I said, frowning theatrically while Simon wriggled with delight. 'Put it on *what!*'

'Please. Put it on, please.' He came across and sat at my feet. 'Dear Karen.' He stroked my hand and knew that his look was angelic. 'Please, *dear* Karen.'

'All right. Look, you can plug the record player in. There. That's right. Now, I'll put it on. You look at the cover. Look at all those people playing in the country. Now. Listen. You'll hear the thunder very quietly at first, building up and up and *up*! And then it goes gradually away again, as it always does.'

'Karen says the thunder always goes gradually away,' Simon informed the gas fire *sotto voce*, while we listened to the first chords of the storm sequence of the Pastoral Symphony.

At first I acted as a commentator. 'Listen, you can hear the raindrops. Now – there's a first rumble of thunder.'

'R–u–u–mble,' Simon echoed entranced, but after a few minutes he waved me to silence imperiously and for once I did not insist on a 'please' or 'thank you'. He sat at my feet, swaying thoughtfully to the music, conducting it with, I noticed, a perfect sense of timing and rhythm. 'Whoosh! There goes the lightning! Bang, there goes the thunder,' he intoned with a real sense of drama, and as the storm faded away he sank back against my knees with a histrionic expression of relief. As the first chords of the last movement soared out joyfully, Simon spread out his arms to the room: 'Now it's a–a–ll – over!' he whispered peacefully and swayed ecstatically in time to the music. At the end of the record, he turned to me quickly. 'Now, I want the other side on – please!' he added hastily.

'Okay, you'll hear a cuckoo this time and some people dancing.'

At the end of the evening I was as spellbound as Simon. With him, watching his delight, I rediscovered not only the Pastoral Symphony but also the whole of Elgar's Cello Concerto, which was another hit with Simon. He dubbed the cello 'the deep violin' and when he heard Dvorak's Concerto the following Saturday that became the 'new deep violin record'. His comments were extraordinarily sensitive. 'Listen, Karen, the violins are asking a question.' 'Oh dear, this is so sad. Somebody's crying!' But most of the time he listened quite silently, his face taut with concentration.

As we got up to go to his bedroom a little after nine he stood at the door of my room and bowed solemnly.

'Thank you, Karen,' he said formally, obviously imitating one of his parents' dinner guests, 'I enjoyed this evening very much indeed.' He almost clicked his bare heels together in appreciation. 'In fact,' he nodded sagely and consideringly, 'it was the best evening we've had yet, don't you agree?'

'Yes, I quite agree,' I said with perfect truth. The time had flown by. 'I enjoyed it too.'

'So, can we listen to your records every time I come into this room?'

'Of course. Whenever you like. Next time, we'll hear something different.'

'Something different *and* the thunderstorm again, please.' Then he snapped out of his courteous pose and became a child again. 'And now, off to the lavatory!' he yelled, and then, mimicking me, 'And don't forget to pull the chain.'

'Karen! Can you just come in here a moment?'

I had just come downstairs to wash up my supper things and heard Judith calling me from the dining room. She was standing in front of the mirror that covered the far wall, examining herself carefully.

'What do you think?' she asked worriedly.

There was nothing new in her asking my opinion. During the months I had lived at the Stanleys' I had come to know her well. She never came into my room – that she would have regarded as an intrusion on my privacy – and I rarely went into her study, or the sitting room, but we did have many conversations on the stairs or in a whisper beside Simon's bed when she came up to relieve me at night. In many ways I felt more at ease with her than I did with anybody I had met since leaving the convent, which was odd because she was a generation older than I, an atheist, an ex-communist, a free thinker. We could not have had more different backgrounds. She would offer me the latest titbits of college gossip, filtering the characters and personalities through her highly critical mind, or talk to me about her children or her work.

She was dressed ready to go out to dinner.

'That's from Campus, isn't it?' I asked, naming the fashionable and expensive boutique that had recently opened. Judith nodded and continued to turn this way and that in front of the mirror frowning slightly. She was wearing a gorgeous garment of many colours that swept the ground.

'It's lovely,' I said, 'the colours are great.'

'Yes, but,' she smiled nervously, 'don't you think it's a little risqué, perhaps?' she asked, turning to face me.

'Oh Lord!' The garment was split right up the middle, almost to her waist. 'Judith, I think you're supposed to wear that with trousers underneath.'

'Ssh!' She looked nervously over her shoulder. 'I don't want Edwin to notice. No' – she returned to her anxious scrutiny in the mirror – 'trousers would be much too bulky, don't you think? And anyway I haven't got any the right colour.'

She turned back and looked worriedly at me. I sighed and laid my supper tray on the table. 'What about a black skirt?' I suggested.

'Oh, no! no! That would ruin the line. No, it'll be OK. I can stand with my handbag here. Look.' She stared defiantly into the mirror. 'That's fine!'

'But you *can't* clasp your bag in that position all night.' We both started laughing.

'Is that all you've had for supper?' Judith was looking at my supper tray. 'One boiled egg? What did you have with it?'

'Oh, some Ryvita,' I said quickly, 'and a coffee.'

'It's not enough, Karen.' I could see that she was dying to ask me what I'd eaten for lunch, but that would have been an unwarrantable invasion of my privacy. 'You're getting terribly

84

thin,' was all she would allow herself. I smiled my distancing nun-smile. This time I was pushing someone away on purpose.

'Look,' Judith said quickly, 'I've been meaning to ask you. Why don't you have lunch with us on Sundays? It's the only meal we all have together and as you're a full member of the household it's odd that you should be upstairs on your own.'

Strangely enough the idea was appealing. 'Thank you,' I said, 'that would be lovely.' We returned to our viewing of the dress.

'Look,' I said at last, 'why don't I put a few stiches in it here? Just a few; it would make all the difference.'

'Ssh! Edwin's coming! Don't call his attention to it and he won't notice.'

Dr Stanley threw himself into the room looking untidily elegant in a dinner jacket. 'Are you ready?' he asked. 'Are you driving or am I?'

'Oh, I'll drive.'

As they walked through the hall, I heard him ask in a resigned voice, 'Haven't you forgotten your skirt?'

'I'm mad!' Charlotte exclaimed. 'There's no other word for it. Quite mad!'

We were sitting, crammed closely together, in Charlotte's tiny bed-sitter in South Oxford, up the Iffley Road. There was just room for a bed, a desk and a washbasin. An old-fashioned electric fire scorched our legs. It was very different from Jane's sophisticated room at Cairncross Hall yet I enjoyed coming here. Charlotte seemed to fit into the world less easily than Jane, for whom it seemed, in so many respects, tailor-made. Indeed if I wanted to see Charlotte I had to come and visit her in her room; she could scarcely ever be persuaded to leave it. She was in love and her man, Mike, whom nobody was ever allowed to see, dropped in on her sporadically. She was not permitted to know where he lived or his telephone number. Mike, a drifter, who roamed the countryside aimlessly in his van, eschewing the lures of security and an organized job, had to retain the initiative. It seemed monstrous. Yet Charlotte was in love and was in a mortal terror of leaving her room lest he called and she missed him.

'But he is terribly attractive,' Charlotte went on. She smiled up at me. 'I know you've never seen him, but he is amazingly good-looking and as charming as hell! God rot him!' she added cheerfully. 'But I agree. Something's got to be done. I'm not going to let myself go on like this, which is why I've asked you round tonight. But how are *you*?' she asked suddenly. In desperation I'd confided to her the secret of my hallucinations; like Charlotte I knew I'd have to do something about myself. I couldn't go on as I was, either. 'You look ghastly, Karen. You must take yourself off to see a shrink, you know. You really must.'

'I suppose you're right,' I said gloomily. Deep inside me, I felt a pang – of regret? disgust?

'It's not that I think you're mad – no madder than me at any rate,' she grinned. 'It's just that I think you'll miss such a lot.'

'I'll go. Okay, okay.' I smiled sheepishly back at her.

'Good. Well, go *soon*. More coffee?' I shook my head. 'Well, there's something I've been meaning to ask you.' She settled deeper in her chair and took a deep breath. 'My uncle has just been to Paris for the first time in his life. He was bowled over by it, bless him, and he's written me this lengthy, lyrical letter about it all. Look at it!' She waved sheets of thick cream note paper in front of me, covered closely with a neat script. 'He's told me I've absolutely got to go myself! That I'm not to leave it till I'm fifty-eight like him. I've just got to get up and go. As soon as possible. Have you been?'

'Not since I was a little girl.' I had a brief kaleidoscopic vision of the Eiffel Tower, the Champs Elysées and the Galeries Lafayette. And *Jane Eyre*. 'I was ten, I think, and I was reading *Jane Eyre* for the first time. My poor parents were furious! I had my nose in that book the entire time! I didn't see a thing!'

'Well, how would you like to see it now?' I looked up swiftly. Fear had shot through me.

'You see, my uncle has sent me twenty quid to go for a weekend,' Charlotte sighed. 'I've got a moral obligation to go really. And I wondered if you'd come too.'

We sat in silence, looking at one another.

'Why don't you want to go?' I asked.

'Travelling, for one thing. Aeroplanes scare me rigid. I've got a real phobia. And I'm almost as bad about boats. It's no good telling me the statistics and how much safer you are than you are in a car or a bus, because I just don't believe it – Well, that's

86

my first reason! Now tell me yours.'

'Money!' I said. It fell out quite spontaneously before I'd had a chance to think about it. I listened to my reason, turned it round in my hands, examining it carefully.

'But, Karen, you've got plenty of money: you haven't got to pay for your room; you've got a graduate grant. You're rich!'

'Yes . . .' I said carefully, 'that's part of the problem.' I was thinking hard. 'You see, I've never had any money up till now. At home I was too young to handle anything more than pocket money. In the convent I didn't have any money at all and I never had to think about it. I find it so difficult to forget these patterns of behaviour, much as I want to. The conditioning was so powerful.'

'A nun in woman's clothing!' We looked at one another and started to laugh. Everything was so hopeless that it seemed ridiculous. We rocked helplessly back and forwards, hurting with mirth.

'Oh dear!' Charlotte wiped her eyes and leant weakly back in her chair. 'What a pair we are! Phobias about aeroplanes, money!' And we were off again. Every time one of us started to sober up she'd catch the other's eye. As I laughed I felt the tension bleed slowly, warmly out of me. Nothing seemed quite so bad suddenly.

'Look.' Charlotte suddenly sobered up and sprang to her feet. 'We've got to go to Paris. Even if we loathe every minute of it, we've got to go. Just to prove that we can do it.'

'You've got to prove to yourself that you can leave Mike for a few days?' I asked.

'Yes! Because if I do it once the spell will be broken. And I'll be free. And you've got to stop living like the Lady of Shalott, locked in your ivory tower, cowering away from the world outside. And don't tell me what happened to the Lady! That's what we're both afraid of, really.'

'You're right.' I stood up facing her, raising my coffee cup in salutation, feeling in her company absurdly heroic and conquering. 'No more discussion, Charlotte. We're going. This trip is for our survival!'

It's difficult for me now to recreate the sense of terror that the prospect of a weekend in Paris held for me. Travelling has since become one of my major pleasures. I've been across America, travelled from the top to the bottom of the Soviet Union as well as through most of Europe. But then, like the Lady of Shalott, I'd enclosed myself in a system of thought that excluded the world. As with the convent, so also with Oxford, that strangely solipsistic city that ignores the rest of the Universe. Both of them alluring and seductive in their beauty and idealism. Outside Shalott there was only a shadow world, holding no reality for me.

Somewhere I was convinced that I too, if I flung myself into this teeming world outside Oxford, would die. Going to Paris – a symbol, surely, of worldly sophistication and good living – would be casting my lot in with the ungodly. I felt that if I embraced such a way of life – even for a few days – I would cease to be the person I was, the person I had striven through the fire to become. I didn't know of any other mode of being.

Yet I was 'half-sick of shadows'. I knew that a whole wealth of experience was only a few feet away; all I had to do was reach out and take it. But I couldn't be sure that I could.

'Mummy! I'm going to tip the water jug right over!' Simon leant the jug over at a perilous angle and waited, his eyes fixed on Judith.

'No, Simon, don't do that,' Judith whispered ineffectively, as she carved slices of roast lamb onto my plate.

Simon filled his own glass and then slowly continued to pour. The puddle on the table grew until Judith and Nanny managed to prise the jug away from him, when he muttered a hollow groan and flung his face down into his meat and gravy. Nanny and I flew for dishcloths to repair the damage.

Sunday lunch with the Stanleys was not really a peaceful affair. With a large audience Simon acted up, feeling the need constantly to call attention to himself. Judith, whose attitude towards all her children had been permissive, was reluctant to correct him.

'Where do you go to Mass?' Judith asked politely.

'Of course, you go to Mass! A Papist in our godless home.' Edwin stared at me entranced, his forkful of cabbage suspended inches from his mouth, forgotten. 'Fascinating!'

'I go to Blackfriars, the Dominican church in St Giles,' I explained. I had fled there, a refugee from the parish church with its mechanically gabbled masses and inane sermons. The austere spaciousness of Blackfriars with its unadorned grey stone made me feel spiritually free. 'They have a nice Mass on Sundays with coffee afterwards. It's a family Mass; the children are allowed to wander about if they get bored and no one minds if they make a noise.'

'Don't talk about these boring things, Karen!' Simon yelled, bringing his fork down splat onto his plate so that there was a brief volcanic eruption of gravy.

'Ssh! It's interesting what Karen has to say, Simon,' Judith said quietly, wiping gravy off her cheek.

'NO! It isn't, it isn't!'

'It sounds a good idea.' Judith valiantly steered the conversation back to the family Mass, fighting against the odds to preserve the semblance of civilized conversation. 'I remember being so excruciatingly bored in Church as a child.'

'Most of them actually like coming,' I replied. 'It's extraordinary. It's probably because they don't have to watch what's going on so they don't mind doing so.'

'Extraordinary,' Edwin muttered politely, as though he were listening to the habits of a tribe of Polynesians. 'Are the sermons good? They should be; there are a lot of intelligent men there, I believe.'

'They're very good.'

Edwin chewed meditatively. 'I find it fascinating that intelligent people choose to believe all that. I mean, why? You might as well believe in Jupiter and the Olympian hierarchy. Just as many grounds for belief there. Darling, don't do that!' he pleaded fastidiously, as Simon started licking his plate and barking loudly.

'I'm like a dog,' he announced aggressively.

'Simon!' Nanny momentarily restored order.

'Most people don't bother to think,' Judith said dismissively. 'It's a habit, I should think. They can't all seriously believe that mumbo-jumbo.'

'Born in a stable, virgin births, three kings, rising on the third day, eat my flesh and drink my blood. Magic, pure magic,' Edwin murmured wonderingly to his roast lamb. 'Fascinating!'

'And does Catholicism make you happy?' Judith asked, ducking as a boiled potato was hurled by Simon across the room and splattered steamily against the mirror. 'Simon! Eat up now! You don't look ecstatic to me, Karen. Catholicism sounds a monstrous system – a terrible suppression of the intellect. More lamb?' She pushed another piece on to my plate. I had eaten more already than I usually ate in a week. It was free, of course, and I didn't have that sickening dread that overcame me every time I paid for something for myself. But, far more than that, it was the company.

Edwin smiled slowly at me. 'Terrible things the Catholic Church has done over the centuries.' He was teasing me now, gently. 'The Inquisition, the suppression of Luther – and quite incorrect too. As far as I can gather he was quintessentially orthodox when he started,' he went on.

'Yes, he was. You're quite right. Then there was Galileo,' I suggested.

'The Jesuits and equivocation. Don't forget that.' Judith was joining in now. 'Pure hypocrisy, of course. The appalling scale of indulgences.'

'The immorality of the Popes.'

'The sedition under Elizabeth.'

'And you can believe in the Catholic Church,' Edwin nodded with a pure detached interest: 'Fascinating.'

'This conversation has been going on for too long! Talk about something else,' Simon commanded portentously. 'We're not interested in Churches and Popes and all that stuff.'

'Okay.' Judith turned to him. 'You start a conversation.'

'Let's talk about Bonfire Night.' Simon relaxed, now that the conversation was within his grasp. 'Tell me about it, Mummy. Karen, tell me about Bonfire Night.'

Bonfire Night was one of the landmarks of his year. He watched the fireworks with mingled terror and joy, but his real pleasure lay in anticipation, going over and over its rituals in advance – even, as now, six months in advance.

'Daddy, tell about how it will get dark and you will light the Bonfire.'

'And the flames will start to crackle in the twigs,' Edwin obliged.

'Snap, crackle and pop!'

'And you'll be so excited, Simon,' Judith joined in, 'when the fireworks start.'

'Whoosh! But, Karen, *you* may be a bit frightened, but I'll say to you, "It's all right. There's nothing to be frightened of".'

'Thank you, Simon. I'll feel much better then.'

'Daddy! Who was Guy Fawkes?'

'He was a Catholic!' Edwin shouted in glee as he pushed his chair back from the table and the meal ended in laughter.

'I'll do the washing-up, Nanny,' I offered. 'You go on up.'

'Oh, no, Karen, there's far too much for you to do all by your – '

'No, Nanny,' Simon said masterfully, seizing a heaven-sent opportunity to have Nanny to himself a bit sooner than usual and starting the ritualistic words which would now finish every meal I attended at the Stanleys', 'Karen insists on doing the washing-up! She absolutely insists. I'm sorry, Nanny, but there's nothing you can do about it. Karen absolutely insists!'

As I carried the dishes out I glowed with a sense of luxury the intimacy of teasing brings with it. I was happy because the teasing meant that the Stanleys accepted me as one of themselves, despite all my differences. The acceptance I was beginning to encounter in the world, from Charlotte and Jane as well, was novel to me; in the religious life there had been such a toll taken on my smallest fault that this new respect was balm to me. I was not a guest here who had to be pussy-footed around and for whom a special effort was made. I belonged. But how strange that I should feel this sense of belonging in a household that so casually and completely rejected the most important thing in my life – my religion.

Though I would not allow myself to realise it at the time, something in me was reaching out towards the Stanleys' view of the Church. It was a pretty appalling institution – I'd read enough Church History to realize that. And it was so lovely, suddenly, after years of straining seriousness, to laugh at important things. Laughing with the Stanleys had suddenly eased the burden of worry I felt about the Church, just as my laughter with Charlotte had released other tensions. As a nun I was often chided for my 'unreligious laugh' and I had worked hard to acquire the suitably mirthless tinkle. With the Stanleys I was developing quite a giggle.

I couldn't admit openly to myself my worries about my religion. To bring all these worries into the open would endanger my equilibrium, because I knew that I was only just coping. I was enjoying living with the Stanleys, and my research, but so much else was wrong. For a start I was beginning to feel seriously weak. I was now well under seven stone. Frequently if I stood up too quickly the world swam in front of me; often I had to sit down suddenly in the street and riding my bicycle was becoming more and more of a problem. Then there were the hallucinations and the frightening periods of depression that often succeeded them. It was obvious, even to me, that I was on the edge of a crisis.

Provided I kept within the confines of what I could easily manage I could cope. It only needed one rude collision with the world to knock me off balance.

'Karen!' Judith shouted up the stairs. 'Phone.'

'Thanks!' Surprised, I walked down the long corridor into the end bedroom where the second telephone was.

'Robin here.'

'Who?'

'Robin. Don't say you don't remember me.'

'I'm sorry, I – '

'Alas! the vanity of human wishes! I was at Jane's – ages ago now, but I've been in London. You were rather charmingly drunk.'

'Oh, yes.' I remembered. Pre-Raphaelite face. Green eyes.

'I want to take you out to dinner.'

'Oh.'

'Come on. You must have one evening free in the next three months. What about next Friday?'

'No. I'm sorry.' Friday was the day of my first appointment with Dr Piet, the psychiatrist I'd been referred to by my GP.

'Saturday, then.'

'I'm on duty here, with Simon.'

'Good Lord. You are difficult. Monday, then?'

I could, in decency, protest no further. 'All right,' I said grudgingly.

'I'll pick you up at eight. We'll go to the Luna Capresi.'

'Oh. . . . Look, I don't eat very much.'

'No, but you drink, don't you? Eight on Monday.'

Panic-stricken I looked into the receiver. Perhaps I could get measles, flu, break my leg. Anything at all to escape this. Slowly I walked back to my room and put on a record. I shut my eyes and forced myself to breathe calmly. I didn't want to go out. Most emphatically I didn't want it. Don't be a fool, I told myself firmly. I knew I'd got to go. It was like going to Paris with Charlotte. It was a necessary step to survival. I couldn't spend my days locked in my bedsitter, reading Tennyson by day and listening to music with an autistic child by night. And for God's sake, it's only dinner, I reasoned angrily. He hasn't asked to sleep with you.

The very idea made me feel ill. Why was I so terrified when on the other hand I was so painfully lonely? I looked at myself in the mirror. My face was still relatively plump, though I had heavy circles under my eyes from lack of sleep. I turned sideways and looked at myself. Better. Much better than I was. But I was still too heavy. It suddenly seemed vital that I weigh myself again, now.

Seven stone. I looked at myself in the mirror. How could I cut down? I confined myself to a budget of forty pence a week for my food: that got me half a dozen eggs, a carton of cottage cheese, a packet of Energen crispbread. I also got the odd pint of milk which I transformed into yoghourt in my thermos flask. Coffee for breakfast. Four crispbreads for lunch with a scraping of cottage cheese and a cup of yoghourt, and a boiled egg for supper. On Sundays I didn't need an egg because I had lunch with the Stanleys. Supposing I stopped having lunch with the Stanleys? No. They would be offended and, anyway, that was all right. It wasn't all wrong like having dinner with Robin.

Perhaps I could manage with only two crispbread for lunch? It was worth a try.

Later that evening, when the terror came, it wasn't snakes and spiders that I saw. It was the disembodied face of an old man, a senile old man with his head niddle-noddling, his eyes vacant and bleary, a strand of saliva running from the side of his mouth. There was the usual stench and as I felt myself rushing slowly but inexorably down the long dark tunnel that always ended the experience, I felt as though I were slipping off the edge of the world.

'God help me!' I was crying, when the terror stopped and the sadness began. And it wasn't just a conventional expression of helplessness. It was a prayer. But would God answer it?

*

'So you say you have these hallucinations about three times a week?'

Dr Piet looked interrogatively across the table.

'What do you see, exactly?' He pushed his spectacles more firmly on to his nose. A good-looking man, blond, lean-faced and clever-looking, with an expressive curving mouth. Dutch? Flemish? I sat back in the red armchair. No couch, I was relieved to see.

'What do I see?' I took a deep breath. Here we go. Out come the classical Freudian horrors. 'Spiders, snakes sometimes, and lately a man, a senile old man. Just his head.'

'Hmm.'

'Sorry they're so unoriginal and archetypal.'

'Not at all, not at all.' He smiled companionably at me. And wrote them down. 'Spiders . . . Snakes . . . This old man – have you seen him before? Is he someone you know?'

'Yes, I have seen him before, actually.' Objectively I found this interesting. 'About a year ago I was watching a dramatized D. H. Lawrence short story on the television – a very bad short story actually' – Dr Piet smiled at my effort to remain detached – 'called *The Princess*. The last shot showed the senile old man the heroine married in the end. The shot only lasted for a few moments and it was my old man.'

'Right.' Dr Piet scribbled furiously. 'And what do you feel while all this is going on?'

'Terrified. Quite terrified.'

'That figures. But you know they're not real heads and snakes.'

'Oh, yes. But it doesn't make it any better.'

'And in the past you've had fainting fits, which started while you were in your convent? And the eating difficulty started then too?'

'Yes.'

'Anything else?'

'Afterwards – after my visions – I get terribly depressed. And then I'm depressed because of the visions, because I think I'm losing my mind. And my mind's the best thing about me.'

'Why do you say that?' Dr Piet looked up, hawk-like and pouncing. 'Why is it the best part of you?'

'Well,' I spread my arms comically. 'Look at me!'

'What am I supposed to see?'

'I'm not an oil painting!'

'Well, your hair is covering most of your face so I can't see much of that. When did you last go to the hairdresser?'

'1962. Before I entered the convent.'

'Not since?'

'No.'

'Hmm. And then I see you're grossly underweight. But then when I ask you what you eat, I find that you're causing this to happen.'

'So?'

'We'll leave it there for now. Think about it.'

'Is there anything you can do to help me?' I hated the sound of tears in my voice.

'You've got to do the work, Karen. For yourself. Tell me. Do you ever see the man's body in your vision?'

'No. Just the head.'

'You've got quite an obsession with heads and brains, haven't you? The other parts of the body don't seem to count.'

'How clever!'

'And you must be upset about all this.'

'I am.'

'But you're not showing it to me. You're talking about it as though we were discussing a Bergman film. With bright, intellectual detachment.'

'Well, you don't want me weeping in here.'

'I'd much rather you did. When did you last break down and cry in somebody else's presence?'

'I can't remember.'

'I see. The only time you let yourself cry is when you're hallucinating. Right? Or when you're half concious?'

'Right.'

'Think about that.'

'But control's a good thing. If I could control my life I wouldn't be having all this trouble. I wouldn't be here.'

'Well, we don't know that, do we?'

'You haven't told me yet why I see spiders and snakes.'

'No, I'm waiting for you to tell me.'

*

95

On my way home, I stopped off at Blackfriars for Mass. It was the evening Community Mass and because it was a weekday the church was rather empty. Here and there in the half-lit church, a shadowy figure knelt, head in hands, praying silently. On the floodlit altar the Dominicans stood in a huge semi-circle round the altar, celebrating the Mass together.

I knelt down, breathing in a world I knew. The cut and thrust of Dr Piet's questions had been quite clear in their drift. I could see quite clearly where they were going. I didn't want the body; I didn't want emotion. I wanted the austerity and chastity of that ritual at the altar.

The priests in their white vestments and white habits started to say the words of consecration together. Pointing to the white disc of bread in the Prior's hands they proceeded to change it into the Body and Blood of Christ. A rite that for two thousand years Christians had done in memory of Him.

Hoc est enim corpus meum. This is my body.

The disc of bread looked just like a piece of bread still. I could see what Edwin meant by the Church's magical element. As in magic rites all through history, we would all soon walk up to the altar and eat that bread, to make ourselves one with the God-head. The comfort I had received in the purity of the Mass drained slowly away. Was it really true or was it just beautiful? Simon used ritual to hide from the darkness, to grab at comfort when life proved impossible. How could I be certain that the Mass was not just another delusion?

No. I buried my head quickly in my hands to cut out the thought. Yet for a second I felt with anguish the cold breath of a world without God.

CHAPTER FIVE

Dicing with Death

THE LOBSTER LEERED pinkly and evilly at me from the white plate, smothered in a violent terra-cotta sauce. I felt a sprinkling of sweat erupt on my face, which had suddenly gone cold.

'I told you,' I smiled pleadingly across the tiny table for two, 'I just can't eat this.'

Robin smiled back, bland but determined.

'But *I* say you can.'

His small green eyes glinted challengingly as he dug his fork into his own pink mess, right in the belly.

Robin lifted a slab of shell-like flesh to his lips. A drop of sauce was left on his thin, lower lip and I watched his tongue flicker out to retrieve it. He lifted his glass of straw-coloured wine to me in command.

'Cheers.'

'Everything all right, sir?' The waiter hovered respectfully.

Robin tasted, his head on one side, and nodded back discriminatingly.

'Fine. Thank you.'

'It's such a waste of money!' I protested, thinking of the alarming figure on the menu. It was a sum that would have kept me in food for three months.

'Nonsense.' Robin addressed himself to the lobster again. 'You'll eat it, if we sit here all night.' I watched him, mesmerized as he dug his fork into the strong-smelling gunge again, conscious of the light tinkle of conversation from the other tables, the ripple of civilized laughter. 'It's absolute rubbish to say you can't eat,' Robin continued, his mouth full and a strand of lettuce just visible, clinging to the side of his mouth. 'It's pure masochism and self-indulgence. Come on, drink up.'

I raised my own glass to my lips and felt the ice-cold liquid slide effortlessly down my throat. The wine was good, very good indeed, and I waited for the beginning of that glow and security that drink always brought me. There seemed more than a hint of threat in the air as though for some reason a contest had begun. I took another sip of wine and a mouthful of salad. Salad would not make me fat.

'Anyway,' Robin sounded suddenly vulnerable, 'I wanted you to enjoy yourself. I've saved up for quite some time to bring you here.' He shook his dark red hair off his face and looked directly at me, his eyes clouded with the beginnings of a boyish hurt. 'Please eat a little bit, Karen. It's no fun eating by yourself, and a man,' his voice suddenly became husky and serious, 'a man', he repeated, his green eyes studying the table as though he were suddenly bashful, 'hates to have his gifts flung back at him.'

Instantly I felt guilty and in the wrong. 'Sorry,' I murmured, rather puzzled that I was apologizing – after all, I had pleaded with him not to order anything for me – and resolutely raised the warm, pink flesh to my lips.

In my mouth the hot fish mingled with the salt wetness of nausea that sprang up. I spooned more into my mouth and swallowed hard, blinded suddenly by tears of physical distress that flooded my eyes.

'Good girl!' Robin beamed at me in delight. I felt instantly better. After all, it *was* kind of him to take me out. And he was right. I had to make the effort to get well. I took another mouthful and, when I gagged, took another draught of wine.

'So.' Robin's former arrogance and charm were restored and I felt lighter, as though I had somehow restored his equilibrium to him. 'Our mutual friends look as though they are actually taking the plunge.'

I nodded, feeling, after three mouthfuls, off duty for a while. 'Yes, it looks like it. What do you think about it?'

Robin sighed and shook his head. 'Don't misunderstand me,' he said carefully, 'I like Jane; she's a nice, sexy girl. But, my goodness, I'm worried about Mark.'

'Why?' I asked in astonishment. 'Mark seems perfectly well able to take care of himself. He's known Jane for years, he's a tough character. I just hope he really appreciates her. Why are you worried about *Mark*, for goodness sake?'

'Because,' Robin leant across the table earnestly, 'Jane is going to emasculate him if she's not careful.'

'What on earth do you mean?'

'Here, have some more wine. And eat up.'

I bravely took another mouthful, feeling ridiculously under orders. 'Well. Explain yourself.'

'Jane *is* clever. She *is* cleverer than Mark, but she makes no effort to conceal it.'

'But why should she?'

'Because a man,' and again I watched, fascinated, that same serious bashfulness, heard the voice descend to throaty reverence, 'must feel he's in control. If Jane wants to marry Mark she must make him feel superior. Otherwise he'll lose a sense of his manhood.'

I barely noticed the next mouthful; this was all so extraordinary.

'Do you mean that Jane must suppress herself for the rest of her life in case Mark feels his image of himself threatened?'

Robin smiled and filled our glasses again. 'You modern women,' he said softly, smiling to show that he was aloof from a problem which to him was purely academic, 'are going to emasculate a whole generation of men.'

'But what's so special about a man's masculinity?' I asked curiously. 'Why is Mark's masculinity more important than Jane's integrity? Surely Mark would rather have an intelligent wife than not? Surely he doesn't want his ego to depend on Jane playing an elaborate charade with him?'

Robin beamed at me, indulgently. 'I agree with you, of course, it's just that most men aren't able to cope with people like Jane, or women like you for that matter.'

'Women like me?' I echoed, laying down my fork thankfully and praying for the waiter to come and collect the débris. 'I'm not a bit like Jane.'

'No, you're not. But you're quite a challenge, you know, Karen.' Robin looked approvingly at my plate and signed to the waiter. He spoke teasingly. 'At seventeen – yes, I've been checking up on you, doing my homework – you turn your back on the male sex and flee to a convent. You come out, years later. Okay. Not surprising, really, it's a most unnatural life, cooped up with a load of women. *But*,' he leant across the table, his eyes alight with the pleasure of his argument, 'do you make a beeline for men? No! You go on, living a life as pure as the driven snow.'

I found myself laughing back at him. 'How do you know?'

'Well, you do! You are a virgin, aren't you?' Taken aback, I found myself nodding.

'And you're twenty-seven. Yes. I can tell you're a virgin. You're all closed up like a clam. Tight and impenetrable whenever a man comes into the room.' He grinned, boyish again. 'You're not offended, are you? You see, my point is that this is almost intolerable for a lot of men.'

'Why? Do you mean I'm a walking insult to the male sex?'

'Something like that. Christ, if a man had been locked up away from women for seven years, he'd be out sniffing round, furiously randy afterwards. I know a couple of blokes who've been priests. The women they've got through since! But not you! You walk round telling us by your sheer lack of interest that we're absolutely irrelevant to you.'

'I suppose you are, really,' I said thoughtfully. The wine was loosening my tongue, and despite some strange sensations in my stomach, I felt more at peace. 'There have never been any men in my life and I've survived, more or less.'

'Less rather than more, judging by the look of you. Pudding?'

'No, thanks,' I gulped.

'I'll let you off. You were a good girl and ate quite a bit of your lobster. Tell me.' Robin leant back in his chair and surveyed me curiously. 'Did you nuns have lesbian affairs with one another?'

'No!' The surprise in my voice caused several other diners to look our way. 'Sorry. No, we didn't.'

'Why not? There you all were, after all. Frustrated as hell, I should imagine.'

There was a prurience in his eyes that was beginning to upset me. 'It wasn't like that,' I said wearily, 'not at all. The whole emotional tempo was very cold. We never spoke to one another except in a group of three or more. It was the Rule.'

Robin nodded. 'I expect that Rule was designed to prevent just that. So you never saw one another without your clothes on?'

'No.'

'And what about flagellation? Did you do that?' His voice was harsher now, and his eyes narrowed.

'Yes.'

'Till the blood ran?'

'No. Why do you want to know all this?'

'Sorry.' His voice warmed suddenly. 'Have some more wine. I'm not trying to prove anything, love. But it is interesting. You know, we've all read books about nuns but you've done the real thing. You've had such an interesting experience. You mustn't be prickly and over-sensitive.'

'Sorry.' Again I felt strangely rebuked. After all, there was no harm, really, in what he was asking. I made an effort. 'No, not until the blood ran, but it was meant to hurt.'

'Did you have a whip?'

'Only a tiny one, made of knotted cords. We called it a "discipline".'

Robin nodded and I felt his knee momentarily brush against mine. Quickly I drew my legs away, my stomach heaving.

'Did you do anything else in that line?'

'We wore a chain round the top of our arms with tiny spikes in it.'

'Christ, that must have hurt! Did you wear it all day?'

'No, only for four hours a day.' I paused, alarmed at the expression on his face. 'But that's all changed now, I expect, since the Vatican Council,' I added, feeling the need to destroy the image that was clearly building up in Robin's head.

'Let's have the bill.' Robin's voice was husky and his neck was stained with a dark red blush. I breathed more easily and smiled at him. Liberation was at hand.

'Thank you!' The relief that it was over flooded my voice, making it sound warmer than it had all evening.

Robin did not smile back, but solemnly held my eyes with his own steady stare. I felt my muscles constrict in alarm.

'Well,' he said softly. 'What about it?'

'What about what?' I capped foolishly in panic, groping round for more time to find a firmer exit line.

'You know what,' Robin went on tonelessly. Even in my dismay I noted with one part of my mind how clichéd he sounded, how his voice and expression were guying Humphrey Bogart. And not doing it very well. 'You've been asking for it. Begging for it for the last quarter of an hour, love. You don't fool me. You need a good screw. Come on, we're going to my place.'

The room swam and I gripped the tablecloth with both hands. Obscene images flashed through my head and, in my stomach, the lobster cried out in protest. 'No,' I said quietly, feeling the tears at the back of my eyes. 'No.' I struggled to find more words but none would come. Every bit of me was stuttering just one word. 'No.'

'Why not?' Robin leaned back in his chair, smiling a lopsided smile. He still looked confident. One lock of hair fell, like a dark red scar, down his forehead.

Because I don't like you. The words flew unbidden to my brain. I don't like you because you feel superior, because you seem to hate women, because you've made me eat a lobster. Because this evening has been an exercise of power. Because, and here I shut my eyes and breathed deeply trying to still the nausea that threatened to overwhelm me, because I don't like your body. It has nothing to do with me. I hate it when you touch me. Because I hate my own body. The last thought stunned me softly with the force of its impact.

'Well?' Robin was still smiling.

'I don't want to,' I said, noting with relief that none of the revulsion or fear I felt showed in my voice. 'I'm sorry,' I said, 'but I just don't want to.'

There was a silence while Robin studied the tablecloth. Then he looked up and nodded pleasantly.

'Fair enough,' he said. 'Okay, I'll walk you home.'

'There's no need for that –' I began, 'I –'

'I'll walk you home,' Robin repeated quickly. 'Provided that you can bear my company for just a few moments more.'

Guilty, I nodded dumbly and tried to smile slightly and reassuringly, like a woman of the world to whom this kind of invitation was commonplace.

'You're still into masochism, aren't you?' Robin remarked as we turned into the Stanleys' road. I looked up, bewildered. During the short walk home we'd discussed the production of *Look Back in Anger* at the playhouse last month. He made no attempt to touch me. I felt easier with him than I had all evening. 'And sadism,' Robin added gently.

'What do you mean?' I was beginning to feel very sick now. The lobster was getting its revenge.

'This.' With a grip that made me cry out in pain, Robin pulled me over to the Stanleys' garden wall under the old-fashioned lamp-post. His mouth came forcefully down on mine with such impact that our teeth jarred noisily; his breath was coming raggedly in brutal puffs of rage and his knee kicked me hard between my legs. Numb with shock I stood there frozen and, almost as though I were no longer in my body, I noticed his hands kneading my breasts and felt my blouse strain at the seams. Robin was no longer the sophisticated diner-out. He became a thing that clawed and mauled, a tongue that scoured the inside of my mouth and teeth, that bit the side of my neck. Suddenly he released me. Dazed and trembling, my mind wiped of every thought, I leaned back against the wall and closed my eyes.

'You little cunt.' Robin spoke breathlessly and gripped my shoulders, shaking me slowly and deliberately. I opened my eyes and stared up at him blankly, my heart empty, my mind now bleeding. How ugly he is, I thought with a strange objectivity; his mouth hung slackly at the corner, his eyes were round with outrage. 'You cock-teasing bitch. Leading me on. Large blue eyes ever so innocent. Turning me on with your talk of whips and spikes and naked nuns . . .'

'But it was you —' my voice broke through thinly.

'You were laughing at me!' His voice trembled with rage. 'You don't laugh at a man ever. Do you hear me?'

He's mad, I told myself.

'You don't tease me with your cool, clear voice leading me on, eating my food! I will not be teased sexually, do you hear?' There were tears in his voice now and he struck me hard across the face. 'I've just done you a favour, you tight little virgin. Do you understand? That's the nearest you'll come to a man, you frigid bitch.' He slapped me hard on the other cheek and vanished down the road, a figure of trembling righteousness and outraged dignity in the silvery, romantic moonlight.

My head reeling, I listened to his footsteps die away and then turned to the gutter and began to vomit. My body felt unclean and I wanted to purge it of the gross amount of food I had gorged that evening. It was my body that was at fault. How I hated this odd female body of mine, with its curves and secret, hidden mysteries. This body that bled and smelt that was suddenly, after years of decent secrecy, on view for all to see. It was women's bodies that drove men mad, as I had made cool, clever Robin lose his mind this evening. I thought of women's bodies in magazines: the long legs, dark cleavages, luscious breasts. I wanted no part of it. If I stayed safely in the confines of my ivory tower of study and friends, I was all right. But if I went outside that, the world kicked me in the teeth, recognizing me as its sworn enemy.

'Karen, I'm going to say a word that you don't want to hear,' Charlotte warned me gloomily. 'Believe me, I don't want to say it, either. Paris.'

'Oh Lord.' I stared at her dumbly. 'All right. Paris.' I swallowed hard and nodded seriously.

'What about July?'

We sat, staring at each other. Charlotte's large copper alarm-clock ticked loudly, marking the inescapable passing of time.

'You said you had another reason for not wanting to go,' I said tentatively, 'apart from boats and aeroplanes.'

'Mmm.' She nodded and stretched herself lazily.

'Is it anything to do with Mike?'

'Yes, of course it is. Wait a moment.' She sat up in her chair, taut and alert. Down in the hall, three flights down, the communal telephone was ringing. We listened. Charlotte's face was suddenly closed, blank with the effort to suppress hope.

Then she smiled bleakly. 'That's why I don't want to go to Paris.'

'How long is it since he phoned?'

'Three weeks. I know it's crazy! I know I should either drop him or just not let myself be so vulnerable. He's treating me badly. But I can't! I'm afraid that if he comes and I'm not here, he'll never come back again. Which would be a bloody good thing.'

'But we *must* go, mustn't we?' I felt my own heart sinking.

'Yes.' Charlotte spoke firmly as much to herself as to me. 'Oh, it's not just Mike. Really it's not. It's the writing too. I'm stuck in this novel and, you know, I find myself living it sometimes. I feel it's all locked up here with me in this room and that if I go outside or leave it for a while it will crumble away to nothing. Mad, isn't it?' she sighed. 'Here, have some more wine.' She filled our beakers with the cheap, red plonk I'd brought with me.

I didn't understand why I encountered such a strong veto in myself every time the Paris project was raised. 'The spider plants are coming along well.' They festooned prettily down the walls, over the books, hanging from shelves and mantelpieces, giving the tiny room an illusion of life and growth.

Charlotte raised her eyebrows and grinned at me helplessly. 'Who'd water the plants?'

We giggled feebly.

'I know,' I sighed. 'You can make up more and more excuses for not going. I don't know *what* I'm afraid of, really.'

'But we've got to go, haven't we?' She spoke firmly. 'We can't do much more tonight than look into one another's eyes and say "We're going." But next time – *next* time – we'll have to book it.'

We stared at one another solemnly. And nodded.

'This way,' the nurse said, 'down the corridor and it's the small ward on your left.'

The hospital smell, the glimpse of blue bedspreads, a trolley, a wheelchair. Another nurse walked briskly past me, giving me a brisk antiseptic smile. I turned left, afraid of what I might see.

'Karen!' Rebecca's voice was unchanged. '*Thank* you for coming! It's so good to see you. And so quickly too.'

That morning I'd had a postcard from her. She'd been in Oxford Street, on an errand for the community, and collapsed. They'd brought her swiftly to an intensive care unit and now, not quite out of danger, she was in the West Middlesex Hospital.

'Well!' I sat down on the bed. 'How are you?'

In the thin nightdress her frailty was only too evident: the little bones at her wrist which I could almost count, the horror of her profile and the shallowness of her chest. Her skin had a bluish tinge, her eyes bulged even more than when I had seen them last, the flesh around them having wasted away. She smiled at me. For the first time in our friendship, I could see her hair. It was like straw.

'Much better, thank you, really much better. It was awful but they're really good here!'

A nurse bustled in with a tray, laying before Rebecca a plate of baked beans, sausages and chips. 'Here you are, Sister. You eat that up now and I'll be back for the tray in a second.'

Obediently Rebecca lifted her fork and plunged it into the steaming, smelly mess. I suppressed a shudder.

'I'm awfully sorry.' I looked at my watch. 'Have I interrupted your lunch? It's three o'clock and I thought that was the Visiting Hour.'

Rebecca grinned, a death's head grin, and shook her head.

'No. I'm given something to eat every hour, more or less. You see I've got to put on weight quickly. They won't let me out of here until I've reached at least six stone and I've an awfully long way to go.'

My mind reeled. How much could she weigh? Five stone, a mere seventy pounds. And she was so tall. At least five foot ten.

'What about you?' Rebecca eyed me professionally. 'I think you'd better have some of this!'

We looked at one another and smiled ironically. What was it Mother Frances had said: 'You and Rebecca! What a pair!' And here we were, both in our different ways wasting away.

'Don't you find that disgusting?' I asked. I was fascinated to watch the unconcern with which Rebecca was spooning the stuff down. Baked beans, sausages and chips! The calories there must be astronomical.

'No.' She spooned another chip, moist and soggy with grease. 'You see, it isn't like that with me. It never has been. I've always been able to eat. It's just that I don't absorb the food.'

'It's much worse for you, then, isn't it? I mean, it seems as though something inside you has taken you over and is eating you away?' I frowned sadly in an effort to understand. 'At least I'm in control of it.'

Rebecca carefully wiped up the last of the tomato sauce with a piece of sausage.

'It's odd, isn't it?' she said detachedly. 'With all this food I ought to be putting on some weight.'

'But you're not?'

'No. At least I'm not losing any, though, let's look on the bright side. Thank you, nurse.' Two fruit yoghourts and a glass of milk had just been carried in. With cheerful resignation, Rebecca started to spoon in the pink, sticky stuff.

'But what about the Order? They'll have to do something about you now. Now that it's got to this pitch.'

Rebecca nodded and lifted her glass of milk. It seemed almost too heavy for her. 'Yes. I'm going to see a psychiatrist regularly. Ghastly, isn't it? I know! I do feel ashamed, but I must. I can't go on like this.'

'Have you seen him yet?'

She nodded. 'Yes. Several times. This is his ward, in fact, which was why I was moved here. He's a Catholic, which should help.'

'What have you talked about?' I asked curiously. 'Sorry, do you mind my asking?'

'No, of course not. Not you. I know you understand. We've discussed my childhood, really. What I was like before I entered the Order.' She smiled reflectively. 'It's funny. I'd completely forgotten.'

'What were you like?'

'Terribly passionate, violent. I was always losing my temper and shouting, locking myself up in cupboards to make my point. I was a real rebel!'

'Good Lord!' I stared at her in amazement.

'I know!' She sighed slightly.

I thought of Rebecca as a novice. The cool, gentle voice, the downcast eyes, the absolute submission. 'You were perfect!' I breathed. 'When we were postulants, we used to say you were the perfect novice. You were the perfect scholastic, the perfect young nun! You never lost control, never. Custody of the eyes, silence, obedience, religious reverence – you could do the lot! I used to think you were born like that! Where did all the passion go?'

'Aha!' Rebecca shrugged. 'I suppose that's the sixty-four thousand dollar question. It's still there, I suppose, somewhere. Only I don't know where it is. And until I find it, this will just go on and on. I mean, it's not as though I *still* felt angry, passionate and rebellious. What I am,' she said wryly, 'is me *now* – quiet, obedient and all the rest of it.'

The nurse bustled in with a wheelchair. 'I'm sorry,' she smiled at me, 'but it's time for your X-ray, Sister.'

Rebecca pulled at her dressing gown and stood up, uncertainly, beside the bed. Instinctively I averted my eyes from her shrunken form, from the shoulder-blades and hip bones that stuck out like knives through the white nightdress, at the emaciated body that for a second I glimpsed in silhouette.

'Can't you walk?' I asked in horror as she settled herself in the chair.

'She's got to conserve her energy,' the nurse explained matter-of-factly. 'We can't have her burning up all those nice calories she's just eaten by running up and down stairs, can we?'

'I suppose not,' I agreed, frightened suddenly at the lengths they were going to to save Rebecca's life. I studied her serene, impassive face as we made our way towards the lift. Did she want to get better? Or did she want to die?

'I'll come again soon.' I took Rebecca's hand and squeezed it gently. 'Goodbye, Sister.'

And for a moment the title and its full significance sent a chill through me.

'But, of course, you've got the same illness as Rebecca.'

'Not so badly! Not nearly so badly.'

'Depends on how you look at it.'

'I'm in control of my body! She isn't.'

'I'm not so sure of that.'

Dr Piet raised his eyebrows and smiled slightly. His hands were folded neatly together on the blotter. After the first few moments of each session he no longer troubled to take notes.

'But she's going to die if something doesn't happen soon!' I protested. Dr Piet's quiet and imperturbable refusal to see the obvious always annoyed me. Surely he could see how, for all the surface similarity, Rebecca was in a worse state than I. For me to think otherwise for a second would be gross self-pity on my part.

'And how much living are you doing at the moment?'

I looked back at him suspiciously. What was he arguing me into admitting?

'Come on, Karen. Remember what we were talking about last time. Your Lady of Shalott image. You're not living at the moment in any real sense. You're breathing, yes. But that's about it.'

'But I'm not dying?'

'Not physically. No. But why do you think you and Rebecca, in your different ways, are turning away from life?'

There was a pause while he changed tack. 'Karen, do you ever get angry?'

'No. No, I don't.'

'When was the last time you lost your temper?'

'I can't remember.'

'When Robin slapped you the other night, did you slap him back?'

'No.'

'Turned the other cheek, eh? Did you yell "You dirty-minded motherfucker, I hope you rot!" Well? Did you? Or words to that effect?'

'Certainly not.'

'Did you feel angry?'

'No. Not really.'

'What did you feel?'

'I can't remember. If anything I felt a bit guilty somehow, I suppose. Ashamed. Dirty.'

'Don't you think that's surprising?'

'Well, no, not for me. I'm not like Rebecca, you see. Even as a child I never lost my temper or anything. You're on the wrong tack there, really. I wasn't a passionate, rebellious child who got suppressed in the convent.'

'You've never got angry or gone in for emotional rows, then?'

'No.'

Dr Piet leant back in his chair and looked at me. He smiled and nodded slowly.

'Why are you looking all superior and significant?' There was a silence.

'Well?'

'I'm just thinking. I have a young woman here of twenty-seven. She never weeps in front of others, nor indeed at all unless she is in the grip of hallucination or semi-conscious. She never gets angry even though a lot of things have happened in her life that would make other people feel very angry indeed. She has never been in love, she never loses her temper, she never feels the slightest tremor of sexual attraction for another human being. She has a friend who, due to the extremely ill-advised training they have both received, is dying of *anorexia nervosa*. The girl I am looking at is not weeping, she is not angry about this.'

I stared back at him. My lips felt dry. I shivered.

'And you have the nerve to tell me that you're not dying,' Dr Piet said lightly. He smiled. 'It sounds like *rigor mortis* to me.'

I ran my finger over the polished surface of the teak desk, tracing the contoured grains.

'But I *am* emotional,' I protested. 'Far too emotional. I had a nervous breakdown, don't forget. I do have feelings! Lots of them. That's why I couldn't stay in the convent.'

'Yes. But they're not expressed, are they? Or if they are, very rarely.'

'But – '

'Don't tell me. You're going to talk about "control". It's a constant theme of yours. Well,' he paused, 'you were going to hold forth on the glories of self-control.'

'But that's why I went into the Order in the first place,' I argued. 'My feelings were too strong, too powerful. I wanted to get above all the mess of feelings and find God.'

'They were so powerful that you never lost your temper, never rebelled, were never passionate?'

'They *were* powerful. Potentially. I knew that. Look how strong they are – they're driving me mad because they're out of control.'

'Ah. Yes. Now you're talking.'

'What do you mean?' I asked, checked.

'I mean I don't doubt that you have very powerful emotions. Very powerful indeed, but you won't admit it. Do a bit of lit. crit. on yourself for a change. "Mess of feelings", "get above them". God as the supreme passionless, intellectual orgasm. You hated those feelings enough to push yourself through seven years in a Convent to get rid of them.'

'Is that why I have hallucinations, then?'

'You said it. Those feelings of yours have to get out somehow. You can't go on like this, Karen. You've had one breakdown. That didn't work – your emotions erupted and then you put them tidily away. They'll have to find another way to break out of that convent you've got inside yourself. And it will be a much more painful exit than it was physically walking out through the convent gate. You can't go on like this much longer.'

Dr Piet was right. In another sense, like Rebecca, I was dying. Even though at the time I dismissed his words as over-dramatic, I'd been trying to die spiritually ever since I entered the religious life. In the Early Church the best way of following Christ perfectly was martyrdom. After all, He had said that if anyone wanted to be His disciple he had to take up His cross and follow

Him to death and the martyrs had a chance to do that literally. When the persecutions stopped monasticism was developed as a substitute for martyrdom. Even when I entered my Order in the early 1960s I learned that I had to die: my mind, heart and body all had to die so that Christ could live in me instead. On my Profession day I lay under a funeral pall as a symbol of this death to self that I was vowing to practise every day of my life. Now I thought of life in terms of death.

Jane was a perpetual source of amazement to me at this time. Quite often she rang me up to say 'Karen, Mark and I are going to take a drive and a walk in the country and have a pub lunch. Do come!' and I'd go, thawing in the presence of so much enjoyment and marvelling at the way she organized her life for pleasure. It would never have occurred to me to pick up the phone and ask her to meet me for a drink and a film, or even to invite Charlotte round for a cup of coffee. I'd assume that they wouldn't want to come and that they'd got plenty of more attractive things to do. But even more than that I just couldn't deliberately contrive pleasures for myself. Yet by watching Jane, and watching the Stanleys in their holiday house at Cornwall, I was learning how to do it. Without realizing it, I was taking lessons so that, much later, when the crisis was past I too could manufacture delight for myself as well as anyone else. Bemused, I'd sit with Jane while she was cooking and gasp as she poured a whole bottle of wine onto pounds of expensive steak. 'Mark and I have just discovered that two thirds of our income goes on entertaining!' she'd say cheerfully, concocting enjoyment for herself and her guests. I was storing up these things in my heart for future reference, but, then, I couldn't begin to imagine putting them into practice.

Life can be grim – there's evil, war, poverty – but I didn't know then that the way we all go on, if we do, is by attaching ourselves to life by manufacturing happiness. It is so obvious that most people never even think about it; they just go out and do it. All the things I'm looking forward to while I write this make me anticipate the future with pleasure.

But in the early '70s I didn't see such a future for myself; I didn't in fact see any future at all beside loneliness and madness. Mother Walter had once said to us while we were novices that if we weren't finding the Noviceship unbearably hard it meant that we weren't trying hard enough, and indeed during our training it wasn't pleasure that was deliberately manufactured and contrived but pain and humiliation so that we could embrace the Royal Road to the Cross. I would one day learn to ransack life of its potential happiness and create life-enhancing circumstances that would make me want to go on living.

But as I watched my spectres that promised me a life of insanity, as I looked at Rebecca lying in her hospital bed, I knew that I was exactly like her. I didn't want to live; I wanted to die.

Standing on the college lawn, I shrank into myself, terrified of the scene before me. All round me women stood, mouths gaping and contorted in obscene smiles, their arms waved in frightening and exaggerated gestures. They were covered in clothes which only hid the rottenness inside, the colours hurt the eye with their violence and bruised the spirit. Faces, legs, arms, brown, white, pink, lips scarlet and cerise and eyelids loaded with thick blue and green powder made a strange ballet in my head. One of them came close to me. I watched her thrust her face into mine, saw her pink lips open. Her teeth menacingly bared themselves in a grin and her tongue flickered as she spoke unrecognizable words in my face. I ought to know her, I should be able to understand what she was saying. I watched her voracious vivacity fade into puzzled and offended incomprehension and I turned away, walking quickly to get away, to get anywhere. In the small shrubbery strange brown and grey beasts trotted backwards and forwards, their hooves wounding the soft green turf. There were squeals of the damned everywhere, and children bounded around terrifying in their swiftness, running and stumbling over the lawn in uncertain circles, their legs stiff and mechanical. I shut my eyes to escape from a world gone mad.

Then suddenly the clouds of incomprehension cleared. I was on the College lawn. It was the summer garden party. Dons and old girls strolled across the lawn chatting easily, greeting each other affectionately. In the shrubbery the donkey rides were proceeding calmly, little coloured flags fluttered cheerfully, festooned from tree to tree. Yet for a moment all these things had lost their identity and been revealed as foreign phenomena. The normality of the world had for a moment been peeled away.

Weakly I leant against a tree and tried to get my bearings. What happened to my mind during these periods of disorientation? I was meant to be going somewhere. Somewhere specific. Oh, yes. Quickly I looked at my watch and set off briskly for the marquee. Judith had asked me to meet her and Simon there for tea and then take care of him for a bit. I was late.

I heard him before I saw him, recognizing the shrill screams.

'No, Mummy, no! I don't like it.' He stood, his face red, his hands clasped over his ears as though the noise was intolerable, tears pouring down his face. Judith stood, tense and agonized beside him, shifting her weight nervously from one foot to another, muttering ineffectual consolations. All round people self-consciously averted their eyes, talked more loudly and animatedly and then glanced back, embarrassed by their own curiosity. I hurried over. 'Sorry, I'm late,' I whispered apologetically.

'Are you? I hadn't noticed,' Judith said distractedly. 'Look, we've got to get him out of here. Fast. It's the noise, I think, and the crowds. Look, Simon!' she said brightly with false cheer. 'Here's Karen! Isn't that nice?'

'Hello, Simon!'

'Take me away!' Simon's voice rose to a roar, shattering the civilized conversation around him. 'Mummy! Karen! Take me out of this tent!' His horror of the world about him rose to a crescendo.

'Yes, come on, Simon.' Judith took his arm hopefully but Simon stood rooted there, screaming with terror and frustration.

'You see, he can't move,' she explained to me. 'It's panic, I think. But he just can't move!' We looked at one another helplessly.

'Come on, Simon,' I whispered coaxingly. 'You can do it. Let's just get to the car and when we get home it will be lovely and peaceful. Won't that be nice?'

Simon screamed more loudly than ever. People were looking more and more askance. A frightening reality was being thrust under their noses and they resented it. The crowd thinned away leaving us in a circle of the damned, apart.

'I'll get him some tea,' Judith whispered, 'that might help. With some sugar. For shock.'

I nodded and put my arm around Simon's shoulders only to

113

have it shaken off as though the touch burned him. I wondered about these terrors of Simon's. Were they like mine – the world suddenly stripped of its consoling familiarity – but worse, far worse because he had no easy rationality to fall into?

'Here, darling. Drink this.' Judith stood with a cup of steaming tea in her hand. With a roar of blind rage Simon dashed the cup from its saucer. Its contents emptied themselves in a brown, scalding stream down the front of my dress. I yelped in shock. More heads turned.

'Oh, my dear, I *am* sorry.' Judith sounded distraught. 'You must let me pay for it. I'm – '

'Never mind, Judith. It doesn't matter, for goodness sake, it really couldn't matter less!'

'Mummy! Please! Come on!' And Simon, released by his action from his trance of shock, pulled at Judith's arm and we bundled ourselves out of the marquee, an undignified and disgraced trio.

We parked the car outside the front gate and Simon rushed out ahead of us, running awkwardly down the garden path and disappearing round the corner of the house into the back garden. All the way home, he had huddled away from us, muttering angrily to himself. 'Stupid old garden party! Stupid people. I told Mummy I didn't want to go. It's too much. I find it quite intolerable.' He was furious with us, still shivering with shock.

'Perhaps I shouldn't have taken him,' Judith sighed, as we got out of the car and hurried after Simon. 'But last year he did *quite* enjoy it, though crowds aren't usually a good idea. He didn't want to go today. But, then, you can't just give in all the time to him or he'd never go anywhere.'

'No, of course not. And he did enjoy it at first,' I reassured her quickly.

As we rounded the house into the back garden we were greeted with a roar from Simon. 'Mummy!' he yelled, 'I despise your existence! Stupid garden party! Horrible people!'

Then a blast of cold water hit us, soaking us in an icy jet and taking our breath away. Simon had turned the garden hose on us, spurning the punishing world that had made him suffer.

'Simon!' Judith ran forward, laughing weakly, soaked to the skin, her dress clinging to her. She held her arms up in a ritual gesture of surrender. We both laughed hysterically as the water continued to pour over us. 'Pax! All right! Revenge! Yes, okay, we're very sorry. Edwin!' she yelled into the living room, where Edwin Stanley was reading, peacefully oblivious of the chaos outside, 'come and get the hose off him! Simon, all right, you've got your revenge now. We're very sorry!'

Lindsey walked, elegant in a chignon and pale mink-coloured suit, across the lobby of the Crossroads motel and perched on one of the bar stools, talking to Sandy in his wheelchair.

'Off duty, at last!' she breathed, and accepted a gin and tonic. 'Thanks, Sandy. How was your day?'

She had landed a part in Britain's most popular soap opera and appeared nightly on the television. I had become an avid watcher of the serial. She was the secretary and had originally come to Crossroads to spy for another motel, but, seeing the error of her ways, she had broken down, confessed all and been forgiven. Lindsey herself had been delighted about this as it meant that her time on the serial was extended indefinitely.

'It's not Shakespeare,' she had said, 'but oh boy, the money's good.'

It was indeed. I paled at the sum. In a month she earned more than I got for a year on my DES grant. Now, sitting in Nanny's bedroom, *Crossroads* introduced me to a whole new world. I watched it every evening, ostensibly to watch Lindsey, feeling rather guilty to be looking at something so unintellectual. But soon I started watching even when Lindsey wasn't going to be on. I was hooked.

I became engrossed in a world which was a foreign country to me. This was what life must really be like. For me the normal was either the Looking Glass world of the convent, where all ordinary values were turned on their head, or it was the eccentric world of Oxford. In *Crossroads* the characters did not put each other through extraordinary tests of willpower and virtue. They seemed content to live and let live.

Once I went to the studios in Birmingham to have lunch with Lindsey. One of the directors, in the course of making polite conversation, suddenly became riveted.

'You mean you're an ex-nun, now a graduate student, looking after a braindamaged child in your spare time. Wow!' He turned round quickly to one of the script writers. 'Can't we use this?

Wouldn't it make a great story in *Crossroads*!'

The other man demurred and I could see why. My Gothic horror story – and he didn't know the half of it – would have split *Crossroads* down the middle. Watching it I felt the way an anthropologist must feel when he is studying the habits of an obscure tribe. The fact that one of the characters was really my own sister made the whole experience even more bizarre.

Simon slept peacefully, turned on his side away from me. I took out my book and started to read in the small circle of pale light that came from Judith's bedside lamp. I was doing the late-night shift, sitting with Simon until his mother came to bed. She would be late tonight, she'd warned me; there was a dinner at College at which she had to put in an appearance. I didn't mind particularly. Sitting in the long attic room at the top of the house I felt peacefully away from things. An owl hooted outside and I looked nervously across at Simon. He was a light sleeper and if he once started waking during the night I knew that he and Judith would have very little sleep. But no, he slept on. Time ticked peacefully by.

Suddenly Simon reared up in bed. He gazed ahead, his eyes fixed and frightened, yet, I sensed, also unseeing. He began to make strange animal noises in his throat. Oh, no. I felt cold inside and panicky. Was he going to have an epileptic fit?

I picked up the child's rubber teething ring that Judith kept by her bed, hurried across to Simon, inserted the ring between his teeth and pushed him gently over on to his side. Then we both waited together. I had no idea what I would see. The books I'd read and the prejudices I'd inherited had prepared me for a hideous sight; the responsibility, too, seemed enormous. Simon was a big child. He was taller than I already. What if in his convulsions I could not control him and he damaged himself still further?

He was still moaning strangely from his throat, his eyes locked in that unseeing stare. Then suddenly his breath stopped for what seemed like hours. His face became distorted and his eyes brutish-looking and angry. The colour drained slowly from his skin, leaving it mottled, a dead marble colour, then finally the hue of dirty stone. It went on for what seemed ages and then suddenly his teeth locked on the teething ring and his body started jerking wildly and convulsively while a shuddering cry came from him that sounded weird and inhuman. Please let it stop, I prayed, holding his head firmly in a sideways position on the pillow, probably quite needlessly: I'd heard dreadful warnings about epileptics choking because they had swallowed their tongues. It went on and on. . .

Then, just as suddenly, the convulsions stopped and Simon relaxed, the teething ring fell sideways out of his mouth, and he feel directly into a heavy comatose sleep, snoring in rattling, ugly breaths. Gradually the colour seeped back into his face. It was over.

Nevertheless I stayed, sitting on his bed beside him. If he should wake up suddenly, he would feel awful. Judith said he could be enormously distressed and confused afterwards. There was also the danger of a second fit, closely following the first. If that happened I was to send for an ambulance immediately as it was an emergency. But it was all right. For about half an hour the comatose rattle continued. Then, imperceptibly, it merged with a more natural breathing rhythm and Simon slid into peaceful sleep.

Shaken, I returned to Judith's bed. Poor child. I felt suddenly immensely angry with someone. Presumably with God, as it was He who was ultimately responsible. Wasn't it bad enough that Simon should have this brain damage at all? Did he have to have epilepsy on top of everything else? I thought of Simon's gifts – his sharp sense of mimicry and repartee, his extraordinary sensitivity to words and music. Certainly, had that senseless birth accident not occurred he would have been brilliant. And now all those gifts were crippled and maimed; they could never come to fruition and Simon himself was hampered at every turn by huge and overwhelming fears. On top of all that, I'd lived eighteen months now with the Stanleys and had seen how Simon had dislocated their lives and the suffering that they too endured, watching him day by day.

Suddenly the significance of what I was feeling hit me. Anger had swept through me. But it was anger directed against God. One of the first movements of spontaneous passion I'd felt for years was sweeping me away from Him.

Outside I heard the stairs creaking cautiously and knew that Judith was coming up to bed. I watched her slim figure shadowed against the frosted glass in the door, concentrated on opening the door with the minimum of noise. She stole into the room with painful caution, wincing when she stood on a creaking board. If Simon woke when she was there, he always refused to go back to sleep and plagued her all night.

'Everything all right?' She stood there in one of her extraordinary evening dresses. This one was Indian and had little jewels of mirrored glass sewn all over it.

'He had a fit, I'm afraid. But he's all right now.'

'Oh, no!' Dismayed, she sank onto the bed and looked across the room at her son who was now sleeping heavily. Her face, which had reflected the stimulation of a good evening, suddenly collapsed into the familiar lines of strain and worry that she so often wore at home. 'Oh, no! He hasn't had one for such a long time. What can have caused it? Are you all right? It didn't upset you too much?'

'No. No, of course not. Don't worry about that!'

'Oh, good.' Judith sat in silent thought for a while, as I got my things ready to leave.

'Karen,' she said suddenly. We were whispering, of course, but I could tell by the tentative tone of her voice that she was nervous about what she was going to say. 'Karen – do you think you – please feel free to refuse, that goes without saying. You do more than enough as it is, more than any of our other lodgers ever have and Simon's so fond of you. I always feel happy when he's with you. But do you think – I mean –'

'Come on, Judith,' I said, amused. 'Let's have it! What is it?'

'Well, I wonder if you'd consider taking Simon to Mass with you at Blackfriars.' Judith always spoke swiftly and nervously but in her present embarrassment the words positively tumbled over one another.

'What!' I was astounded.

'Yes, I know.' She grinned at me, aware of the strangeness of her request. 'It's funny, really – I mean, Edwin and I are such staunch atheists. But I've often thought that Simon ought to have some kind of religion; it's a comfort isn't it, and the ritual and all that part of it is right up his street.'

'But Judith,' I said, still amazed. 'What will Edwin say? I mean, yes, I'm perfectly happy to take Simon and I think he'll probably like it, but it is a bit of a surprise, to put it mildly.'

'Oh, Edwin won't mind,' Judith shrugged, 'he'll think it's rather a joke, really. Which it is.' She giggled. 'Can you just imagine what all our friends will say after my nasty remarks about Christianity in the past?'

'You wouldn't feel like coming yourself, I suppose?' I asked with irony. 'You haven't seen the light?'

'No! No. Good heavens, no!' Judith started laughing, warding off the idea of her conversion with nervous little gestures. 'No, but seriously that Blackfriars Mass sounds ideal, because presumably no one would mind if he made a noise or any kind of scene. And then he'd get to meet lots of new people in your coffee meeting afterwards. And religion would do him good.'

She sounded as though religion were some kind of spiritual iron tonic – a regular dose once a week would automatically induce peace of soul.

'He won't understand any of it, of course,' I said. 'I presume you don't want me to instruct him or anything.'

'Oh, Lord, no! No, he doesn't have to *understand* it!' Judith said dismissively. Well, why not? I asked myself. Lots of Catholic priests would say the same thing.

'Anyway,' she continued, 'I don't want him getting any odd ideas that'll upset him – you know – guilt and all those strange "moral" ideas you Catholics go in for. But, you see, I can trust you, you wouldn't do that, and judging by your account of them the Dominicans wouldn't do that, either.'

'No, no, of course they wouldn't.' For Simon it would be just another fairy story, like Goldilocks or Jack and the Beanstalk – and, unless I could find some rhythmic or onomatopoeic words, a rather disappointing fairy story. 'He wouldn't be able to distinguish it from a fantasy,' I explained to Judith. 'And he'd never grasp the *point* of all the stories, except on a very simple level. You know: Jesus loves me and is my friend.'

'Well, I suppose that won't do any harm,' she said doubtfully. 'You see, I just think he needs some kind of comfort in that way and religion is supposed to bring comfort.' Who was I to say Simon would get nothing from it at all?

'You see.' Judith turned her worried face to me and I had to admire what she was doing. This was a sacrifice of all her cherished principles, her friends would ridicule her mercilessly, but she really was trying to see what would be best for Simon.

'You see, Karen, it's all very well for people like Edwin and me doing without religion. But Simon isn't strong or well enough to be an atheist.'

'Karen! Where are we going this morning?' Simon demanded, sticking his head round the kitchen door the following Sunday.

'We're going to – ' I looked at him questioningly. 'Blackfriars!' Simon roared with genuine delight. He certainly seemed enthusiastic.

'Do I look smart?'

'You look very smart indeed!' He did, too. White jersey, brown trousers, and his hair brushed and curly. 'Now, Simon, you go and look at the papers next door while I make our toast.'

'Moon rises!'

'Karen,' he put his head round the door. 'You won't be angry, will you, if I spill my coffee all the way down my white jersey?'

'Not if it was an accident, no.'

'But if it was on purpose?'

'Then I'd be very angry indeed!'

'Because, Karen, I'm going to do it!' He picked up his mug and regarded me hopefully, waiting for what he knew would be my reaction.

'Don't you dare!' I thundered predictably.

'Oh, don't be severe!' Simon beamed.

'I shall be very severe indeed, if you're not sitting in your place in the dining room in two seconds flat!'

'Oh, don't be displeased!' And on his way back to the dining room I heard him mutter, 'Karen was extremely oppressive with Simon. "Don't you dare do it!" she cried angrily. Simon looked crestfallen and pleaded with Karen. "Oh, don't be displeased!" he begged wistfully.'

During Mass, an hour later, Simon behaved perfectly. He stood with his eyes closed and his hands joined, the fingers pointing heavenwards. Who on earth had taught him to do that? It must be his school. 'You don't need to stand like that all the time,' I whispered. He looked back and nodded solemnly. During the hymns and music, he listened hard with head averted, a strange half smile of approval on his lips. Rapturously he flung his head back and sniffed the incense like a drug. 'Karen,' he whispered, still sniffing luxuriously between words, 'I like coming to Blackfriars. I really do.'

I was pleased and relieved, but as we sat for the sermon there was something nagging at the back of my mind.

Did I really believe in any of this? Really *believe* in it? Of course there was a man, Jesus of Nazareth. So much was historically proven. But did I really believe that He had risen from the Dead, that He was the Son of God? Never mind the rest of it. The Doctrine of the Trinity, for example, Consubstantiation, the Sacraments, the Infallibility of the Pope . . . to name just the obvious central articles of faith. My theological studies seemed now a hindrance to belief: I knew too many of the very human and often disedifying ways that these dogmas had been developed and elaborated. Indeed, the likelihood of there being any sort of God seemed ludicrously remote. If Jesus, a nervous, passionate young rabbi living in some obscure province of the Roman Empire two thousand years ago, could see this mountain of intricate theology that had been developed in his honour, would he recognize it?

The Sermon was over and we all rose to our feet. Simon looked around expectantly hoping for some more incense. 'I believe in One God: the Father Almighty and in Jesus Christ, His only son, Our Lord, who was conceived by the Holy Ghost, born of the Virgin Mary. . .' The congregation repeated these extraordinary words mechanically, as I'd done so often myself. I remembered a Jesuit telling us during a retreat that Faith was not a matter of the Intellect but of the Will. A Christian could only accept the essential incredibility of his faith by choosing to believe in it. Somewhere along the line I knew that I'd abandoned that choice. The only way Christianity made sense was when it was lived at the highest level of intensity. It then acquired an emotional logic of its own. And I realized now that for it to acquire that logic for me personally again, I had to return to a fervour of prayer and commitment that I could no longer manage. The thought of meditation, examination of conscience and the rest of it filled me with an enormous weariness.

As the others filed up for communion I remained on my seat next to Simon. How could I, in all honesty, go to communion when I no longer really believed that the wafer laid reverently on each communicant's tongue was anything more than flour and water? The only way I could get my faith back was by an effort of will, a choice that expressed itself in every single moment of my life. No, I thought, as I had done three years ago when I decided to leave my Order, I cannot do it. Gradually I felt myself loosen my unquestioning grasp of the faith I had been born with; one by one I uncoiled the tentacles of fear and habit and felt my faith slide away, leaving me even more exposed and vulnerable than I felt at first without the protection of the habit.

'Karen! Will you bring me to Blackfriars again next week?' Simon asked after coffee as we crossed St Giles and hurried past the Lamb and Flag.

'Yes, of course,' I agreed calmly, without a second's hesitation. Without God the world was a terrifying place and, for all the confusions of my post-convent days, it had been a comfort to know that He was there, albeit increasingly in the background. Now there was nothing; the world was only a small planet hurtling pointlessly through space.

I had to leave the God I knew who dragged around with him the rags of my own past life with all its mistakes and misconceptions before I could really find Him again. I had created this 'God' in my own image and likeness and in the likeness of a mistaken system. Now I had to let Him go so that He could become Himself for me. If I wanted to find Him I had to lose Him first; this is – and I should have known it – a law of the spiritual life. Heaven knows I'd read enough books about it. This was, though I couldn't see it then, a positive step towards myself and towards God at the same time. But the loss was a real one and all I could feel at the time was the pain of the parting and, in a very real sense, a death.

'Karen!' Simon tugged at my arm to pull my attention back to him and beamed into my face so that our noses nearly collided. In spite of myself I found I was smiling back. 'Karen, we will be going to Blackfriars again next week, won't we?'

Yes, I knew even then that I would continue to go. It was like putting some money on the pools each week. By lingering in the environs of the Church I might get the spiritual energy back which would enable me to choose Faith again. I shook myself impatiently. Most unlikely. Mere self-indulgent day-dreaming in fact. No, religion was over for me and in some sense that meant that my life was over too. But Simon had enjoyed the morning and it was a way of helping the Stanleys.

'Yes, of course we're going,' I said.

'Karen! We're getting married.'

I looked at Jane and Mark, who stood, like a conventional engaged couple, raising glasses of champagne to one another and smiling teasingly into one another's eyes.

'I've even got a ring!' Jane said, with self-mockery in her voice as she held out the austerely platinum-encircled finger.

'I'm so pleased!' I embraced them both and accepted a glass of champagne from Mark, who wrapped me in a fraternal hug from which, woodenly, I extricated myself.

'I really recommend being engaged,' he said seriously. 'God knows how I'll find the married state! But being engaged is nice.'

'Yes, it is.' Jane leaned against him proprietorially. 'There's a certain peace in throwing in the towel! Human beings aren't meant to live alone, Karen; the world's a bleak place. You need someone to curl up against to keep the dark out.'

'You make me sound like some kind of duvet, darling,' Mark grinned. 'Or we sound like a couple of animals, curling up together in the forest.'

'Bears and squirrels!' Jane exclaimed caustically. 'I know, I know!' She took his hand and pressed it reassuringly, then waved her champagne glass at me. 'You need somebody, Karen. It's time now. You get yourself a man to keep the dark out.'

As I watched them that evening, effortlessly close and loving with one another, I felt yet again how ill-equipped I was for survival. Their mutual involvement underlined my own loneliness and I felt them receding from me into a world of light and normality, leaving me to my own demons.

'I can't go!' Charlotte spoke the words breathlessly down the telephone. 'I'm sorry to let you down. Or perhaps I'm letting you off the hook – I suspect I am! But it's Mike. He seems to want me around at the moment – actually wants me around! It seems like a chance I mustn't pass up. And the novel's at a point where – look, I just can't!'

'No, Charlotte.' I found myself smiling grimly to myself. How had I ever for a second felt it possible to break out of my own self-imposed cloister and leap freely into a world I knew nothing about and to which I was dead anyway? Dead to love, dead to feeling and passion, dead to enjoyment and fulfilment. 'I can't go to Paris, either,' I said. 'Absolutely not.'

As I locked up my bicycle one evening in the Stanleys' bicycle shed, I felt all the usual signs coming on. The tight feeling around my head, pressing down on my temples like a steel clamp, the flutterings of panic in the pit of my stomach that I knew would rise to a powerful torrent, draining my sanity, and an overpowering desire to sleep. Dr Piet had warned me about that. 'Sleeping during the day is just another way of escaping involvement,' he'd said, 'resist it as far as you can.' I glanced at my watch. Only 6.30. Another evening of the terror and hallucinations that were plaguing me with ever-increasing frequency.

I don't know how long I wrestled with my subconscious that night before it happened. During those strange periods time ceased to have much meaning anyway. I don't remember which horror exactly led me to the glass shelf over my wash basin and made me pick up the pink barbiturates which my GP had given me as an antidote for my insomnia. But I do remember pouring a large tumblerful of the sherry that Jane had given me as an end of term present. I wanted to lose myself. Somehow. What was the point of going on like this, with a mind that was diseased and which one day might plunge me into incurable insanity? I didn't want to live in the world any more, yet there was nowhere else I could live. I wanted to block out the horrific series of hallucinations once and for all, find finally some peace and rest. I do remember dimly the powdery taste and the stickiness of the sherry and I remember clearly the sudden rush as I fell down a long, precipitous corridor, further and further from life, with a giddy exhilaration and a heady feeling of release. Ahead, far, far in the distance, was a tiny pinprick of light. And I remember that point of light suddenly being extinguished and the relief of the velvety darkness.

CHAPTER SIX

For Dear Life

JANE STOOD UNDER my window, hands on her hips, head thrown back.

'Karen!' she yelled, her clarion tones shattering the peace of that quiet little Oxford backwater. In the pale dusk of the summer evening, her calico cream dress glimmered prettily making her look like an urban milkmaid. 'Karen!' she yelled again. There was no reply. Should she go and see Charlotte instead perhaps?

Mark had gone back to London after the weekend. He had a job now in a teacher training college, a job he was lucky to get, and she'd nearly decided to go with him to his smart, bijou house in Greenwich. She loved London, was out of love with her thesis, and her engagement had made her fall in love with Mark with renewed thoroughness. She almost packed an overnight case and went down with him for a few days, just for the hell of it. Oxford was so dreary during the long, summer vacation; the libraries were empty and there were no real queues for books in the Bodleian, but that only deprived you of an excuse for not getting on with your work. She threw her toothbrush into her bag and then she passed her desk and saw her latest notes and cards neatly lined up there. It was no good.

'Bloody Baudelaire,' she muttered forlornly, and Mark laughed and agreed that for her conscience's sake, she must stick to her original plan and get in a few weeks' solid work before he began his own holiday.

Her room seemed doubly empty after he'd left and, on a sudden whim, she walked over to the Stanleys' to see me and have some coffee. But I didn't seem to be in my room.

Jane went round to the back door, which she knew was always left open. In the kitchen, under the glaring light of the one unshaded bulb, Edwin was concocting his supper. Unlike Judith he was extremely interested in cooking and on the rare occasions when he ate at home he experimented elegantly with the left-overs that Nanny left out.

'Ah, Jane! Hello!' Jane was a frequent caller and well known to the household. 'You're a cook, aren't you? What do you think of this?'

Jane looked into the pan where some slices of cooked ham and cold chicken sizzled round in a dark, aromatic sauce.

'Mmm,' she sniffed appreciatively, 'what have you put in it?'

'Just a spot of red wine and a few herbs.' Edwin threw the long white mane of hair off his face and grinned his clever-monkey smile. 'For God's sake don't tell Judith, will you? She'll think it a terrible extravagance.' He looked furtively down the long corridor that led to the sitting room.

'What did she have for her supper?' Jane was still intrigued by the solitary lives the Stanleys led under their communal roof.

'A fried egg on toast, of course.' He gestured towards the frying pan that stood, greasy, beside the sink waiting for Nanny to wash it up in the morning.

'A shade more oregano, perhaps?' Edwin dived back to the recipe book, which was propped open on top of the fridge. 'This man believes in improvisation. Do listen: "Go wild with the sauce to your taste".' He laughed throatily and Jane joined in, charmed with the incongruity of the slang on Edwin's usually precise lips. His laughter followed her as she went up the stairs. 'Priceless, isn't it?'

'Hello, Jane! Nanny, look. 'It's my friend Jane!' Simon walked shyly up to Jane and touched her red curls. Jane was a favourite of his because of her constant cheerfulness and her inability to be frightened or disconcerted by him.

'Hello, Simon. Are you going off to bed now?'

'Yes, of course! It's nine o'clock. *Stupid*. It's very foolish of you, Jane. You must know by now that this is my bedtime!' Simon exclaimed amicably, baring his teeth for Nanny for inspection.

'Hello, Nanny!'

'Hello, Jane. Karen is in, I think. She came in some time ago!'

'Oh, good. I did call but she didn't answer. She must be immersed in her book.'

'Immersed! I'll soon un-immerse her.' Simon threw down his

toothbrush and started off down the passage that led to my room shouting commandingly. 'The Royal Arms! Wake up! Jane has come to see you!'

Nanny grasped him firmly from behind by the cord of his dressing gown. 'Simon! Don't interrupt Karen. Her room is private and we don't go inside unless she's looking after you.'

'On Wednesdays, Saturdays and – ' Simon paused, smiling sideways at Nanny.

'Sundays!' she completed patiently. 'Up to bed now, Simon!' She pushed him gently towards the spiral staircase that led up to the attic bedroom. 'Say goodnight to Jane.'

'Goodnight, Simon.'

'Goodnight, Jane. I think you're a very nice girl.'

'You're very nice too.' Still smiling to herself Jane rapped a cheerful tattoo on my door. Listened. What she heard made her push the door open quickly.

I was lying in a coma, breathing in long, gravelly snores. On my bedside table was an empty barbiturates bottle and half a bottle of sherry.

From a long way off I could see my body quite clearly, stretched lifelessly on the narrow table. I could see the tubes, hear the squelchy pumping and gurgling, could see the nurses tight-lipped with concentration, the doctor issuing curt orders. My face – what I could see of it – was grey, shrinking into itself, the skin clinging starkly to the bones. I didn't look like myself at all. Was I dead, then? This must be my soul or my spirit up here, free at last of my body with all its anarchy. A strange, detached peace – at last I'd achieved it. It was what I'd striven for all my life – to leave the body and the conflict of life far behind me and soar freely in spirit. Curiously I looked down at all the undignified struggle going on over my body. Why on earth was anyone bothering with that absurd shell that I'd left behind? And now what? I wondered, and was aware of a gathering up of all my spiritual forces for some new dimension of experience. I was on the brink of something else. Something unimaginable. . .

Then a sudden explosion of sensation. A harsh white light assaulted my eyes, a stench of vomit and excrement, loud, angry voices, unkind fingers jabbing the tender places between my shoulder blades. I was back in my body – a struggling, panting animal fighting for breath against the intrusive tube that grazed my throat and violated my squeezed and bruised stomach, pumping life back into me. I felt a howl of protest rising inside my head. No more life. But my body was saying something different. It was fighting blindly for air and for space.

'Don't struggle, dear. You'll only make it worse.'

'That's it, I think. Pulse better?'

'Yup.'

A gulp of air and the beginnings of a blissful slide into peace. A stinging slap on my cheek. The world rushed back and I was catapulted cruelly into a sitting position, jerked and cranked up noisily from behind. A large face with pink, mottled cheeks thrust itself into mine.

'Karen!' Another slap on the cheek. 'Can you hear me? You mustn't sleep now. Not yet. Keep awake, dear.'

The 'dear' was a rebuke.

I looked up at the white cap, the dazzling blue dress and Persil-bright apron.

'What fool prescribed barbiturates? The girl's undergoing psychiatric treatment, apparently. Some people just like making work for us if you ask me.'

'Wake up, dear! How many did you take?'

I stared at her. And turned away. Another nurse was fiddling with my arm. A tube. Bandages. I looked at my arm in faint surprise. How had they got that tube in without my feeling it?

'What's your name? Can you tell me that and can you tell me where you live?'

Uncertainly I drew breath and a voice, not mine, scraped through my bruised throat.

'I – I –' It was too much trouble. Wearily, I turned away and gazed at the chrome rail on my bed. It gleamed brightly, like a revelation. A revelation of what?

'We're taking you up to the ward, dear. Your friend can come with you, but not stay for long.'

My friend?

'How are you, Karen?'

It was Jane, her face bleached with shock, and when she reached out to take my hand I felt too tired and too bewildered to pull it away. As I stared at the endless succession of ceilings and as we raced through corridors, my stomach churning with sea-sickness, her hand became the only stable thing in my world. My grasp got tighter.

'Here!' A different voice broke through the laconic comments of the nurses. 'She'll need another blanket, nurse! Overdose, is it? I was the same last week, remember? She'll be cold! Get her another blanket. She'll be cold.'

The word entered my brain painfully and joined with the discomfort I felt. My strange, hoarse throat tightened. A croak came out uncertainly. 'I'm so cold! I'm so cold!'

'Get back to bed, Brenda, you'll wake the others. Get back to bed. This is none of your business.'

Another nurse's face loomed over mine, dramatically lit by the dim light.

'Where's your sponge bag, dear?'

I stared back. Bewildered.

'Your sponge bag. You must have brought one with you when you came into hospital. Didn't you pack a case?'

Sponge bag? Case?

'What? Didn't you bring it? Oh, for crying out loud!'

And dimly as I sank at last to an exhausted, dull sleep, I heard Jane's voice.

'She didn't think she'd need her sponge bag in the hereafter, nurse. When you're trying to kill yourself, sponge bags are not one of your top priorities.'

Next morning I opened my eyes and stared straight into the rose-pink depths of the curtain round my bed. From outside came a medley of unfamiliar voices, the tinkle of crockery and the officious squeaking of rubber soles on a smooth floor. My head was throbbing painfully, my stomach was wounded inside and my arm was tethered to a drip. Through a crack in the curtains I could see a nurse wheeling a trolley. Her voice cheerfully called instructions to someone beyond my line of vision.

Jane's words flashed into my stunned brain. 'When you're trying to kill yourself. . .' And I remembered it all.

Not the details, not a complete cycle of events, not the full chain of cause and effect. But the central fact was there.

I lay there, listening to the words. 'When you're trying to kill yourself.' Incredulously I tried to fit them to myself. Could I possibly have done such an extraordinary thing? Suicide belonged to the pages of literature or to the newspapers. Not to me. Desperately I tried to recall the moment of decision, but could not. The evening before was lost in a swirl of hallucination. But something, some deep recognition, told me that that was what I had done. I remembered the peace of that long slide into death, the detachment at last from the world, the endorsement of every one of my endeavours during the last few years. Of course it was true. And I should have died. They shouldn't have brought me back. What use was my life either to myself or to anybody else? I had wrenched it away from religious life and this violence had unhinged my mind. I recalled the anger in the nurse's voice last night. The way she spat out the word 'dear'. Outside the cubicle I could hear the nurses chatting cheerfully as they hurried round the ward, preserving life. How could they feel anything but contempt and anger for one who had tried to throw hers away? I felt a rush of shame. I ought to be dead.

But as my thoughts tossed miserably round, my body was telling me something very different. And, when my brain finally sank into drugged torpor, I found myself listening to it. I watched the clear liquid in the drip slide down the glass tube and disappear into my arm. My heart was knocking urgently in a nervous but insistent rhythm. As I cautiously took a breath I felt my lungs greedily expand to suck in fresh air. My innards were juddering with shock and I remembered that sudden awakening into my body last night, that painful rebirth of the senses. My body didn't want to die. I had hated it, whipped it, starved it, last night poisoned it, but still it went on. It was determined to resist me. That liquid was vanishing into a vast network of veins and arteries. And now I noticed how very pink the curtains looked, how brilliantly blue the blankets. The smells of the ward sprang at me – the Dettol, the floor polish, the soap. A complicated symphony of noises resounded outside. My senses seemed to be rejoicing and celebrating their reprieve by a sharpened appreciation of the world around them. And I remembered how my hand last night had not drawn away from Jane's but had, involuntarily, clung on for – I smiled wryly as I finished the phrase. For dear life.

Tiredly I felt the familiar spiritual sensation of guilt seep through me, spoiling the first moment of physical ease my body had known for years. Just think – this morning I might have been in Hell.

Then I remembered that strange sensation of looking down on my body as if it no longer really belonged to me. And the breathless feeling of being on the brink of something unimaginable. I must have been near to death at that moment. Was it God I was expecting then? Surely not. I shook myself impatiently. There was something familiar, now I came to think of it, about that feeling of being about to tip over into a new dimension. It happened when I hallucinated. And sometimes when I 'fainted' I seemed to be poised and waiting in terror for an experience which would divide me irrevocably from everything I'd ever known. But last night there'd been no death-fear. Only peace and a girding up of my forces to meet this unexpected Thing.

Look, there's no God, no Hell and certainly no Heaven, I told myself tiredly. All this is just a hangover after a lifetime of belief. And yet somewhere I knew I'd have to think again about this. Later. When I wasn't so tired.

The curtains round my bed squealed and slithered round the rail and a nurse strode in.

'Well,' she said, brightly, gimlet eyes checking the drip. 'You've been lucky, haven't you?'

'How are you feeling, then? Come on, it's no use pretending you're asleep!'

Unwillingly I opened my eyes. The speaker was right. I was wide awake, but lay, my head turned away from the ward, unable to meet the inquisitive eyes. The shame I had felt persisted. Half the time I lay there, listening to my breathing, feeling the convulsions of my stomach, counting my heartbeats with an astonished respect for the way this machine kept on and on functioning. But it was not enough for my body to want to live, if my mind could, in its insanity, almost kill it in a moment of unconsciousness.

'Come on! Let's have a chat. You'll feel better for a chat. I did!'

Wearily I turned in the direction of the voice, not feeling at all ready to face the outside world. A girl in a red dressing gown, wispy, mouse-coloured hair and a round, rosy face, grinned cheerfully at me.

'That's better! You don't feel like seeing anyone at first. I

131

know, because I did what you've done. In fact I did it twice!' She giggled. 'You're an overdose, aren't you?'

I nodded feebly. She'd tried twice! I studied her for signs of despair or instability and found none.

'Right! We ODs must stick together, you know. There are two others in this ward. The nurses don't like us! They try and hide it but they don't like us at all!'

'Well,' I croaked uncertainly, trying out my voice. My throat was still scraped raw from the tubes. 'I can see their point, can't you? It must seem so self-indulgent.'

'So – what did you say?' She was clearly balked by my vocabulary. 'Oh well, never mind,' she shrugged. '*I* had complications, you know,' she continued, with a hint of pride. 'That's why I'm still here. They don't usually keep you in long for an OD. Just a day or two. But I got bronchial pneumonia after mine.'

'Are you all right now?' Brenda's body too seemed ruthlessly bent on survival, against all possible odds.

'I've been in here a week. My poor husband! He's been going round the bend! You know, he's got a job and we've got two kids – '

'Kids!' I exclaimed, amazed. She looked barely eighteen. 'Have you got children?'

'Yes, why shouldn't I have?'

'You look so young!'

'Thanks! I'm going on nineteen. Yes, I've got two kids – worse luck! – boys – two and a bit and ten months. We had to get married, me and my husband, but it's all worked out fine. Only thing is I get so depressed. Funny, really. I don't know why. We've got a nice council house and everything. Anyway, my poor husband'll be glad to see me coming out tonight. Hope he comes early so we can take in the Bingo on the way home!'

'Good,' I said weakly. 'Yes, I expect he will be pleased to see you back.' Poor Brenda, poor husband. And poor children.

'Only thing is,' she lowered her voice, 'I'll have to go and see my psychiatrist tomorrow. I'm so scared because he'll be really mad with me.'

'Brenda, I'm sure he won't be!' I sat up to emphasize my point but fell back onto the pillows and the room spun round alarmingly. 'He won't be cross!' I repeated.

'Feeling dizzy?' She nodded knowledgeably. 'Yes, I was dizzy at first. You know, these nurses don't know nothing really and they don't care too much, either. Like last night. I knew you'd be cold. But would they bother? No! I said to them, "She'll be cold, you know," and they didn't take a blind bit of notice, not until you started up "I'm so cold!" Your friend – the one that brought you in – she had a laugh about it!'

A nurse bustled up to the bed, took my pulse and temperature, and fluffed up the pillows.

'Nothing much the matter with you this morning!' she said reprovingly. 'Dr Piet is coming in to see you later.'

'Dr Piet? How does he know?' How fast the hospital machinery worked.

'Oh, I expect the doctor phoned him.' She adjusted the drip. 'No food yet and plenty of fluids,' and she was off, squeaking busily down the ward, giving me my recipe for survival.

'Who's Dr Piet? Your psychiatrist?' Brenda looked genuinely sympathetic, wrinkling her nose on which there was a fine dust of freckles. 'Aren't you scared? Isn't he going to be mad?'

'No! Of course he won't be cross.' It seemed impossible to convince her. For her a psychiatrist was an impatient schoolmaster. How could she hope to get better when she had so little understanding of her problems? But, then, for all my education, was I any better?

'Oh, he will, you know.' Brenda grimaced disconsolately and bent over to examine the nail polish on her toes. She sighed. 'You see, when I did this before he said to me then: "Now don't you dare do it again! You've got your children to think about!"' She looked up from her toenails and shrugged at me.

'But why did you do it before?' I probed.

'Well, that's the funny thing, really. I just don't know. I just get so depressed at home with the kids that it seems the only thing to do. But I don't know why. You know, Dr White – he's my psychiatrist – he asks me if I get on with Mike, my husband, and about how I got on with my Dad when I was little. Well, we got on all right, you know? What I can't understand is what that's got to do with *now*. I mean, it stands to reason I wouldn't be depressed *now* about something that happened fifteen years ago, would I? And nothing did happen, anyway. I'll tell you one thing.' She lowered her voice again. 'I got some more of them pills at home. I'll take them again, you know, if I get low. I mean, why not? It seems the only sensible thing to do, I mean – '

'All right, Brenda. Back to bed!' A nurse appeared from nowhere. 'You'll get cold and we'll have you ill again! Karen's got to be washed now before the doctors come round.' She swished the curtains round my bed, shutting me off from the world in a pool of pink silence.

'It seems the only sensible thing to do.' I watched Brenda cheerfully giving out cups of tea to the other patients in the ward. What was the thing people said about a suicide attempt? A cry for help. Had I been crying for help? I turned the question over in my mind. No. I didn't believe that help was possible. 'From whence cometh my help?' the psalm had asked, and always over the years I'd had only one answer. 'My help comes from the Lord.' God was the only one who could provide lasting or effective succour. And right now He no longer existed for me.

I looked back at Brenda, who had her earphones on and was grinning away at a radio programme while sipping a cup of tea. Perhaps she was crying for help. But no one could help her: neither her husband, nor her children, nor her psychiatrist. Yes, we could all provide superficial help to one another. But real sickness of soul no human being could assuage. I knew that. And if there was no God there was no possibility of help.

And yet how was it that I was not more devastated by what had happened? How could I be sitting calmly, sipping lemon squash, smiling at Brenda across the ward? The anger with myself that I'd felt when I woke this morning had gone. There was fear. Fear, of myself. Of my sick mind that could so rule my consciousness. There was sorrow for the God who seemed to have vanished. Loneliness and apprehension were there too. But none of these emotions was as strong as one might expect. I sighed and let my limbs sink heavily into the pillow, smiled gratefully as a nurse bustled up and took my blood-pressure. Underneath the fear and the depression there was something else. Something new. But I couldn't work out what it was.

'You see? What did I tell you?'

Dr Piet sat on the end of my bed looking at me inquiringly.

134

'Sorry, I know it's maddening to have someone say "I told you so" but I did, didn't I?'

'Told me what?' I asked anxiously, marvelling at the *sang froid* of his greeting. Suicides must be everyday occurrences for him.

Dr Piet clasped his forehead in mock-anguish. 'Great,' he said. 'I pour out the gems of my wisdom on her and she doesn't even remember them!' He straightened up, suddenly, and his voice became more serious. 'You know, you do remember. One thing you do have is an exceptionally good memory. You just think about it for a while.'

'You did say that my emotions – '

'And passions – don't forget about them, will you? You don't like your emotions much but your passions you like even less. Sorry,' he patted my foot through the blanket, 'I have to bring them up, if you won't. Go on. Your passions and emotions – ?'

'Had to break out. You said I couldn't go on like this. And you said that the next time they broke out it wouldn't be a breakdown because that hadn't worked. It would be worse. . . .'

'Mmm. How do you feel?'

My head ached, my stomach still felt squeezed and violated and my throat and nostrils were raw and painful. But I knew that my physical state was not important to Dr Piet; he left that to the doctors and nurses in the hospital.

'I feel – ' I sighed, 'ashamed, I think.'

'You would! Why?'

'Because it seems such a selfish, pseudo-dramatic thing to do. An attention-seeking device. A time-waster for the nurses. People will say it was weak-willed and histrionic.'

'Yes, I expect they will. Some of them will say you're a spoiled hysterical cow. But in the circumstances they'd be wrong, wouldn't they?'

We discussed the fact that I'd taken the pills when I was barely conscious.

'In a way,' Dr Piet said, 'I'd feel a lot happier if you *had* done a Madame Bovary – if you had made a lovely hysterical, self-conscious and self-indulgent suicide attempt. That's much easier to deal with – for you and for us. But you – you'd never let yourself consciously do anything in such bad taste, would you?'

We laughed. 'Suicide is awfully vulgar really, isn't it?' Dr Piet went on, 'so emotional and overt. No. The only way you could bring yourself to take your life is when the conscious part of your mind has freaked out and the subconscious is given a chance. You'd consider it appallingly bad form to take an overdose while you were fully conscious.'

'But this is awful!' I wailed. 'If I can do this – ' I waved vaguely round with my left hand (my right arm was still tied to the drip) 'what could I do next? I'm not in my own control any more. And anyone who isn't that is mad!'

'Your trouble is that you exercise such cast-iron control and will power that your subconscious and emotions have to go to these kinds of lengths to get any kind of innings at all,' Dr Piet said quietly.

'But it's not a fully human act if it's not willed and rational.'

'Oh, come on, come on. You're supposed to be the Eng. Lit. specialist. Look at Lady Macbeth. You can't say she wasn't expressing herself in that sleepwalking scene. But look, Karen, I told you something else, didn't I? Something when we were talking about your friend Rebecca. . . .'

I looked at him and shook my head.

'I told you you were dying,' he said quietly. 'It looks as though I was right, doesn't it? And not just metaphorically. It was pure chance that Jane found you when she did.'

There was a silence. Outside the cubicle I could hear the normal life of the ward going on. Trolleys being wheeled to and fro. Nurses laughing. Instruments clattering. I might have heard none of this. I might be dead.

'Are you afraid?' Dr Piet asked softly. 'Afraid of yourself?'

I nodded, unable for a moment to speak.

'Good.' I looked up puzzled. 'It shows that the woman in you who is trying to come out wants to live. Wants to live very much indeed. We'll have to stop this – this – what for want of a better term I'll call nun-part, who's fairly hot on mortification, doing you in.'

He watched me, shrewdly.

'Do you think you'll do it again?'

'How do I *know*?' My voice rose in despair.

'Just let yourself feel for a moment. Lean back and shut your eyes. Relax.' He laughed. '*Try* and relax. Okay. Now – behind the embarrassment and the shame, behind the fear of yourself,

136

behind the depression even – is there anything different about you this morning?' I groped down inside myself and kept coming up against it. A new sensation. I'd had it when I was lifted onto this bed last night, just for a moment. I'd had it in snatches during the morning, and now it surprised me again. A certain stillness. Exhaustion? Perhaps. But a stillness too. Something in me had been calmed.

I looked up at Dr Piet. He smiled. 'You see?' he said. 'It's there. After a suicide attempt – and that's what this is – after a suicide attempt there's a period when it is most unlikely for the patient to try again. For a while, anyway, the destructive energy has used itself up in the immense effort it has taken to do anything as unnatural as self-destruction. Something has been put at rest. So,' he leaned forward speaking vitally, 'we've got a respite. You're right to be afraid. But we've got a period of time to work with when you should be okay. We're going to have to work hard at it. All right?'

Jane perched on my bed, systematically eating the grapes she'd brought me. She had, of course, taken the whole episode completely in her stride, waving aside my embarrassed thanks.

'For God's sake! It was a marvellous piece of luck for me! I feel tremendously noble and resourceful, though it was just a question of dialling 999, really. And dealing with the Stanleys.'

My heart sank. 'How did they take it?'

'They looked pretty aghast, I must say. Judith hopped from one leg to another, looking like an anguished stork, and Edwin was put right off his supper. Pity, really, he'd gone to quite a lot of trouble with it.'

'But Simon didn't know?' I asked. 'That would have been dreadful.'

'No, no. He was in his room. Slept through the whole thing. The ambulance was quick. And I'm afraid I didn't do anything really heroic, like trying to make you sick. I tell myself that I was afraid of doing more harm than good. But really I was just too squeamish. I must say,' she grinned at me, 'it's never dull knowing you!'

'I expect the Stanleys feel the same,' I said hollowly. They'd been so kind to me and how had I repaid them?

'They're amazingly fond of you, Karen, in their own funny way. I mean they'd die rather than show it. Like me, really. But, you know, we're all terribly concerned. Judith rang up the hospital to make sure you were okay.'

'All the same, Jane, I can't go back – not yet, anyway. I've got to give them a chance to get over it. It's a dreadful breach of hospitality, after all.'

'Would you like me to ask them?' Jane asked. 'For heaven's sake, eat some of these grapes. I bought them for you, and I've eaten half of them already!'

Absently I took a small bunch and forced a grape down. 'You see, if you ask them now what can they do, they've *got* to say: "Come back – all is forgiven". Anything else would sound so heartless. It's emotional blackmail really. No, I think the thing to do is to go off on my own, positively, do you see? And then – when everything has simmered down a bit – let them take the initiative.'

Jane considered. 'I do see what you mean. Will you go home, then? To your parents?'

'They're away at the moment, on holiday. Anyway,' I paused, trying to make my thoughts clear, 'I don't want them to know about any of this. What can they do about it? It would only worry them sick and make them feel guilty. Also – they're too – involved. I thought I might ask to go and sleep in one of the student's rooms in the Convent.'

'In the Convent!' Jane exclaimed incredulously. She coloured and paused. 'Sorry. You never talk about it, so I never know how you feel about all that part of your life. But don't you think that part of your troubles may well be due to those years you spent there?'

'Not really,' I said. 'I mean, the nuns certainly didn't intend any of these difficulties. And, oddly enough, even now after all that's happened, it's the place where I feel most at home. At least I'd have a rest from endlessly trying to fit into the world again.'

'I can see your point,' Jane said doubtfully, abstractedly watching Brenda emerge from her cubicle, dressed up and ready to go.

'Mike's not here yet,' she yelled cheerfully across the ward. 'I don't know where the Hell he is!' She wandered across to the window to watch the ambulance drawing up in front of Casualty in the yard below.

'But, Karen,' Jane went on, 'how would the nuns feel about having you around? After all, aren't you a renegade or something?'

'No, they don't look at it like that,' I explained. 'I met the new Superior in the street not long ago and she did say that if ever I wanted to come and stay for a few days – "to get away from it all" – I'd be most welcome. I think they feel friendly towards me and a bit responsible. Especially after what happened to my friend, Rebecca. That gave them all a shock. I told you about her, didn't I?'

'Yes,' Jane said. 'I must say the two of you seem to be a right pair! How is she?'

'On the mend, thanks. I had a letter from her a few days ago saying she'd put on a stone. Apparently she suddenly felt that she *wanted* to put on weight and the weight just – happened.'

There it was again. The immense power the subconscious had over us both.

'Well, there's one happy ending,' Jane said, and suddenly, impulsively, she took my hand and smiled at me. 'Now we've got to make sure that there's another.' Yet again I found I did not want to draw away from her.

The subdued hubbub of visiting-hour chit-chat was suddenly shattered by a strident yell from Brenda.

'Oh, there you are! You're late! What've you been up to, then?'

Involuntarily we both turned to look at a pale youth, awkwardly carting two sticky-looking toddlers into the ward. He was wearing a suit which had either never fitted him properly or which had ceased to fit him due to a sudden weight loss. One glance at his face – his eyes narrowed and strained and circled with the huge, purple bruises of insomnia, his cheeks haggard with a responsibility too great for his years – inclined us at once to the latter view. He couldn't have been more than eighteen.

'My God!' breathed Jane in horror. She and Brenda had had a cheerful reunion when she arrived at the evening visiting time and when Brenda went to change I'd told her her hopeless little story. 'He's the next one for a nervous breakdown! How on earth will they manage?'

139

'I wanted to go to the Bingo on the way home!' Brenda cried loudly as they left the ward in a grisly, disorganized quartet. 'But we're too late. We'll have to go straight home!'

'Bingo!' Jane echoed in wonder, and we looked solemnly at one another. 'Karen, you've got a hell of a lot more going for you than they have. Just you hang on to that!'

The next morning I stood by the pay phone in the ward and dialled the number of the convent. I asked to speak to the Reverend Mother.

'Karen, how lovely to hear from you!' The words came down the line in cool and measured tones, but there was a genuine warmth and concern there. I asked if I could come and stay, to which she agreed pleasantly. I could have one of the rooms in the hostel, could come and go as I wished. And, of course, it would be free. There was to be no question of payment. 'Just look on us as another home, dear.'

'Thank you, Reverend Mother.' I felt my heart swell with astonishment at the generosity and kindness.

The pips broke in and I hastily thrust some money into the slot.

'Where are you phoning from, Karen?' Reverend Mother asked. 'Are you in a call box?'

'I'm in the Radcliffe, Reverend Mother. I've spent a couple of days in hospital.'

'My dear! I'm so sorry. Are you ill? What's been the trouble?'

I stammered out my story.

There was a silence at the other end of the line.

'Reverend Mother? . . . Are you there?'

It never occurred to me what she might feel. I'd heard so many times: 'Nuns are never shocked, any more than Christ was. We are here in His place – not partaking of the sins of the world but understanding them. It should always be said "You can say anything at all to a nun".'

I had heard it so often and still believed it. So when there was that pause down the line I thought only that it was a silence of sympathy.

'Reverend Mother? . . . Are you there?'

'Karen,' the words came over thinly, coldly, 'I'll have to think about this. It's a terrible, terrible thing you have done. Some theologians would say that suicide is the greatest of all sins. I can't take the responsibility for this alone. I shall have to take advice, to pray about it. I'm just so appalled. . . I don't know what to say to you. . . But I can't just say come back here. . . '

The voice was still speaking when I replaced the receiver. And I felt tears of anger pour down my cheeks.

Mesmerized with horror I watched the woman make her slow, crab-like progress down the corridor. Her limbs bent like squidgy rubber in all directions. On her face there was an expression of exaggerated terror, as she took each painful step forward. While both her hands and feet were in contact with the wall she was all right, but each time she took a new step and broke the fearsome attachment to the walls nameless horrors assailed her.

'Come on, Mrs Saunders, you can do it!' the nurse said encouragingly every thirty seconds. It was plain to me that she couldn't.

When I'd telephoned Dr Piet, he had decided that I had better be admitted to his psychiatric hospital for a while.

'It's not ideal – in fact it's far from ideal,' he had said ruefully, 'but frankly it's better than the convent. That was a crack-brained scheme, if ever I heard one. No –' he cut short my protestations – 'I can see the advantages *you* saw in it. But I just think "fresh woods and pastures new" is the order of the day from now on. As a literary specialist you will doubtless recognize the quotation.'

'One good thing has come out of that phone call,' he remarked just before hanging up. 'You're furiously angry, aren't you? You're weeping with anger! Congratulations! Keep up the good work.'

Now as I sat in the long ward day room, I wondered how I could endure an hour of this place, let alone a few days. I held onto my suitcase – a guarantee that, for the moment anyway, I could still walk out. The other inhabitants of the day room, I was glad to see, looked less ill than Mrs Saunders, but they seemed strangely quiet. Drugged to the eyeballs, probably.

'Hello, then? Come to join the loonies?' A short middle-aged man with glasses and a five o'clock shadow came and sat next to me. 'Ah, cheer up, darling. It's not so bad. Quite like home it seems after a day or two.'

'That's what I'm afraid of,' I said, unable to take my eyes away from Mrs Saunders. 'Still,' I added firmly, 'I'm only here for a few days.'

'That's what we all say,' the man replied cheerfully. 'What's up with you, then. *Anorexia*? Looks like it, if you don't mind my saying so! Suzie's got it too – she's not here at the moment – so you'll have company. And you'll join us in the weigh-in brigade every morning. Drag you out of bed at half-past six, they will, throw you on the bloody scales. Pour a cuppa tea down your throat and send you back to bed. For a rest. For – a – *rest*.' He groaned with exaggerated ridicule. 'Fat chance of *that*, after they've woken you up, good and proper! Well, what do you make of the old place, then?'

'It's a lovely room,' I said weakly, and indeed it was, having once been the drawing room of the house. Huge french windows looked out onto a terrace, the walls and ceilings with their elaborate cornices were painted a gleaming white and the doors were beautifully proportioned. There the beauty stopped, however. The institutional armchairs, the floral, hide-all carpets and the dismal, undefinable smell of illness swamped the room's original elegance. Resolutely I turned back to my companion. He at least looked cheerful.

'Oh, we've got it all here!' he exclaimed cheerfully. 'Ping-pong in the next room, the telly, the garden – *if* you're allowed outside, that is. It's not so bad! Just waiting for Nurse to register you, are you? Thought so!'

A woman in a cerise knitted dress, her shoulder bones sticking through the material painfully and her greying hair pulled neatly back off her face, walked uncertainly towards us, threading her way aimlessly through the maze of armchairs.

'Who am I?' she asked, bending down so that her lost worried eyes gazed directly into mine. Her skin was white and crumbly-looking. 'I don't know who I am.'

'You're Mrs Sims, dear,' my companion explained patiently, with the air of one who has repeated himself many times. 'Got that? *Mrs Sims*.'

'Oh!' she cried with an air of discovery. 'I'm Mrs Sims!' she said to me, happily, before she wandered off.

'Barmy! Quite barmy!' my friend commented equably. 'Still, we're not all like that. Not by a long chalk. No. You'll soon feel at home in no time. A right old giggle we have sometimes!' I smiled weakly at the prospect. 'What's wrong with you?' I asked curiously. He seemed the epitome of normality to me. Still, I looked round nervously, perhaps he was schizophrenic. Nothing would surprise me in here. I felt panic mounting; the strain of the last few days was obviously beginning to tell. It was no use my feeling superior. If anyone was mad here it was me, for all Dr Piet's squeamish avoidance of the word. Visions, hallucinations, depressions, suicidal tendencies, Lady Macbeth sleepwalking scenes! Mrs Sims had nothing on me. I've got to get out! I told myself desperately.

'Me, dear! Not a sausage if you ask my opinion.' He settled down happily to tell his story. 'I had headaches, see. Went along to the GP. I get these headaches – terrible! I told him. Well, I had the lot – tablets, diets, X-rays. Nothing would touch the buggers. Went into the Radcliffe – suspected tumour on the brain – that was a nasty moment, I can tell you. Weeks I was in there, being investigated – tests, brain scans, the lot. Did they find anything? Not a dicky bird!'

In spite of my gloom I was beginning to get caught up in the story and in his jovial acceptance of it all.

'So what happened?' I asked.

'Well, the doctor comes along. "Mr Cooper," he says, "we can't find your trouble. Doesn't seem to be anything physical. So, we're transferring you to the Warneford for investigation in case it is of psychological origin." "You think I'm a nutter, then?" I asked. "Never had no trouble in the family that way before." "Certainly you're not a 'nutter', Mr Cooper," he said. "No, no. That's not a word we use. No. I'm sure you'll find that some – depression – anxiety – that you perhaps don't realize you've got is causing these headaches of yours." So, here I am, sweetheart, six months later.'

'Six months!' I exclaimed in horror. 'But are you any better at all?' I asked him. 'I mean, how are the headaches?'

'Shocking,' Mr Cooper sighed and shook his head in some perplexity. 'I don't know. I really don't. Nothing's shifted them.'

'But have you found out that you really are depressed?' I asked.

He certainly didn't look it. Perhaps it was something physical after all.

'No, darling! I mean, I see the doctor twice a week here and we've talked things over. But, like I say, I'm all right. Had a good job, before this lot started, got on all right with the wife and kids. Went to the football and the pub with my mates. No trouble except these flipping headaches. But the doctor – ' he laughed shortly, 'will he take no for an answer? Not on your life. "Mr Cooper," he says, "did you have a difficult birth?" I ask you! Where's the sense in that?' He suddenly burst into the wheezing laugh of the heavy smoker and dug me in the ribs with his elbow, inviting me to share the joke. 'How about you, darling? Did *you* have a difficult birth, then?' His laughter was infectious. Psychological niceties on the lips of Mr Cooper did indeed sound ridiculous. One thing seemed quite clear, however. The psychiatrist had clearly not been able to get through to Mr Cooper any more than Brenda's psychiatrist had been able to make her understand his role and the nature of her depression. What were they all playing at? Was psychiatry really any more than a verbal game for people with a particular kind of education? I decided that it was my job to try and make Mr Cooper understand the bearing of his doctor's question, even though it did seem a shame to spoil his joke.

'Did you have a difficult birth?' Mr Cooper was still laughing. 'Well, darling, I said: "I dunno, Doctor, I don't remember it, do I?" and do you know what he said? – this is a good'un, wait till you hear this – he said,' Mr Cooper paused dramatically, '"Are you sure?"'

'Karen.' A nurse stood at my elbow and picked my suitcase up. 'Would you come this way, dear?'

'See you later, I expect, sweetheart,' Mr Cooper's voice followed me as I hurried past Mrs Saunders after the nurse. 'I'll see you eat your chips at supper tonight, like a good girl!'

I rounded the corner of the corridor and there, hopping from one foot to another and standing as near to the ward entrance as possible, was Judith Stanley.

'My dear!' She hurried forward and took my suitcase from the nurse. 'What were you thinking of? You can't possibly stay here – it's absolutely ludicrous!'

I stared at her, feeling my mouth go dry with sudden hope. 'Do you mean –' I began to ask uncertainly. Judith was pushing open the big doors resolutely. She looked appalled at her surroundings, even though she tried to smile nervously at the nurse who nodded briskly at both of us and bustled officiously back into the ward.

'Come on!' Judith said impatiently and, in a daze, I followed her out of the ward, through the hospital entrance hall and out into the mellow summer afternoon. 'What an extraordinary thing to have done,' I heard Judith saying. 'I telephoned the hospital to ask when you'd be coming out and they told me that you'd come here.'

'Dr Piet –,' I began again. The air seemed gloriously fresh after the stuffy smell of despair in the ward and the sunlight was warm and golden. I felt a flicker of exhilaration as I hurried after Judith, who was unlocking her battered and ancient Morris Minor. It seemed a chariot fit for the gods.

'Yes, I've spoken to him.' Judith stared at me after she had flung my case on to the back seat. 'He told me that you didn't feel you could come back to us. And that you'd asked to stay in the convent! My dear, I've never heard anything so insane in my life. You must be mad!'

'Yes,' I said meekly, smiling now at the irony. 'Yes, I sometimes think I am. Mad, I mean.'

'Here.' Judith scrabbled in the glove compartment and brought out an opened packet of after-dinner chocolate mints. She threw them into my lap and started the car. 'These were left over from a dinner we had at college last night. There are quite a lot left. I thought they might cheer you up.'

As we drove into Oxford I felt a glow of returning life. The dark green trees, as we sped down Headington Hill, seemed lush and mysterious, Magdalen Tower once again beckoned to me as a sign of a fresh start, as it had on the day I'd left the Order, three years ago. I felt an excitement at the bustle in the streets and a surprising fondness for the people we passed. It was Judith who'd done that for me. She'd made me feel that there was a place for me in the world after all. She was bringing me home. I knew there would be no maudlin discussion about my depression, my abortive suicide. The subject was closed now but the box of mints on my lap – dear Judith! how typical of her to pinch a half-used box from College, but how appropriate, the gift of a

145

new one would have been so uncharacteristic that it would have been embarrassing – was a sign that something extraordinary had taken place but it was accepted and absorbed.

As I humped my suitcase up the stairs to my room I could hear the television blaring from Nanny's room.

'Does Simon know what happened?' I whispered to Judith swiftly.

She shook her head. 'He knows that you haven't been well, and has his suspicions that something strange has been going on. That's all.'

I tiptoed past Nanny's room, feeling suddenly shy. The door was flung open and Simon barred my path. He stared firmly at the floor, his eyes fixed.

'The Royal – ' he said quietly, with an experimental intonation.

'Arms!' I smiled back.

Simon beamed and awkwardly shuffled across towards me, put an arm stiffly round my shoulders and solemnly touched my forehead with his in a formal salute.

'Karen,' he said, 'you're my best girl friend.' Then flapping his hands impatiently he waved sentimentality aside. 'But enough of all that kind of stuff. Nanny!' His voice had recovered its usual number of decibels. 'The Royal Arms has come home! And now we're all complete!'

CHAPTER SEVEN

Guy

'How about coming out for a coffee and a quick fuck?'

Astounded, I wheeled from my pile of books. The words were not whispered but rang out cheerfully and clearly. A disapproving chorus of throats being cleared and papers being rustled by my neighbours in the Upper Reading Room in the Bodleian Library broke out in the musty stillness.

'Well, what about it then?' He stood grinning down at me and I realized I'd often seen him there. Lately he'd taken to sitting in the desk opposite mine and when I looked up from my work I found him looking at me thoughtfully. Twice he'd winked and I buried myself in my notes again hastily. He was always surrounded by huge, dusty tomes that looked as though they had not emerged from the stacks for years and he either stared in puzzled meditation at the cramped print or covered sheet after sheet in tiny, hieroglyphic handwriting. I suddenly realized in some confusion that I'd noticed quite a lot about him. One leather boot was stuck in the rung of the chair next to mine in a slightly swaggering gesture and, with a loud scrape, he pulled it back and sat down next to me and our faces were more on a level. Dark hair, a slightly darker beard, thin face with dramatically hollow cheekbones, he looked like a Nordic subject in an El Greco painting. A pale blue shirt was tucked into his jeans and I found myself looking at the hairs on his forearm. Turning away quickly I looked into his eyes which were pale blue with tiny, deranged-looking pupils.

'Ssh!' One of my neighbours hissed reprovingly.

'Sorry, mate!' my companion whispered equably, raising his hand to the stout, dowdy woman don, making her bristle even more.

'Ssh!' I too tried to be disapproving but his cheerfulness was infectious and I found myself smiling back.

'Missed you last week when I was in here.' He raised one eyebrow inquiringly. 'What happened? Fall into the Cherwell or something?'

'No. I – I was ill,' I said. It was only a week since the day Judith had collected me from the Warneford and today was my first day back in the Library. It was strange to be back in this long, passionless room, taking notes as though nothing had happened. That sense of stillness and calm that I was aware of the day after I swallowed the pills still made me feel as though something was laid at rest. For the moment.

Not a shred of concern crossed my companion's face, and if I'd expected a conventionally polite inquiry I was disappointed. 'Still alive, I see,' he whispered. Then he smiled back at me again. 'You're not coming out, I take it?'

'No. I've got far too much work to catch up on.' It was not true, but to go out with him was unthinkable. Yet still I found myself giggling slightly. The Bodleian seemed an odd place for a pick-up.

'Not even for coffee – just coffee?'

I shook my head. I'd felt, this last week, a new surge of life somewhere, but this encounter threatened to be too life-like at the moment.

'See you next week?'

Again I shook my head. 'I'm going to Cornwall for the summer.' I was going with the Stanleys to their house.

Unperturbed, he stood up, nodded and stretched. He was, I noticed, thin but muscular.

'Well, be seeing you in September.' He rumpled my hair as though I were an old acquaintance. 'So long, honeychild.'

As I watched him stride down the long room with a seaman's roll he looked incongruous. My notes on Chomsky's linguistic theory seemed, for a moment, unreal. The sun beat in through the tall windows in huge slabs of light and the dust of many books spiralled purposelessly, imprisoned in the airless library. Odd, I thought. I must be getting better. There was none of the usual fear or panic that approaches from men usually brought with them.

The door swung creakily behind him and smiling to myself I settled back to my books, feeling the disturbed silence heal and lap me round again, fold by fold.

*

I'd been to Cornwall with the Stanleys before, but this year it was different. One thing I'd noticed since coming out of hospital was that my visual sense was heightened, as though the world, which I'd so nearly lost, were given back to me more intensely than before. I'd always been aware of the extraordinary blue of the sea beyond the red slash of the Stanleys' fuschia bushes on the terrace, the tang of the salt air and the warmth of the sun seeping into my skin as I lay, book inevitably in hand, on the terrace looking at the bay below. This year, though, I found I was reading less and would often catch myself staring out to sea, listening to Judith's guests hard at work in the grounds, bashing down the thistles that had grown up during her absence in Oxford, and watching the horses from the nearby riding school who grazed in Judith's cliff paddock silhouetted nobly against the sea. Before I had read feverishly to allow no time for thought. Now I felt more a part of the Stanleys' summer ménage. They did not entertain much in their Oxford house but, instead, invited their friends to stay in the huge house on the Cornish cliff that Judith's father had built for her mother as a wedding present. There was one evening when Edwin and Isaiah Berlin had us all weeping with laughter as they read Beerbohm's *Savonarola Brown* together and another afternoon when I came across Edwin with two other philosophers sitting solemnly in the kitchen round the dishwasher which one of them had attempted to mend.

'It has just completed its second cycle,' Edwin informed me gravely. That year too Felix, one of the Stanleys' older sons, came down with half of his London commune and a grand piano, which he had picked up cheap. The whole household turned out to push the piano up the winding path on a rolling procession of broom handles and into the music room. For the rest of our stay he and Judith played pieces for two pianos, he scruffy and wild-haired, she lean, intense and dry, calling encouragement to one another above the Mozart and Beethoven. In the evenings Felix and his friends made their own music, loud, weird and deafening, while the rest of the party tried to read in the adjacent sitting room.

Life was not always so indolent. In the afternoons everyone was expected to bathe under Judith's eagle eye, but no one was allowed to utter the word 'cold' for fear of putting Simon off.

Tight-lipped and muscles clenched, we strode into the icy water calling strangled cries of encouragement to Simon, who stood gingerly at the water's edge or else sat huddled miserably on a lilo which Edwin would dutifully tow, wading up to his thighs in the freezing blue water, his hair streaming patriarchally in the breeze. 'How are you getting on?' I asked once, swimming briskly past. 'I am unaware that I have legs,' he replied calmly, adjusting his spectacles.

It was the year, also, of the Anti-China Clay campaign which Judith was leading in the area. The clay authorities had proposed to dump deposits of refuse out at sea, ruining the Stanleys' cliff by a hideous pipe line which would stretch far into the water. Edwin took a mildly satirical amusement in Judith's involvement with the cause and at dinner in the huge kitchen he and his allies among the guests tried to compose slogans for car stickers.

'Bathe while you may
   Before the clay.'
'Ambiguous and inaccurate.'
'Don't be fey
   Stop china clay!'
'Obscure.'
'Keep china clay
   From beach and bay!'
'Brilliant, Edwin.'
'Karen,' from Simon, 'do you insist on doing the washing-up so that Nanny can come upstairs with me?'
'Karen's done quite enough – she cooked the supper!'
'No, but Karen, do you insist? I'm sorry, everybody, but Karen absolutely insists!'
'Anyway, we've got the washing-up machine.'
'Edwin! I absolutely forbid you to use the washing-up machine.'
'Mummy absolutely forbids the washing-up machine but Karen absolutely insists!'
'It's a ludicrous waste of water and electricity.'
'Ludicrous! Ludicrous!'
'And you use far too much electricity anyway, Edwin. You had the fire on this morning, just because it's a little chilly. Ludicrous! If you want a fire there's plenty of wood – '

'Ludicrous!'

'The same,' Edwin beamed round at his audience, quite unabashed, 'is going on in boarding houses in Worthing.'

And that summer too, of course, I no longer got up at the crack of dawn to walk the five miles over the cliffs to get to Mass on Sunday mornings. The walk could be quite pleasant, even though it meant braving a field full of heifers and getting scratched to ribbons as I crawled through hedges and over barbed wire fences. The fly in the ointment was Mass and a sermon, soullessly gabbled by a priest who seemed bored and irritated with his congregation of holidaymakers. This year I could no longer make the effort; I still continued to go to Mass at Blackfriars, haunting the place where my faith died in the forlorn hope that one day I might get it back. To stop going to Mass altogether was such a final break with God that as yet I could not make it. At present, still numbed and made passive by the suicide attempt, I could no longer question myself about my faith.

'Karen,' one of the Stanleys' guests said, one Saturday evening over dinner, 'I'm going back to London early tomorrow morning. If you like I could drop you off at Mass, so you'd only have the walk home.'

My heart sank. I felt strangely bashful about telling this houseful of atheists that I no longer really believed in God.

'It's very kind of you,' I began, 'but – '

'Oh, for God's sake, don't take her to Mass,' Judith exclaimed, helping herself to more lasagne, 'she always comes home in such a bad temper.' She smiled at me and waved the dish in my direction.

'Do I really, Judith?' I asked, disconcerted, refusing the food, as a matter of course. 'How awful!'

'You're not like that after Mass at Blackfriars,' Judith considered, 'but here you're gloomy and jumpy for the rest of the day.'

'The sweet unction of religion,' Edwin murmured. 'Is it much worse here than Blackfriars?'

'Yes, it is,' I explained. 'But religion isn't just a matter of taste.'

'But of course it is,' Edwin retorted. 'It must be a matter of taste. *Your* taste!'

'It shouldn't make all that difference, though,' I insisted. 'But how dreadful that I've always come home from Mass in a foul mood. I'd no idea!'

'I thought the whole point of your religion,' Judith answered, 'was to make everybody charitable.'

'It is.'

'Well, then, you mustn't go if it puts you at loggerheads with the human race for hours afterwards!'

I found myself smiling. Her own instinctive charity over my suicide attempt compared very favourably with that of the professional Christians. I looked round the table. Her ex-son-in-law was sitting with his new girl friend next to Judith. 'They'll be sleeping together, of course,' Judith remarked casually when she asked me to make up their room. When Felix and his friends had arrived she had waved her hands vaguely. 'Oh, just make up all the beds in the cottage – God knows who's sleeping with whom! Let them sort it out themselves!' Nothing in my past life had matched it. In Catholic circles an ex-son-in-law would never be welcomed over the threshold again, let alone with his lover. Yet why ever not? They were far from being a wicked couple. And it wasn't just sloppy liberalism, either. Their tolerance extended to me too and my shameful, albeit accidental, abuse of their hospitality.

Besides all that, the thought of religion suddenly made me feel weary. A lassitude of spirit started to spread through me, like a stain, tainting everything. I'm tired, I told myself. If God exists, He will understand that I need a rest. But, of course, he didn't exist. I couldn't deceive myself any more.

'No, I'm not going,' I smiled sheepishly round the table.

There was a chorus of cheers, wine glasses were waved in the air in mock salute. Simon, who had been preternaturally quiet during the last five minutes, bashed his spoon noisily on the table.

'We'll have her an atheist yet!' Edwin remarked to the table. 'She's coming on nicely, isn't she?'

That summer was a turning-point. I was literally and spiritually on holiday. I was resting from both religion and *angst* and learning to enjoy life, seeing that it could be both beautiful and funny. When the time came for us to leave Cornwall and return to Oxford, I was, although I didn't realize it, ready for even greater changes which would embed me still more deeply in a world I was beginning to appreciate.

'So you've had a good summer?'
  'Yes, thanks! Very good.'
'I can see that.'
  'How?'
'You're a good colour, you're more relaxed. Been out in the open air? A bit plumper.' Dr Piet sat back in his chair after he'd said the last word with emphasis, looking at me steadily.
  'Am I?' A dart of pure fear shot through me.
'What?'
  'Plumper?'
'You should know. Do you weigh more? How much?'
I sat and looked at him dumbly. My mouth was dry.
'Well? How much?'
  'Six and a half stone.' The words spilt out, shamefully.
'Yes, that is better. Good. Before you went away, when you were in hospital, you were six stone three. Splendid. Excellent progress!' Dr Piet sat looking at me quizzically. 'Isn't it?'
  I was silent.
'What did you eat in Cornwall? Don't you want to tell me? Okay. Then what have you been eating since you got back?'
  'Oh, the usual stuff. You know.'
'The forty pence regime? Ryvita, cottage cheese, yoghurt and an egg a day.'
  'Yes.'
'Is it less than before you went to Cornwall? Or more? What you've been eating.'
  'About the same.'
'You mean you don't want to tell me. Isn't that right? All right. Just say it. Don't hedge. I can tell what you mean, anyway. . . Have you been making yourself sick?'
  'Only once or twice.'
'After you've eaten more than usual?'
  'Yes.'
'Okay. Now look, Karen. Will you do something? For me or for yourself. Will you promise me one thing?'
  'What?'
'Eat as you are doing, if you want. Okay? I'm not going to force

it yet. But I'm going to ask you every time you have coffee or tea to stir a teaspoon of Complan into it. You know what I mean? That invalid food. It won't make you fat, I promise you that. But it'll give you some protein.'

I looked at Dr Piet and he looked frankly, honestly back at me. I smiled and relaxed.

'All right.' It was only a small concession.

'Good girl. Now, let's talk a bit about why you're doing this to yourself.'

'I think it is to do with money. I can't bring myself to spend money on food. It's so expensive!'

'But you've got enough money. How much do you get a year? On a graduate grant?'

'Seven hundred a year.'

'And you don't pay rent, you don't really go out much at all, do you? Not *out* out – theatre, cinema.'

I shook my head. 'I'm afraid that it will all go – get whittled away, bit by bit, and suddenly it'll all have gone.'

'I don't think you need worry,' Dr Piet remarked drily. 'Forty pence a week on food and virtually no other expenses! I think you'll find seven hundred pounds has quite a lot of forty pences in it. As far as I can calculate you've got about four years' delicious eating stretching ahead of you at this rate, even allowing for the inflation, which the economists say will be upon us any day now. No, wait. Hang on! You've *had* two years of your graduate grant already, haven't you, on this regime. My God, Karen, you'll be a millionaire at this rate! I bet that money's piling up beautifully in the bank. Got it on deposit? Yes? Thought so. You'll be a girl worth knowing soon. Put you on an ordinary salary and you'll be a tycoon!'

'No, stop.' I was giggling weakly. 'You mustn't laugh! The money stops this time next year.'

'There's another reason why you're not eating. Think. Why did you get so upset when I told you that you looked plumper? Go on. Think about it. You came in here, looking tanned, a little rosy, smiling and relaxed. Happy – dare I say it? – you looked happy. And as soon as I say you looked plumper, you freeze up. You feel sick now, don't you?'

I nodded weakly. My mouth was dry and I felt panic crawling at the pit of my stomach.

'Could it be,' Dr Piet spoke slowly and looked meditatively at his blotter, 'that you're afraid of looking sexually attractive?'

There was a silence in my mind. Quietly I listened to a truth that had reached beyond it. After a few moments, stripped for once of any quick answers, I turned back to Dr Piet, who was watching me patiently.

'I wasn't sure that you were ready for that yet,' he said at last, 'but you are, aren't you?'

I looked back at him. The panic was beginning again, a fear of what he was about to tell me and its implications.

'Look,' he leaned forward, speaking softly and swiftly, 'how long is it since you menstruated?'

'Over a year,' I said after a moment, the beginnings of an unwelcome understanding glimmering.

'Right. And look at your body. Better still, look at it properly when you get home. Take your clothes off and look at yourself in the mirror. But for now just look and think as honestly as you can. Where are your breasts, your hips?'

I smiled weakly and gestured.

'And you're not having periods any more.'

'Do you mean,' I said after a moment, 'that I've made myself into a neuter figure?'

Dr Piet smiled at me, and shrugged. 'Thou hast said it! What you've done is make yourself quite sexless. Just think for a moment, and you'll see that it's not surprising. Think of the way you were dressed as a nun.'

I thought back to the enveloping yards of black serge, the cape, the veil, the bulky skirts.

'You see? All covered up. Monks are just the same. As a protection for their vows of celibacy they all cover themselves up so that the shape of the body is hidden, so that the body becomes, to all intents and purposes, sexless. That's all very well for them, but you're not a nun any more, are you? You're a woman out in the world, fair sexual game for anybody.'

'But I don't want sex!' It came out as a wail. I could feel tears forming and shook my head impatiently. The words came out choked and clotted with an emotion I felt ashamed of. 'It frightens me!'

'That's hardly surprising, is it? No, don't try to pretend the emotion isn't there. Let the tears come. This is good. You're honestly reacting now. With your guts, instead of taking refuge in a purely cerebral response.'

'The Catholic attitude to sex isn't healthy,' I said.

'No, it isn't. Sex is for breeding, not for pleasure. But I'm sure a lot of your respective schoolfriends are happily married Catholic mothers of three by this time. Could be genetic – something you've inherited from your parents, your randy grandmother. Who knows?'

'But I'm *not* randy. I don't want anything to do with it.'

'That's what you think!'

I looked at him, appalled. 'I'm *not*! Really!'

'Well, you're not exactly happy with the *status quo*, are you? All right! You go into a convent! You take vows of celibacy! You try and make yourself like an angel! You thrash your body into submission with a whip! Then you leave. At first everything's easy. You give yourself – quite sensibly, you've got a hell of a lot on your plate – a limited objective. You get your First Class Degree. Then what happens? Once you haven't got a goal any more?'

'Suicide, madness and despair,' I sighed.

'And *anorexia*. You suddenly wake up to the fact that your body is on view – legs, thighs, breasts, hips – in a way it hasn't been for years. And you don't want sex! So you start to starve yourself.'

'But I'm *not* randy!' I was angry now and sounded it.

'That's just where you're wrong!' Dr Piet leaned back in his chair. 'If you're not, why get so het up? Why not say quite calmly, "Actually, Dr Piet, you're quite mistaken. I'm not keen on the whole idea of sex – its sounds pretty distasteful, actually. I've got my work, which is perfectly satisfying. I don't need it." If you were happy with being celibate, you wouldn't be starving yourself to death to make sure sex didn't come your way. There'd be no need to go to all these lengths. If you were happy with being the sexless object you are, would you be trying to bump yourself off? Come on, Karen, use your head! Think!'

'I don't want it,' I mumbled desperately.

'Of *course* you don't on one level! You never have. Being a nun satisfied that part of you very well. But it's not satisfying the woman in you now, is it? Look, drastic measures are needed. You've got to smash your way out. You're doing well. Already you're beginning to think for yourself *and* feel all kinds of emotions you never let yourself feel before. Great. But another issue is the sex issue. The *anorexia* is a symptom: it's no use my bringing you in here and force-feeding you. But it's equally no good sitting waiting for love's young dream to ride up on a white charger. He won't. If he did you wouldn't recognize him at the moment. You've just got to get on with life sexually, now – no point in waiting till you're ready. You'll never let yourself be ready.'

'What do you suggest I do, then?' I asked bitterly, really frightened now. 'Stand on a street corner? Or advertise in the Lonely Hearts' Column?'

'Neither,' Dr Piet smiled calmly. 'No need. Because you are responding sexually, in a very rudimentary way. You're responding to me. Now.'

'What!' I stared at him aghast, feeling appalled and – suddenly – disgusted.

'Of course you are. Conversation's one of the sexiest things there is. An articulate woman like you ought to learn that, for your own good. Look, week after week I'm penetrating your mind like crazy. Of course sex is in the air. Oh, it's all right.' He laughed at my horrified expression. 'I'm not imagining that you're burning with desire to tear your clothes off and drag me down onto that mud-coloured rug. I'm pretty conceited, but I'm not that conceited. But you like me, I like you. We both enjoy these sessions – even you do on some masochistic level! The old hostility and resistance have gone. There's a spark in the air. A charge. It's sex. Nothing very scary in that, now, is there? If we weren't in a professional relationship, who knows how this might end!'

'Stop!' I had my hands over my ears now. I didn't want to hear any more.

'It's all right,' Dr Piet laughed gently and tapped on his blotter with a biro to regain my attention. 'I'm only teasing you. I'm a happily married man with two kids. Karen? Look at me. All right?'

I raised my burning face and saw him through a fog of embarrassment.

'But I'm not backing down on the rest of it. You've come a long way, Karen. The world is coming through to you at last and you're beginning to go out to meet it. But this is an essential step. Passive measures won't do. You've got to smash your way out of that cloister of yours. However painful it is.'

I sat there, fighting to regain my former calm, which had vanished in the chaos of my feelings.

'It's the only way,' Dr Piet went on inexorably. 'You do want to get better – don't you?'

A sudden screech of brakes broke roughly into my reverie and, startled, I watched a white van shudder to a halt a few yards further down the High, amid the honking of a dozen outraged horns.

'Hi!' A dark tousled head thrust itself through the window and grinned in my direction. It was several seconds before I recognized my friend from the Bodleian. 'Want a lift?'

I found myself smiling up at him. 'Well, I – '

'Get in.' The door was thrust open and to my astonishment I found myself climbing into the van and sitting in the rough passenger seat. Foam rubber spewed from various rents and tears in the black vinyl and the air in the driving compartment was heavy with nicotine.

'Not seen you recently. Had a good holiday in Cornwall?'

'How clever of you to remember!'

'I'm a genius. No problem,' he smiled. 'I've not been able to get to the Bod myself recently.' He tapped the steering wheel. 'Pressure of business.'

'Business?'

'My job. I drive this bloody thing for a living.'

'I go left here.' I indicated the slow climb of Longwall Street.

We skidded to a stop and a hard, lean arm broke my rapid progress towards the windscreen. Brakes squealed again. There was still more honking and swearing around us.

'Wankers!' muttered my companion calmly, thrusting his chin in the air and gesticulating with two raised fingers at a passing lorry. 'You doing anything this evening? Going out? In a hurry to get home for something specific?'

'Well, no, but – '

The gears cranked into operation. 'You are now.' He turned and laughed into my open-mouthed astonishment. 'The name's Guy. You're Karen. Right?'

'How did you know that?'

'Psychic. No, you silly moo! I read your Reader's Tickets, of course. Elementary.'

'But look,' I found myself laughing helplessly, 'you just can't do this.'

'Why not? Look, seriously.' Guy turned round and surveyed me calmly. 'Just a drink. Nothing more. I won't lay a finger on you – your virtue is safe with me!'

'It's not that,' I replied feebly.

'Yes, it is. That's what you're afraid of but I just want to talk to you, that's all. And you must want to talk to me or you wouldn't have got into the bloody van, would you?'

I supposed not.

'Anyway,' he announced pleasantly, 'you're being kidnapped.'

The pub was a rough, bare establishment in the warren of roads behind the High. There were no other women there. The only gesture towards modernity was a juke box in the bar corner which belched forth loud, wailing music. Guy was drinking Guinness, carefully wiping the beige foam from his moustache, and had bought me a barley wine. 'Quickest and cheapest way to get drunk,' he said as he put the unfamiliar dark drink in front of me.

'But I don't want to get drunk!'

'You need to,' he nodded to himself. 'Good piss-up would do you the world of good.'

We exchanged life histories. Guy had been expelled from public school, got his A-levels at a Grammar and graduated at Oxford eight years ago with a Fourth.

'How did you manage that?'

'Never did the bloody work,' he shrugged. 'Oh, I was reading all right. Got a lot out of Oxford in my own way. Only trouble was I never read what was on the syllabus. Did my own stuff, my own research.' He grinned suddenly and looked at me sidelong. 'I got two files of notes and essays for three years' work! Oh, it's all right. My old man paid. He's too loaded for me to get a grant so I didn't waste taxpayers' money.'

'Didn't you mind getting a Fourth?'

'Why should I?' He turned a puzzled blue stare upon me.

'What's the point? I don't want a career. I'm a poet. Got a lot of valuable work done when I was an undergraduate. This job's good enough for me. Keeps my mind free and I can take the odd hour off and get in some research.'

My heart sank rather when he told me he was a poet but it seemed that Guy was not particularly interested in being published. He was writing a lengthy philosophical poem. 'No one'll touch it,' he announced cheerfully, 'far too subversive and obscure for the usual round of poetry readers. Wankers, the lot of them, *Guardian*-readers and silly Hampstead Liberals. Still, never mind.' He drained the last of his Guinness and got up to replenish our glasses. 'I enjoy writing it. It's good. Even if I do say it myself. If you're a good girl I'll even let you read some of it. No, don't worry,' he staggered in mock deprecation, 'I'll spare you that! Unless you want to, that is.'

He greeted the news that I'd been a nun only with the barest nod of interest. I'd offered the information warily, expecting the usual prurient interest. Encouraged by this, I found myself, under the influence of my third glass of barley wine, giving him a brief but accurate account of my life to date. Including my recent visit to hospital. Again there was no spurious concern, just a calm nod while he rolled himself another cigarette, his oil-stained fingers clumsily crumbling flakes of tobacco. I felt suddenly relaxed in this seedy working-men's pub, on holiday from both my past and my present life with their stress on discipline, endeavour and accomplishment.

'No, really.' He leaned forward suddenly serious and intent. 'I envy you. Being a nun, I mean.'

'Envy me!'

'You've had a fantastic life! No, don't get me wrong. I'm sure a lot of it was hell. But the extremes! You've lived in an extreme way – you know; total celibacy, poverty, asceticism. What a start!' He gazed at me, slightly pop-eyed with drink. 'Everything you do now will be an extraordinary sensation, just by force of the contrast. Sex, drink,' he gestured towards my barley wine, 'freedom! The whole thing. The rest of us are so jaded. For you it'll be clean and new!'

It was a novel point of view. I smiled at him uncertainly. 'You don't want to get caught up in this second-hand academic shit,' he was saying. 'You've got your own living to do. It'll be like –

drinking water on a day when you're absolutely parched. You know what I mean?' He tapped my knee again as if to call me to attention. 'You could go now to the extremes of debauchery. No, it's all right, darling, it's not a pass. Just an idea. Christ, what a mind-wobbler!'

Still shaking his head in amazement, he grabbed my glass and rolled yet again, with his lurching, sailor's gait, towards the bar. I leaned back and watched him through the cigarette smoke. No doubt it was the drink, but I did suddenly feel at the start of a new adventure.

'Look,' Guy continued as soon as he reached our table, carefully laying the brimming glasses in front of us. He took a cautious sip, tasted it intently, and then turned his full attention back to me. 'You're depressed. Right? So depressed you nearly bumped yourself off a couple of months ago. That kind of depression isn't a handicap, for Christ's sake, it's freedom!'

'Freedom?' I faltered. But something in me responded to the words.

'Yes, freedom. Because if you're that depressed then nothing matters any more. You've got nothing to lose. Have you? Look. Name me one thing you're afraid of losing when you're really depressed.'

'Next time you're suicidal,' he went on intensely, 'don't waste it. Use it to benefit mankind! You could get rid of some political menace, for example, die in some tremendous cause.' A new record on the juke box broke into the ensuing pause and Guy groaned. 'Shoot Cliff Richard, for a start – do us all a favour!'

I found myself laughing helplessly, relaxed and miles from the rest of my life. But there was something more. The extremity of Guy's views struck some chord in me.

'Don't you feel sometimes,' he was saying, his mad-looking eyes fixed on mine, 'that you're on the brink of something else. Something just out of sight which is absolutely mind-blowing. And terrifying.'

I nodded. 'I always thought it was God.'

'Well, it isn't, of course. You know those times when you sort of clock out of reality – don't know what you're doing?' Guy asked. 'I have something like that too. Not hallucinations. Just blind rages when everything round me blacks out and I don't know what I'm doing. It's all right,' he added hastily, 'I'm quite safe most of the time and I never do much damage. I just throw things around, shout, belt off into the night. And I haven't a clue what I'm doing and I never remember a thing afterwards. That's what I mean by living on the edge. We're both on the edge of bloody volcanoes.'

We looked at each other solemnly over the tops of our glasses. The gaze lengthened and I found I couldn't draw my eyes away. Then slowly Guy reached out and took my hand. To my surprise I didn't want to draw it away. 'We're both in the same boat, aren't we?' he said quietly. He pressed my hand gently and I found myself returning the pressure. For the first time I could see that touch meant connection. I could feel this connection burning in my hand and then running down my arm through the rest of my body like an electric current. Deep within me something turned over and I shivered slightly.

'We're friends, then?' he asked, his eyes solemn.

'Yes,' I nodded slowly.

'I declare the Eynsham Autumn Fair open!'

In seagreen silk and pearly feathered hat Lindsey cut the ceremonial tape with a flourish and the crowds clapped enthusiastically. In her capacity as celebrity of *Crossroads* she had been invited to open the Fair.

'Good for fifty quid!' she whispered conspiratorially when we met up in the tea tent. I watched fascinated as people pressed round her, begging for autographs and signed programmes. To them she was, I realized, a celebrity.

'Kathy – I'm sorry, Miss Armstrong!' an enthusiastic lady beamed at me as she poured me out a cup of tea, 'has some very exciting news for you! It's so difficult trying to think of her as Lindsey – I can only see her as Kathy Lamb!'

'It's not surprising really,' I remarked after she'd left. 'You're dressed up in one of your *Crossroads* outfits.'

'I know!' Lindsey grimaced. 'Nothing of my own was suitable. Anyway, that's the point. They *want* to tell everybody that I look just the same off the screen.'

'Well. What's your exciting news, then?' I refused cakes on the plate in front of me but Lindsey bit into a pale pink bun. Jam spurted out of it inelegantly at either end. 'Shit!' she muttered, wiping her impeccably made-up mouth with a mauve napkin.

'Kathy Lamb doesn't swear,' she looked round furtively. Fortunately no one seemed to have heard her. On the next table somebody was asking the children to guess the name of her Teddy Bear and though many eyes were turned our way, no one would have dared eavesdrop. It was a table of the Gods. I felt decidedly dowdy in my long plaid cotton skirt and cheap velour jacket.

'I've been written out of *Crossroads*,' she announced, having another shot at the bun.

'Oh, no!' I was all compassion again. 'A year of the fleshpots and then back to Life on the Dole. What's happened?'

'Kathy Lamb falls in love with an archaeologist who just happens to stay at the motel for a few weeks, God rot him.' Lindsey helped herself to a piece of anchovy toast. She was obviously out to make the most of a free meal as well as the £50.

'And?'

'And they get married and she accompanies him up the Amazon in a canoe for his next dig. Curtains.'

'Are they filming the dig?'

'You have to be joking! No, I'm just waved off at the airport. Sandy in his wheelchair, Meg fluttering a hanky, David Hunter shaking my hand meaningfully, Uncle Tom Cobley and all!'

'When did you hear this?'

'Oh, last week, when this month's script was given out.'

'Lindsey, I *am* sorry!' I really was. Her life was no more secure than mine.

'I'm not!' Lindsey looked positively delighted.

'Why? Has something else come up?'

'You could say that. Karen, eat something, for God's sake.' She helped herself to an éclair. 'You look like a skeleton.'

'No, thanks. Lindsey, stop being so mysterious! What are you going to do?'

'Well,' she licked the cream from her lips and smiled, as though at a sweeter memory, 'you remember the guy I was telling you about?'

'Which one?'

'How many peas do you think there are in this pot, Miss Lamb?' A little girl, quivering with excitement, stood at her table, eyes fastened greedily on Lindsey.

'One thousand, three hundred and forty-two.' Lindsey smiled

163

with her eyes and deposited ten pence in her saucer. 'Karen? This,' she explained to the little girl, 'is my sister.'

The child barely bestowed a glance on me as I guessed 'One million and three.' Over the loudspeaker a disembodied voice announced that the Tombola was still open.

'A task for me later on. To give out the prizes, I mean.' Lindsey consulted her watch. 'Do you think,' she asked the child, 'that you could get me some more of that anchovy toast? It's absolutely delicious!' Enraptured, the child scurried off. 'I wish we could have a drink,' Lindsey sighed mournfully. 'Did you notice how sharply they guided me past the bar in that marquee into the tea room! It would never do to see Kathy Lamb drinking whisky at this time of day!'

'Lindsey! What man?' I asked impatiently.

'Oh! Yes! Sorry! The peas put me off track. The Canadian I met in Malta last May while I was on holiday.'

Dimly I recalled him. An exotic week-end on a sundrenched shore.

'What about him?'

'I'm emigrating to Canada to find him!'

'What!' I pushed my tea away. 'You can't do that!'

'Why not? Thank you so much!' Lindsey greeted the child all smiles, and forbore to take another slice of anchovy toast until she had signed the child's programme.

'Look,' she leaned across the table talking intently and seriously. 'I'm written out of the serial. Bad news! I'd have liked to have gone on for a while – it's fun and the money's good.'

'Kathy Lamb will never survive in the Amazon!' I said decidedly. 'How will she powder her nose?'

'Oh, I don't know.' Lindsey stopped chewing for a moment and poured herself another cup of tea. 'Kathy's quite a girl, really. I mean, she's tough – not just a pretty face. And what else is there for her? Stooging around in that motel year after year, doing David Hunter's typing for him?'

We looked at one another. 'All right,' I said, 'point taken. Canada might be a new start. Better than stooging, poverty-stricken, round London again. But is the man all that important? I mean, Canada's a big place. How do you propose to "find" him?'

'Oh! He knows I'm coming.' Lindsey stirred some saccharine into her tea. 'I've wired him. He's all for it. What I mean is that week-end was too short and we've got to discover each other properly. Maybe it'll come to nothing. But it's worth a risk.'

'But do you have to emigrate? That's so final!' It suddenly seemed sad that we would be thousands of miles apart. Our lives barely touched. Hers proceeded from man to man at lightning pace. She knew so little about me. We'd always assumed that we would have time later to become proper friends. Now it was too late.

'I have to emigrate to get a work permit,' Lindsey explained. 'But if things don't work out I can always come back. It's not as final as it sounds.' I marvelled at her courage and determination. She was going half-way across the world to try and find happiness. Perhaps there was happiness for me, too, somewhere. It was a strange thought. It would mean change for me. More change. But I wouldn't necessarily have to go to another country. The changes I needed to make were much nearer home.

'I had a fantastic childhood myself. Absolutely fantastic.' Guy smiled happily into his Guinness. We were sitting in our usual place in the pub off the High. It sounded a sad childhood to me. His parents were posted to Africa when he was eight and he went to live on a farm in Lincolnshire with his grandmother and his five unmarried uncles.

'Didn't you miss your parents?' I asked, tracing patterns in the rings of beer on the table.

Guy shook his head. 'Not much. They became strangers very quickly. I think kids live pretty much in the present. And I had a marvellous life on the farm in the school holidays. Ran wild I did.' He grinned at the memory.

'The day before my parents came back on a visit, I'd have a bath, and again on the night before I went back to school. But never any other time. My grandmother would have to chase me all over the farm – couldn't stand the soap!'

'You seem to wash now,' I remarked. His clothes and person were always spotless.

'Oh, right! I mean a bath's a sensual experience, darling, or haven't you found that out yet? But no, really. I hear people talking about *Wuthering Heights* and saying the violence there is exaggerated. Bloody fools! I remember once going into the barn with my Uncle Frank and we trapped a young fox. Pretty little thing it was too. Frank just picked it up, tied a rope around its neck and hanged it, there and then. Just like that!'

'Were you upset?' I winced at the picture that Guy painted for me.

'No! I was eight or nine then. A little savage. I was thrilled. Wouldn't like it now, of course! I've been civilized – a bit.'

'But Guy – how on earth can you say that you had a fantastic childhood? It sounds dreadful,' I said, bewildered. 'All that violence must have done really bad things to you, surely.'

He shook his head. 'Violence is just a part of life. You should know that from your Tennyson – "Nature, red in tooth and claw". It's only civilized places like Oxford that cover it up and pretend it doesn't exist. No. It was the best part of my life. My uncles spoiled me rotten. It ruined me for everything else. It all seemed so tame afterwards.'

'Was that why you couldn't fit into school or Oxford, do you think?'

'Could be.' Guy shrugged and leaned back, his eyes half-closed, scarcely seeing me. He sipped meditatively on the side glass of rum he kept beside his tall pint glass of Guinness, obviously years away. 'You see, once you've lived closely with violence you can't go back and pretend you've never seen it. You should know that, for Christ's sake. Your life in that nunnery sounds violent to me.'

'What on earth do you mean?' I demanded, mystified. 'Everything was terribly polite and civilized.'

'Of course it was, you silly moo!' He reached across and took my hand and shook it in exasperation. Again I felt the connection flowing between us. 'But your life was violent all the same – and much more unhealthy than the farm, if you ask me. Look at the self-destructiveness involved. I'm not just talking about the discipline, though, of course, that sums it up beautifully. But all that number about putting yourself to death. And look at you! You're still doing it now. Stuffing yourself with sleeping pills and nearly kicking the bucket. Making yourself look like a Belsen victim. That's violence, too, Karen. And it's got you. It's caught hold of your imagination just as the farm's caught mine and you can't escape from it.'

I looked at him, startled by his insight. 'But not towards other people! I only feel violent towards myself.' I paused. He had slid away from me again into his past, his eyes narrowed painfully. My hand was being clasped as in a vice and I nearly cried out until I realized that he couldn't hear me any more. There was a sadness on his face that I'd never seen before and I tapped his knee to call him back to the painful present. 'You're probably right,' I said after a while. 'About the violence, I mean. But what do we do, you and I? How do we make ourselves forget and become normal?'

'What's so great about being normal?' he sighed. 'Oh, Karen! You still don't understand, do you, love? We'll never be normal. No. The great thing is to capitalise on what we've had. I tell you – I'm always telling you – we've been lucky to have that insight into the way things are. We've got to explore it.' His voice was suddenly slurred and his breathing heavy. I looked at his face, which was crumpled suddenly with melancholy. 'You've got to come to bed with me one day, you know,' he said quietly. 'It's inevitable.'

I gasped, and shuddered gently. But not with disgust. There was a blurring in front of my eyes and a tightness round my ribs. He was right. We belonged together, bound by our strange yet curiously similar pasts in a frightening present. I felt a flicker of excitement. And a red streak of panic.

'I'm afraid, Guy.' The words came out in a strangled wail. 'I'm really afraid of it.'

'Of course you are!' He spun round and stared at me, his eyes blazing. The pupils, I noticed, were tiny black holes, angry and enraged. 'Of course you're afraid. We're both bloody afraid. You've got to push yourself on!'

Heads turned in our direction but I didn't care very much. He was shouting and the truth of what he was saying echoed in my head. He was holding me by the shoulders and his hands were bruising me with their pressure. I looked up and saw that he was trembling.

'Come outside,' I said gently.

'I haven't finished my drink.' He threw the rest of the rum down his throat and turned back. 'What are you waiting for? Are you going to hang around like this till you become a raving bloody lunatic or a frigid Oxford don, frightened of her feelings?'

'Don't be so angry,' I begged, close to tears.

'I am angry, blast you! But it's not masculine pride. It doesn't matter a damn really who you go to bed with, as long as you stop destroying yourself. Even your bloody shrink agrees with me! Never thought I'd see myself in agreement with one of the establishment.' The words were tumbling over themselves and he was staring straight ahead, blindly. 'I hate to see what you're doing to yourself. Freezing yourself up in fear of something that's so simple and natural.' He stood up suddenly and grasped me by the wrist. His face was white and I could sense that he was losing control. He pulled me after him and dragged me out of the pub to where the van was standing.

'Get in!'

'Guy, do you think you ought to drive?'

'Get in!' He wrenched the door open, picked me up and threw me into the passenger seat and slammed the door shut. I leant back, trembling myself, less from the danger than with the assault of what he was saying. He flung himself into the seat beside me and hunched over the wheel, staring bleakly ahead at something I couldn't see.

'Look, Guy.' I could hear my voice shaking and noticed, with surprise, that I was crying. 'I'm not ready yet.'

'And when will you be ready? Oh, don't give me that bullshit. You *like* suffering. You want to be unhappy and you want to make me miserable watching you dying on your feet.'

'But why on earth should it make you miserable?'

'Because I care about you, you stupid cow. I want to help you. And you could help me. But you won't bloody do it, will you? Just because you're scared.' His voice was coming out in a low rasping cry and his eyes were fixed ahead of him as though he were seeing some horror of his own. How quickly it had happened. It was no time at all since we'd been chatting amicably together in the pub. Terrified, I put out my hand and touched his arm. Instantly he swung round to face me and with a horrified fascination I watched him lift his right arm, shake my hand off his left and grab me round the neck. It was like a slow motion film. 'Wake up, damn you!' he screamed and his right hand flashed down and hit me once, twice, three times across the mouth.

There was an explosion of pain and I could hear myself crying out. Suddenly the van lurched forward and started hurtling violently down the pavement. I could feel the under-carriage scraping along the ground.

'Guy! Stop!' Fortunately we were in a side street and there was no one around. We narrowly missed a lamp post.

'I'm not stopping.' His voice was calmer now; with a jolt the van crashed from the pavement on to the road and started zigzagging back and forth. Brakes squealed. 'Wake up, Karen,' he said, almost pleasantly this time. He was laughing quietly to himself as he turned off, screeching, into another side street. 'When you're with me, you live dangerously. It's the only way to live. Life is dangerous.'

The pain in my jaw was throbbing but I was scarcely conscious of it. Something had cleared in my head; as the van rushed perilously through the darkness, crashing against the pavement, screaming round pillar boxes and lamp posts, I felt a strange sense of release and excitement. There was nothing I could do. He was going to kill us both and I found I didn't care very much. He was right. My life wasn't worth living. This was better. The orange street lighting flared luridly and for just a few seconds I found myself laughing, brushing away the tears impatiently. I was sick of being a good girl. For a full five seconds I wanted to break every rule in the book; an anarchy that I hadn't known existed in me rose to the surface and I reached out and touched Guy's shoulder, as we swung with a final shriek of brakes round a sharp bend and came to a juddering halt.

The sudden silence was a shock. I leaned back weakly, wondering what had happened to me. Sweat trickled coldly down my neck and my body was shaking with reaction. The excitement was gone now and I could feel my mouth hurting badly. But there was also a clean, hollowed-out release, as though something that for years had been pent up was set free. Wonderingly I touched my mouth and found that it was swollen badly. When I drew my hand away there was a dark smudge of blood. I found myself turning back to Guy, calmly. He'd claimed me now, in some strange way I belonged to him.

He was leaning over the steering wheel, spent and shivering. His breathing was painful and laboured as though he were in the grip of a bad dream. I looked at the way his hair grew down the back of his neck and wanted to touch him there, where he was vulnerable, to feel the softness of his skin. The hollows under his cheekbones were shadowed dramatically, imparting a look of suffering, and his eyes, I could see, were full of unshed tears.

'Guy.' I stroked the back of his neck and felt him shudder convulsively. I put my hands on either side of his face and forced him to face me, finding a strange new pleasure in the touch of his skin, the harshness of his beard.

'What have I done? What happened?' His voice was dead and exhausted. 'Where the bloody hell are we? Jesus Christ!' His eyes widened when he saw my face. Tentatively he put out his hand and touched my cheek gently. 'Did I do that? Did I? Did I do that?'

I nodded. Dumbly we stared at one another and I saw the horror fill his face as he struggled to remember. 'Did I hit you?' he asked again miserably as if he hoped there'd be a different answer this time. 'I don't remember! I can't remember a bloody thing. I remember talking to you in the pub. Enjoying being with you. Talking about my childhood, weren't we? And then. Nothing. Everything a complete blank.' There was panic in his voice, but despair as well. A despair I understood so well.

'I know what it's like,' I said unsteadily.

He broke away from me but grabbed my hand. Hard. 'Yes,' he said bleakly. 'I reckon you do.' There was a silence and his voice broke out again, on a higher note. 'I could have bloody killed you.'

'Yes.' It was as though the blow had smashed through some depth of reserve. All I wanted to do was to touch him. And I could. It was so simple really. I tried to smile and winced, remembering too late my damaged mouth. 'It's all right. You haven't killed me. We're both still here.' Again I touched his shoulder. He turned and we clung together, listening to each other's desperation in the silent street.

Even at the time I wondered why I wasn't more shocked by this display of violence. After all, a couple of years ago I'd been sitting primly at community recreation, decorously walking in serried ranks down cloisters, coolly turning the other cheek when criticized – in short, living the life of a Victorian lady. Now, here I was hurtling round back streets with a man who was completely out of control, from whose lips a steady stream of expletives that I'd never heard in my life was flowing. Nothing had prepared me for any of this. Why wasn't I at least slightly repelled?

Both Guy and I hated ourselves, of course. The only difference was that where he smashed out at other people, my habit of violence was directed towards myself. During my relationship with Guy I watched the way his violent attacks worked and slowly, in a tacit process of osmosis, I learned about my own violence. Little by little I faced the fund of anarchy left in myself, released it, externalized it and eventually was able to let it go.

Struggling under my heavy load of files and papers I made my way down the steep hill from the station and stood at the Number 1 bus stop. I glanced at my watch. Seven thirty. The buses were never regular, and though I could easily walk home I felt drained by my day in the British Museum. There were always so many tasks to fit in when I visited the Reading Room and such a pressure to get through the quota I had set myself for the day that I didn't relish the thought of a dark, damp walk through that particularly seedy part of Oxford. Still, it was cold here at the bus stop. We were well into December and I was glad of the furry warmth of my anorak. I just hoped the bus wouldn't be too long.

'Oh, Karen! Am I glad to see you!'

Startled, I woke from my Tennysonian dream and peered at the distraught figure with hair flying in dramatic outline against the orange flare of the streetlamp.

'Charlotte?' I asked uncertainly.

'Oh, Karen! Are you desperate to get home now? Bless you! You couldn't be an angel and come over with me to the Postal Sorting Office, could you?'

'The Sorting Office?' My companions in the queue at the bus stop eyed us both suspiciously. 'Of course I will. But what on earth for?'

'Oh, thanks! Let's hurry! I really need to talk to someone.'

As we crossed the busy road, dodging cars perilously, and hurried down the dreary no-man's-land of Becker Street, Charlotte explained her dilemma. Taking the advice of one of the tutors she'd applied for a year's traineeship at one of the Oxford University Libraries.

'It's a good idea really, I suppose,' she sighed. 'Sensible. A reasonable salary. Nothing too strenuous, so I'll have plenty of energy left for my writing. No obligation to train further but there's the option of a good career afterwards if I do – whoops! careful – watch that bus!'

'So where's the problem?'

'They offered me the job.' Her face looked almost statuesque in the lurid light. Our heels clattered in a brisk staccato in the silent little street.

'And?'

'I just couldn't decide what to do. I wrote two letters, one accepting the post and one refusing. And I posted the one refusing this morning.'

'And now,' we turned into the Office Yard, 'you wish you hadn't.' I was beginning to see what we were doing here.

'No!' Charlotte's voice rose in a crescendo. 'I got *that* one out of the post!'

'How?' I turned to her in astonishment. 'I thought it was impossible!'

'Oh, I just stood by the pillar box all afternoon. The postman was a love. I explained it all, showed him my handwriting, identification and he let me have it back! He thought I was a loonie, I think. Then I dithered some more and posted the letter accepting!'

'And you didn't get that one back.'

'Not such a nice postman. Oh, he was only doing his job! So I just thought I'd try here.'

We looked hopelessly at the impregnable fortress of the Sorting Office. The doors looked decidedly sealed. Lights were on and shadowy figures moved inside like ghosts behind the blinds.

'Well, what do we do?'

'Let's ring – or knock or something!' I beat hopefully on the door. Silence. 'Charlotte, this is useless! They're not going to let you sort through all that mail and get your letter back! And they shouldn't, either. You could be anybody, sabotaging the system. You could be your rival for the job trying to get the post for herself! Come on now!'

Charlotte beat on the door again. There was no reply.

'Do you mind if we just go round the back and see if there's a door with a bell?'

'All right. But I really think it'll be no good!'

We looked at one another and started giggling helplessly. 'Oh, Karen!' she said at last. 'Thank God it was you! You're the only person I know who's mad enough to understand.'

We tiptoed round the yard. Barbed wire blocked our further progress. 'I wonder, if I just climbed over, there might be another way in. . .'

'No!' I was laughing uncontrollably now. Feebly we leaned against the wall. 'The letter's probably gone through the system by now. What post was it?'

'Five thirty! Oh Lord, do you think so?'

'Yes, I do!' I lied with authority. 'And anyway, you'll only want to change your mind again! Look, let's go and have a coffee or something and talk it over.'

Ten minutes later we fell into the glaring normality of the Golden Egg in George Street and ordered coffees, still slightly hysterical.

'What's the trouble with the job?' I asked. 'I'm going to play Devil's Advocate. All right? After all, it's non-arduous, regular employment, doesn't commit you further. Good options. All the things you said. And you know how short you are of money. It'll be more interesting than the tax office.'

'Oh!' Charlotte moaned, stirring sugar into her weak coffee. 'Don't tell me. I know! I know! You're absolutely right. But the die's cast now and I just know it's the wrong decision!'

'The die isn't cast!' I said firmly. 'You haven't got any note paper in your bag, by any chance?'

'You have to be kidding!' Charlotte scrabbled in her battered-looking bag and fished out a pad of Basildon Bond and a packet of envelopes. 'I've been writing different letters all day, all over Oxford, at hourly intervals! And then tearing them up.'

'Or posting them!' We both giggled again. 'All you have to do is write *yet another* letter refusing,' I said, pulling myself together at last, 'explaining that this cancels your letter of acceptance. Apologize politely and I can push it through the door of the library tonight. It's on my way home! All right? Now think about it. It's done. The letter's gone through the box, they read it tomorrow, and say "The girl's mad, just as well she's not coming!" And it's over. Finished. Now think! We'll sit here in silence for as long as you like and then you can see how you like living with the fact that you've refused the job.'

Silence reigned. I studied the menu and watched a young couple chomp their way through the Golden Egg special, watched the waitresses scurry round in their yellow checked pinafores and jaunty caps, and felt extraordinarily fond of Charlotte.

'No!' Charlotte broke off and grinned at me, her face transfigured. 'I do *not* want the job. I feel immensely relieved. I feel mad with joy. Almost mad enough to eat a Golden Egg special to celebrate!' She signalled to the waitress. 'Oh, go on, Karen. Splash out! Have a cottage cheese sandwich at least! It's on me! Bless you! I'm free! I'm free!'

While waiting for our feast, I felt suddenly, inexplicably hungry, and with an unwanted extravagance waved aside Charlotte's offers of payment.

'Tell me, why don't you want that job?' I asked. 'Just testing – you understand? It's secure. It's safe.'

'That's just it!' She shook dollops of vermilion sauce over her plate with abandon. 'It's too safe! We're not meant to be that safe. Life isn't safe. That job would have stifled me with cosy security.'

'Don't you want to be safe?' I asked incredulously. I'd suddenly realized how very much I did. All my life I'd been walled in by rules of behaviour, rules for belief, rules for the heart which had separated me from all the pain of uncertainty and risk.

Charlotte considered, her chin propped on her hand. 'Yes. The cowardly part of me does. But I want to be free more.' She grimaced ironically. 'That's great coming from me, isn't it? Locked up in my room waiting for Mike like bloody Godot.' She shook herself and straightened up, staring straight ahead, her face hard with purpose.

We sat, motionless.

'I'm getting out.' She spoke quietly, seriously. The exuberance of a few moments ago had gone. 'I'm really going to be free, not just free of a cosy job so that I can sit in my prison. I'm going to London, breaking with Mike. I'll get a job there.'

For a few minutes we sat together silently. Charlotte was still looking straight ahead into the emptiness of a Mike-less future.

174

Her hands grasped the pepper pot fiercely, her knuckles were white with the effort of renunciation. Then suddenly she flushed and smiled almost shyly.

'I'm really pleased with myself, Karen. I've done it. Here beginneth the New Life.' She shook her head impatiently to toss aside the rebellious tears that had gathered and looked back at me. Slowly she nodded.

'Oh, Charlotte!' It was on the tip of my tongue to say 'don't go' but I bit it back. She was right. But how I would miss her.

'Come too!' She leaned urgently across the table, her eyes shining. Impatiently she pushed her plate aside, as though she was pushing away all the obstacles to the scheme, all the panic that suddenly flooded me, leaving me breathless with panic, just as I had been when she suggested going to Paris.

'The thesis,' I muttered ineffectually and glanced away from Charlotte's knowing stare.

'You've got to get out, love. You're not made for the academic life. Oxford's like another cloister for you. You need something much freer, much less confining.'

'I don't, you know! I'm not a free spirit like you. I'm much more conventional, I want to be safe.'

'Oh, yes? What about Guy?'

I remembered the car hurtling out of control through the dark, twisting street. And my own exhilaration.

'Think about it.' Charlotte beckoned for the bill. 'Oh, Karen. It's hell being free but it's great too! Don't get left behind.'

'Well, what about it?' Guy asked.

Nervously I turned over the sheets of closely typed poetry. It was a moment I'd been dreading. His poetry, I knew, was his reason for living, and yet with his careless speech I could not begin to see how it could be any good. Hurting him was something I could not bear. But I knew that it would be no use lying. I applied myself to the pages while he ordered sausage and chips. We were in his favourite transport café. 'No booze yet,' he decreed firmly. 'Poetry is serious business.'

It was good. Hardly daring to believe it I read on. All the discipline that Guy so clearly lacked in his daily life was packed into the verse with an exciting intensity. The rhyme scheme was complicated but serenely maintained, the imagery obscure but strictly logical. Soon I found myself asking questions, making suggestions. 'Why this?' 'And here?' 'But why not there?' and he answered cogently, seriously, his usual bullshitting left far behind.

'All right, then?' He looked at me steadily, his pale eyes alight.

'Yes. It's good.'

He tensed a moment and continued to watch me and then relaxed, falling back against his own chair and running his hands through his hair. He smiled. 'I've been dreading showing it to you!'

This was a surprise. 'Why? Would you really care what I thought?'

'Course I would, you silly girl! I respect you, for Christ's sake! Why else do I take you out? I don't get a feel of much else except your mind, do I?'

'No, really,' he went on, 'when we talk I'm never bored. Sorry! I know that sounds rather a lame compliment. But women – I love them, don't get me wrong – but they're so boring! I take one to a pub and within half an hour I'm bored out of my mind!'

'Well, you must take out the wrong sort!' I retorted. 'Oxford's full of interesting women!'

'Yes, I know, but they usually look like the back of a bus. No, I usually go out with blondes! I'm only turned on by good-lookers! God knows what I'm doing with you!'

'Thank you, Guy!'

'Oh, you know what I mean. No,' he leaned across and rumpled my hair, 'you're very nice. You've got a nice face.'

'I'd stop it if I were you! You're only making it worse!'

'Oh, come on, Karen,' he laughed back at me, 'let's face it, you're no film star! Of course you aren't, because if you were, you'd probably be as boring as all the other pretty cows I've dragged into bed.'

'You express yourself so charmingly!'

'Well, you know what I mean! For Christ's sake, you don't want me coming in here and saying "You look lovely tonight, darling".' His voice took on the cultivated drawl that I rather suspected was his normal accent. 'Do you, for crying out loud?'

'No, I don't,' I agreed. 'It wouldn't be true.'

'All it means is the guy's trying to get his hand up your skirt!

It's bloody insulting to women if you ask me! Extraordinary, really. You'd think they'd smell the insincerity a mile off. But oh, no! They lap it up, poor fools. They don't realize,' carried away by his own argument, he was becoming as high on adrenalin as he became on alcohol, 'that all this opening doors, holding up coats and expensive meal crap is a deliberate ploy to flatter you into bed.'

'Well, I must say you've never erred in that respect,' I replied, caustically.

'No, you could say that. Just gave you a bloody clip round the ear instead.' He reached across and took my hand gently. 'Sorry about that, sweetheart. I'm honestly – joking apart – deeply ashamed every time I think about it. But really,' his voice rose again, 'the reason I like going out with you is because I think of you as a man. Whoops!' he grinned, seeing my raised eyebrows. 'No, don't get me wrong. I'm not really homosexual – I don't think,' he added consideringly. 'It's just that I can treat you as an equal. You're not always grabbing your fucking powder puff and patting your hair when I talk to you. I can talk to you like one of my mates. But better.'

'Better? Why?' I asked curiously.

'Because when we're talking,' he answered seriously, 'about my poem, just now, for instance, you smash my mind completely. It's fantastic. I know men don't usually like clever women, but I do like you. Anyway,' his voice dropped and he forced me to look at him, speaking slowly and deliberately, 'because you smash my mind up like that, I know you can do the same with me physically. And that is why, eventually, Karen, we really ought to go to bed!' The last words sounded deliberately plaintive and long-suffering.

I smiled back. 'A novel way of asking, I must say.'

'How would you know?' he asked, reasonably enough.

I looked down at the table and suddenly I knew why – all my training, all my taboos apart – I was so afraid of sex. It meant total exposure to another person. A complete vulnerability that was frightening.

'Come on,' Guy groaned gently. 'The suspense is killing me!'

I stared down at the poem and realized what it meant. By showing it to me he had made himself vulnerable in the most extreme way he could. He had stripped naked first.

Dry mouthed, I smiled crookedly, looking up into Guy's eyes, which were watching me steadily. 'All right, then, let's get it over with.'

A bare, austere room. Ironically it could have been a monastic cell. A mattress on the floor, carefully swept floors, a scrubbed desk and a typewriter. The unmonastic touch – thank God for it – was a huge stereo.

'Therapeutic music, I think, don't you?' Guy crossed the room and carefully placed a record on the turntable while I sank on to the mattress and stared numbly at him. A soothing, anonymous beat filled the room.

'And anaesthetic.' He handed me a glass of barley wine. I downed it quickly; the glass rattled slightly against my teeth and I held it up again.

'Is there any more?'

'Yes. Blimey, you haven't got through all that already. Look, love, sex isn't that bad, I promise you.' He came across and took my hands in his, chafing them gently. 'But if you really don't want this, Karen, we'll stop. I don't want to hurt you.'

I looked at him and touched his face lightly. At the moment he seemed incredibly distant from me, the intimacy of the discussion in the café a long-past memory.

I shook my head. 'If we go back now, I'll never do it.'

'You're right.' Solemnly he filled my glass again and handed it back to me. Formally we saluted one another and again I drained the glass immediately and lay back on the mattress. The strong alcohol seemed to take effect quickly, for the room swayed gently round me. I scarcely noticed when Guy lay down beside me. 'Sure?' he asked quietly.

I nodded. 'Can we have the light out, please.'

'No.' Deftly he unbuttoned my shirt and I felt my flesh shrinking away from him. 'I want to see you.'

I lay there in a dream, as Guy undressed me, lying back passively, raising an arm or leg whenever necessary. I was hardly conscious of him at all. This was, I knew, the final break with my religion, the final break with everything I had been. It was ridiculous that this act, which should be natural and spontaneous, was assuming such vast proportions, but there it was. Instead of holding other human beings away, I was going to let one of them enter me completely. Part of me mourned for the intact self I was losing for ever, together with the ideal such a state implied.

'You're beautiful,' Guy said at last.

'Oh, rubbish,' I answered crossly, lying there, stripped of every last defence. I tried to escape back inside my head.

'I don't mean conventionally beautiful,' he replied gently. 'But you are lovely, you know. You've got a good body.'

A good body. I watched him curiously as he ran his fingers down my arms, touched my breasts lightly and shivered. A tiny pang of desire flared and I reached out and touched his bare arms, ran my fingers over his shoulders.

'You're so pale,' he said wonderingly, 'a real ice maiden.'

I looked at his body, tanned, taut and symmetrical. So alien and yet strangely familiar. Suddenly I reached up and clutched him to me, wanting to lessen the distance that had suddenly opened between us for the first time, lifted my face willingly to his kiss, felt his beard scratch my face. I didn't want to be alone any more.

'Mind you,' he murmured, 'you'll have to put on a bit more flesh. You're a bit sharp in places! I'll cut myself badly on these hip bones if I'm not careful.'

I giggled weakly. 'That's right,' he said. 'It's only your old drinking mate here. Not Jack the Ripper. Now come on, darling. Lie back and think of England or something.' Again I smiled at the absurdity and touching indignity of it all and suddenly the closeness we had shared over the past weeks was there again. That strange electrical charge that melted the coldness inside me was back and as our bodies embraced closely I knew I wanted this new intimacy. It was a break with the past but also a fresh start.

There was a moment of quite acute pain as the last rigid barrier I'd preserved against the world was broken. I pulled Guy's head against my shoulder, ran my fingers down his back, across his thighs and for a second lost myself in a faint premonition of pleasure.

For days afterwards I walked round in a dream of achievement. There seemed to be no guilt at all, and I thought back to what Jane had said. For the first time my body felt used and loved.

How could I have made such a fuss about it?

Yet on the third evening I felt the familiar onset of the hallucinations.

I have no idea how long afterwards it was before I came to. When I did I was standing alone in my room and there was a generalized fog of pain and outrage. I was holding something tiny in my hand. Looking down I saw with a shock that it was my razor. As the clouds of confusion slowly cleared around me and the real world settled down once more, I saw dimly through my exhaustion that I'd taken off my clothes, which were lying emptily discarded on the bed. There seemed to be blood trickling down my arms and my breasts. Just a part of a hallucination that hasn't gone yet, I thought, going over to the washbasin to bathe my aching head. As I passed the mirror I stood rooted with horror. Rubbed my hands over my eyes and saw with a terrible fear that I'd rubbed blood all over my face. When I licked my hand I could taste the sharp salty redness and I knew it was real.

My arms, breasts and stomach were covered with sharp cuts, which were bleeding angrily where in some frenzy of disgust I'd slashed myself with my razor.

CHAPTER EIGHT

Departures

'I'M LEAVING,' said Dr Piet.

It took a few seconds for that to sink in.

'You're doing *what*?' I asked softly.

'I've got a consultancy in the North of England. I'll be leaving here at the end of the month.'

'But you can't,' I wailed, miserably conscious of the absurd and childish nature of my reaction. Of course he could leave whenever he wanted. For him this was just a job, this was a step upward in his career. If I were any kind of reasonable adult I should congratulate him. But however coolly my reason told me this I could feel only anger and a breathless sense of betrayal.

'Why can't I?'

'Of course you can – you must!' I said crossly, loathing my ungraciousness. 'Congratulations! You must be very pleased.'

'But?' he probed.

'Well, what will happen to me? You were the person who egged me on into this situation.' I held out my scarred arms. 'And now you're waltzing off into the blue, leaving me with something I obviously can't handle.'

'What do you mean you can't handle it? I think you're doing very well.'

'Oh, don't be ridiculous!' I snapped.

'I'm not being ridiculous. Look at what you've achieved this last year. The very fact that you're able to tell me what you're feeling is an immense stride forward. That would have been impossible a few months ago. Wouldn't it?'

'I suppose so. But – '

'Wait a moment. Let me finish. You've put on some weight. You're back to seven stone. And you've formed a relationship with a man. All right! So you've been at yourself with a razor twice after sex! But I notice you've been very careful not to do yourself any harm. They're superficial cuts, after all. Your subconscious is angry with you but it's still not angry enough for anything serious. It's far less dangerous than sleeping pills. Frankly I'm delighted you're into razors now. Much safer.'

'A real step forward,' I said nastily.

'You didn't really think you were going to get off scot free, did you? After all that anti-physical conditioning? These razor games are just pathetic, last-ditch reflex actions. Like a chicken scuttling round the yard after its head has been chopped off.'

'Yuck!'

'A repulsive simile, I do apologize.' He relaxed and leaned back in his chair, smiling at me. 'But it's a good one because however grotesque and unnatural that chicken is, dashing round without a head, there's no way it can go on for much longer, is there?'

'No. It drops dead!'

'But you're not going to do that, are you?' He spoke confidently and for all my distress I knew that he was right. 'Life's far too interesting at the moment. Too many new things are happening.'

We sat silently for a while. 'I do wish you weren't going,' I said at last. 'And I feel so angry and humiliated to feel that. That you've got me into the position of needing you, of being dependent. I've never felt that before.'

'It's not humiliating to feel need, Karen. We all need people.'

'But you don't need me! I'm just a case.'

'In a way, that's true, of course. But there are people who need *you*. No! don't shout me down. Simon needs you; the Stanleys need you. Even your friends Jane and Charlotte need you in a way. No, you're not their nearest and dearest but you fill a need in their lives. And you need them too. You and Guy need one another acutely.'

'But it's dangerous to need people!' I said desolately. 'Because they go away in the end and there's nothing left. At least God never went away, which made Him a much better bet.'

'But He's gone away now, hasn't He? For a time at least.'

'For ever.'

Dr Piet smiled and shook his head. 'I think your religion's too deep and basic to go for ever. Just my opinion, of course.' He paused. 'This *is* a rotten moment to break off our work together.

But in a way I think it's no bad thing. I think you need to talk to a woman now. It's probably not a good idea to have a male authority figure in your life, just when you're starting to relate to men. You might start putting us on pedestals and that would never do! So I've asked Dr Webster to take you on. You'll like her, I think, and she's been reading all about you.' He tapped my file with his biro.

'So that's it.' I got up feeling bereft and absurdly close to tears. I realized how much I would miss wrangling with him week after week, having him push me closer and closer to the brink of what I thought I could endure. He was irreplaceable. 'It's odd, isn't it?' I said. 'I've always believed that everyone is dispensable. It shouldn't matter to me that I'm getting another psychiatrist, who'll probably do the job just as well.'

'That's the Hell of it,' he said, his eyes holding mine steadily. 'You see, this is what happens when you pull the barriers down. You're not the detached nun any more. You're getting attached to the world, Karen, and that's a sign of health and recovery.'

I smiled uncertainly. All I could feel was the pain of severance. 'I'll take your word for it. Goodbye,' I said quickly, 'and thank you.'

His eyes were kind as he opened the door to let me out into the rest of my life. 'You'll do.'

'If you lie back and shut your eyes,' Guy said, rubbing Germolene into the cuts on my arms and breasts, 'you can pretend we're lying on a beach in the Bahamas and I'm rubbing suntan oil into your skin. Go on! Use your powerful imagination to some effect, for Christ's sake!'

I tried it. 'It's no use,' I said after a while. 'The smell's wrong. All that antiseptic!'

Guy sniffed morosely. 'Yeah, it is pretty foul. And it makes you all pink and powdery. Just my bloody luck to get landed with a nutter!'

'You don't mind! You like it really.'

'That's true! Makes me feel normal for once. Quite a change! As long as you don't come near me with that razor,' he added nervously. 'I may have a violent streak myself but I'm not into masochism to that degree! How long have we got to go on with this Germolene lark, then, anyway?'

'Only till the cuts have healed, Dr Piet said, to stop infection.' I pulled my shirt on, to cover up the mess.

Guy threw me a spray of cologne. 'Put some of that on. It smells like a hospital in here.' He came across, unbuttoned my shirt, and gently kissed the worst cuts which scarred my breasts in a fine mesh of lines.

'Why do I do it?' I took his head and pressed it against my wounded skin. His arms tightened round me, pressing against my ribs; they felt solid and firm and with a low cry of pleasure I put my head against his. 'Why do I do it?' I asked again.

'Why do I smash you up?' His voice came muffled and indistinct and I could feel the warmth of his breath on my skin. 'I told you. We're both living on the edge. That's why we're together now.'

I rubbed my head against his and suddenly we were lying down together on the mattress, arms lightly round one another, keeping the darkness out. 'Karen!' he pleaded. 'Don't do it to yourself. I can't stand it. Turn all your hatred outwards, like I do. You don't need to hate yourself – you're so lovely.'

'How can I be?' I felt a stinging warmth descend from my eyes into the very depths of my body and all at once there was suddenly no questioning any more, no more analysis. There was only my body and Guy's, searching, exploring in a strange ballet of lips, limbs and tongues working inexorably forwards to a point that could only break and shatter. And just at the moment when I felt I could bear it no more I felt myself falling fully and finally into my body, falling away from my long isolation into the warm muddle of Guy. A strange, new peace infused every part of me.

'You see?' His voice came from far away, sounding blurred and drugged. 'How easy it is really.'

Gently he took me into his arms and we lay quietly together, oddly and temporarily happy.

In one way sex is like riding a bicycle. Once you've mastered the art you cannot understand why there was any difficulty at all, neither can you go back to your former state of wobbling and falling off. Except in peculiar and tragic circumstances you are an adept for life.

It was Guy who taught me to respond sexually. He was hardly

the ideal beau, but by simply bypassing all the traditional forms of courtship and flirtation, he dealt with me honestly and unconventionally and, blessedly, without a trace of the tiresome I've-always-wanted-to-do-it-with-a-nun syndrome. Once he'd aroused me sexually there was no real possibility of my looking back.

It was an important turning-point. It should be abundantly clear by now how much I hated my body. Guy taught me to look at it anew. In that he loved it and took pleasure in it I realized at a level deeper than the purely cerebral that it couldn't be entirely loathsome. Guy was able, because he understood my nature so well, to show me that sex could be an act of mutual tenderness. And because all my buried fear of sex had suddenly surfaced and been shown to be phantoms, I gradually learned that there was no need to go on starving my body to skeletal proportions. Of course it was not an immediate cure. But gradually I made little modifications to my diet, substituting scrambled eggs for boiled, bread for crispbread, butter for the ubiquitous cottage cheese. Occasionally I'd be overcome by extraordinary hunger and eat my way through a Chinese meal with Guy, or a plateful of beans on toast or mashed potatoes, feeling faint with a pleasure that was almost sexual. Once my body started to give me such delight it seemed churlish to go on crucifying it; I wanted to thank it, spoil it a little. As the pounds gradually filled out my bony frame, I no longer felt this a disgusting state of affairs. By responding sexually I had for the first time felt that I fully inhabited my body; that it was not my Brother Ass (the name St Francis of Assisi gave to his body), something stupid and disgusting which was holding me back from the finer, intellectual parts of me. For the first time I discovered that my body was me, that it could express in its own terms what I felt about Guy. And because for the first time I felt identified with my body I no longer had to beat it into submission to prove my spiritual superiority. I was on the mend.

It was a sign of other things too. I had learned to let another human being come really close to me, to allow myself to be completely vulnerable to another person. I had learned that to lose control for a while did not necessarily herald madness. Instead of walling myself up in a tight little capsule of security, I'd let somebody else in, and knew that not only had I survived the experience but also that I'd discovered a dimension of myself I'd never believed existed.

I looked across the desk at Dr Webster and tried to suppress my exasperation. She smiled back amiably at me, a youngish, plump woman with the wide-eyed serenity of a figure in a Dutch interior. Where Dr Piet's name sounded Dutch and he himself was English through and through, Dr Webster really was Dutch and spoke carefully perfect English with strange inflections that probably sounded more dogmatic than she intended.

'And how is your boy friend?'

I grimaced involuntarily. 'I do wish you wouldn't call him that.'

'Why?'

'Well. He's too old. He's not a boy – he's thirty-three.'

'But in many ways he seems very immature. Is that not so? I'm sorry. It's my English.' She smiled apologetically and I instantly felt carping and overcritical.

'No. *I'm* sorry. It's just an expression I don't like, that's all. But it's quite correct and lots of people do use it.'

'Would you like me to call him your lover?'

I sighed. 'That's wrong too. It suggests someone French and "Romantic". No – it's not your fault, it's Guy. He just doesn't fit into normal categories, I suppose.'

'You know,' she put her head on one side, 'it strikes me that you are playing games, you two. You are not trying to come into line with the real world.'

'Neither of us is normal, you mean,' I conceded gloomily.

'And I see your life becoming a bit schizophrenic,' she went on emphatically, her eyes gleaming with purpose. 'So much of your day, Karen, is occupied with the brain all day long. And the rest not with the reason. I'm sorry I put that badly. Do you see what I am trying to say?'

'Yes. You mean there's me in the Bodleian day after day, doing abstruse academic work, and there's Guy and all the anarchic and violent part of me on the other hand. The contrast's too extreme?'

'Quite right. You must see that that's true. And I think it's your academic work that's bad for you – even worse than Guy. It's too rational. Too sterile and narrow.' She hunched her shoulders histrionically to suggest cramped restriction and I felt a pang of fear as I saw the way the conversation was tending. 'It's time now to get out of Oxford, I think, for you. Take a job – any job at all that brings you into contact with ordinary people. Where you are not just thinking always but living too. But go away from Oxford, I think.'

I watched her fling her arms out expansively to create the limitless deserts of freedom that lay outside the cloisters of academe. I felt threatened to the core; the clear confines of a world I had come to know cracking.

'Everyone's leaving now.' The words startled me as I spoke them. Charlotte – now writing happily from London. Jane and Mark would be off soon to the North of England where Mark had a job.

'Except Guy!' Dr Webster raised her eyebrows to heaven. 'You will need some more ballast to balance him and keep you afloat.'

'I know! But I must finish my thesis. I *want* to, don't you see? It's precious to me. Like a child, I suppose. I can't just abandon it.'

'And when will you finish it, do you think?' There was a sudden gleam in her eye.

'In another year.'

'And then?'

I sighed yet again. 'I'd like an academic job, but that's very difficult now.' The expansion of the Universities during the Sixties had stopped and there were rumours of cuts in education that were bound to occur with rising inflation. Jobs were gold dust. And I was a woman, which would count against me. And I was mad.

'Karen,' Dr Webster leaned seriously across her desk. 'You are doing so well now. You're even putting on weight again. Seven and a half stone? That is excellent. But you must have more in your life than Guy, your thesis and the rather – bizarre arrangements at the Stanleys'.' She glanced at her watch. 'Time is up. Pity, because I've thought of another solution. You could continue with your thesis. But it is a big thing to think about.'

'What is it?' I asked cautiously.

'No time now.' She smiled. 'Next time I'll tell you my idea.'

*

Stranded amidst the chaotic jungle of Heathrow I stood with Lindsey and my parents, looking for the one small exit in that confusion of lights, desks and voices through which Lindsey would disappear. My mother's eyes were everywhere. Nervously they darted, bright with tension, from the departure board to Lindsey's luggage and back again to the departure board. My father stood miserably beside her, upset by the confusion, just looking at Lindsey. He was, I realized with a pang, looking older. He never liked to talk about his age but he must be over seventy now, and in recent years he had begun to suffer from the extraordinary high blood pressure that had been a problem for him for nearly thirty years and which, until now, he had managed to hold at bay. Now, as he stood looking at Lindsey, I realized that he was saying goodbye to his favourite daughter. He would, if she stayed long in Canada, probably never see her again.

'Have you got your ticket?' my mother asked for the fourth time that morning.

'Yes, I have. It's here. I think!' Panic-stricken Lindsey fumbled in her bag, failing to find it. 'Where is it? I had it a second ago, I swear I did. Oh God! What can I have done with it?'

'It must be there somewhere!' My mother's voice was sharp with anxiety. 'Go through the bag, item by item.' The voice belied any such calm search. If Lindsey's natural warmth and easy affection made her my father's child, her tension and crackling nerves also made her my mother's.

'Here it is!' Lindsey waved the ticket aloft in triumph.

'Thank God!' and they both subsided in total relief.

'Why on earth you had to go on this crazy route I just do not know,' my mother scolded as she always did when upset.

'We'd have lent you the money,' my father put in. Lindsey, to save money, was travelling to Winnipeg on about six different airlines, making extraordinary detours, and her journey would take nearly two days, provided there were no hold-ups.

'Oh, no! I wouldn't dream of that!' Lindsey squeezed his arm affectionately. 'And I'll be glad of the money I've saved when I start looking for a job!'

'Have you any idea at all what you'll do?' I asked.

'Oh! I don't know. Acting, preferably, but perhaps I might get

188

something on one of the local radio stations with my nice English accent. I'll find something! I always do.'

'You are brave, you know!' I'd been looking at her all morning with admiration. She was taking off into the blue with nothing waiting for her at the end – no job, no security – to a completely strange and possibly alien country. I hadn't even dared to go to Paris for a weekend.

'Have you got your passport?' asked my mother, and there ensued another brief flurry and panic.

'Strewth!' muttered my father in exasperation. 'You know it's in there! Why the hell don't you just put them in the side pocket or something? Sort it out from the rest of the mess. You've no system, Lindsey, none at all!'

The irritation, the tension about trivia, was striking some chord in my memory. What was it? Suddenly I remembered that morning, eleven years ago now, when I had set off for Tripton to begin my religious life. I looked back at Lindsey, who was still feverishly hunting in her bag for the missing documents. Perhaps we had more in common than I thought. Like Lindsey, I'd known nothing of what was waiting for me at the other end of that train journey. In some ways I had travelled into more strange and alien realms than anything that could be waiting for her in Canada.

Her flight was called. All panic over, Lindsey clung in turn to my parents and then, slightly more awkwardly, to me. 'Good luck!' I murmured. 'I hope you find it.' For a moment she looked puzzled. What could I mean by 'it' – I hardly knew myself; the words had just emerged. But suddenly her face cleared and we understood each other. I watched her disappear through the gate, turning back to wave once more, looking very young and vulnerable, in spite of her trendy clothes. She gave a funny little flutter of her hand and then vanished in pursuit of an ideal that was taking her to the other side of the world.

So many people at that time were telling me to move like Lindsey, telling me that Oxford was finished for me. I knew they were right. But some inner paralysis prevented me from even considering the idea. Even today, I often have to be catapulted into change. It's one of the last hangovers from the religious life. A nun never initiates change for herself; to do so would be a grave failing in Obedience. Instead she waits passively in the hands of her Superior 'as a dead body allows itself to be treated in any manner whatever'. Thus St Ignatius. As soon as I become happy in a job, in a house or a particular locality, I become cautious of moving on. I always feel so deeply astonished that I've found somewhere in the world where I belong that it seems a foolish tempting of Providence to give them up. Though it has never proved to be so.

'I think,' Dr Webster said firmly, 'that you should have a baby.'

'A baby!' Even in the extremity of shock I was able to register that I was doing for the word what Edith Evans had done for 'A handbag!' in *The Importance of Being Earnest*. On second thoughts, perhaps the connection was not as incongruous as it had at first seemed.

'You are a normal woman, able to conceive and bear a child. What is so extraordinary about the idea?'

'But I'm not married!' I blustered, trying to find some order in which to place the myriad objections that had sprung up in response to this apparently hare-brained scheme. 'I've got no means of supporting a child. I'm a penniless student – remember?'

'It doesn't cost much money to have a baby,' Dr Webster answered calmly. 'And you have some money saved up from these years of extraordinary abstinence you have put yourself through. There are all sorts of ways – state grants, small part-time jobs – to help you while the baby is small.'

'Stop talking about the baby as though it were already a fact!' I protested. 'I'm not having a baby! It's absolutely idiotic. I'm ill! I have moments – hours sometimes – when I don't know what I'm doing. I've tried to kill myself during them, I've cut myself with razor blades! It would be terribly irresponsible of me to have a baby!'

'If you had entirely dependent upon you another helpless human being – and this is my point – ' Dr Webster replied, 'you would outgrow these hallucinations.'

'You can't be sure of that!' I said after a moment, spent letting this idea sink in, 'I've no means of controlling these things. You can't know that that would happen.'

'We can't be one hundred per cent certain,' she shrugged, 'but, then, you can be that sure about very few things in life. But I am,' she smiled at me, 'pretty sure. Say ninety per cent sure.'

I sat back in my chair and closed my eyes. The idea of never having another hallucination as long as I lived was unimaginable bliss.

'Do you really think it would work?' I asked at last.

'Yes. I do. You know I was saying last time that I fear for you next year when you have only your illness and Guy on the one hand and your cerebral academic work on the other. Well, this way you could get on with your thesis and still have a foot in earthly reality, so to speak. There's nothing that brings one down to earth from one's intellectual clouds more than babies, you know. They need feeding, changing, taking for walks, playing with, planning for. And wouldn't you really like a baby?'

I shrugged, yet at the same time felt a sharp curiosity to see what my baby would be like. That brought me down to earth. A baby, with my incipient madness and with Guy and his instabilities as a father, would hardly be off to a very good start.

'It's too much of a risk,' I protested. 'And how would I cope on my own, without a husband?' I couldn't picture Guy changing nappies or helping with a baby's teething troubles, emotional and physical. He'd find the tableau of mother and child distinctly off-putting. He'd be off like a shot. 'It would be terribly lonely bringing up a baby without any moral support at all from a husband,' I said at last.

'But you will probably marry later. Not Guy, no, that I can see, but somebody else. Men are much better about that kind of thing these days than they used to be. And anyway, you would be a different person. You would, I am sure of it, be quite well again for one thing. And you wouldn't be lonely. There is nothing closer than the bond between mother and child and you need that closeness. You've spent too much of your life cut off from people, forcing yourself to keep them at arm's length. Once you've had your baby you will see in quite a new way what human closeness really means.'

I sat, looking at her. Perplexed and confused.

'And think, Karen,' Dr Webster said softly. 'Just think of being really well again.'

★

'Karen,' Simon leaned across and touched me gently on the arm to claim my attention. He gestured towards the altar. 'Do you think Father Paul will let me make some incense one day?'

On the altar, Bernard, a mongol child a few years older than Simon, was swinging the thurible with cheerful abandon. Clouds of incense hid Father Paul, the celebrant, from view. He was coughing slightly, choking in over-abundant fragrance. I turned back to Simon.

'I'm sure he will, Simon. He said you could serve at Mass like Bernard one day, if you wanted to.'

Simon shook his head. He was getting bigger now; he towered over me and his body was thicker and his features coarser. The pretty child was disappearing now into the more threatening adult. Many people found him less appealing and more alarming, though here at Blackfriars he found complete acceptance. Now he spoke in an elaborate stage whisper. 'No. I don't want to be up there in front of all these people. But one day I'd like to make some incense. In the sac – sac – ?'

'Sacristy? Yes, I'm sure you can. We'll ask Paul, shall we?'

He smiled and leaned against me with a huge sigh of contentment. 'I do like coming to Blackfriars. My pleasure in it is increasing daily. Increasing – not outcreasing.'

It was strange that his enthusiasm for Blackfriars had never waned. He was sitting now, his eyes fixed on the altar as though waiting for something, his face sternly attentive. When the priest lifted the Host, he bowed low, reverently and then turned towards me with a dazzling smile. It was almost as if his damaged brain got straight to the heart of the Mass, and was not short-circuited by too much irritable reasoning about it.

He sighed again and closed his eyes. I looked down at him. 'Are you okay?' I asked anxiously. Last night he'd had another epileptic fit while I was sitting with him. I was used to these attacks now; they weren't dangerous in themselves, just unpleasant, and there were certain practical things to be done. 'All right?' I asked him again.

He nodded. 'Just sleepy. I'm very, very weary, Karen.'

I put my arm round him and felt him slump trustingly against me. Perhaps I wouldn't make such a bad mother after all. It might be worth a try. Anything was worth it. I glanced back at Simon. He was pale and had dark circles under his eyes. I wondered how much he remembered about his fits afterwards.

'Do you want to go home?' I asked gently.

'Oh, no! I want to stay till the end. Of course.'

A fit left him tired the next day. And in fact fatigue seemed to bring it on. Edwin had taken him to London yesterday to visit his aunt, and Simon's wild excitement exhausted him, so that he went to sleep as soon as he crawled into bed.

'He missed his supper, too,' Judith said ruefully when she came up to bed. 'He was too elated to eat. And when he skips a meal the blood sugar gets low and it can bring on an attack. I'm so sorry you had it again, my dear.'

'Don't worry. I really don't mind it.'

'*You* ought to eat more, too,' Judith added reprovingly. 'I'm sure all those skimpy meals don't do your general health any good. Or your view of the world. How can you feel anything but depressed when your blood sugar is as low as it *must* be? God knows what's happening in *your* brain. Look what missing one meal has done for Simon.'

'Oh, I'm all right,' I added quickly. 'I do eat quite a lot really. Now.'

'Yes. You're not nearly as thin as you were, but you should still eat more!' she replied. 'I'm going to make you have a lot for lunch tomorrow.'

Judith's words went home. Now that I thought about it, the attacks did seem to be worse at times when I wasn't eating. It could be that my spirits were affected in just the same way as Simon's brain was by lack of food. And of course the emotions were produced by the brain. It might be worth trying to eat even more.

And, as a last resort, I would think about the baby idea. I really would.

There are now times when I confront my former self with astonishment. It is astounding to me how seriously and literally I took the advice of anyone in any position of authority. Not so now! 'Get yourself a First!' commanded Mrs Jameson, and instantly I adopted the academic life in its entirety. 'Get yourself a man!' Dr Piet advised, and I nodded grimly to myself and let Guy carry me off in his van. And now when Dr Webster said 'Get yourself a baby!' I seriously considered the command.

Charlotte once said to me at this period of our lives: 'It's extraordinary, Karen, how many people leap onto a soap box when they're with you and tell you what to do. I find myself doing it, for Heaven's sake! I'm never so dogmatic with anyone else. You must be asking for it in some way.'

I was. Because I had so little sense of myself I wanted other people to tell me what to do. In some ways my religious life had succeeded better than I knew. Though I seemed so full of self, a part of me was still in a state of coma: my self-respect. The fact that I seemed to be going insane didn't help this, of course. Nor did my pursuit of the cloistral in life: I was only too ready to wall myself up in other people's views of the world. So I allowed other people to offer me the most impertinent advice – indeed I cried out for it. How could other people respect my privacy and right to autonomy when I had no such respect for myself?

I was getting better. So many things, so many people were helping. But in this area I had to act for myself. What I needed was a shock to throw me into a greater self-awareness.

'I'm leaving.'

The words fell heavily into the room. I looked across at Rebecca who was staring ahead, looking into an empty and unimaginable future. She'd had a long, slow climb back to health and though she was now back on her feet she was still painfully thin. Her skin looked transparent and had a strange bluish tinge and her eyes were shocked and wounded.

'I'm leaving the Order,' she said again, more to herself than to me, as though she was trying to convince herself of this new development in her life.

'I'm not surprised, really,' I answered. 'After what happened. Your illness was a sign that something was terribly wrong. How do you feel?'

She sighed and huddled into the bulky cardigan she was wearing, cold, despite the fact that the fire was on and it was a warm day. 'It's the right thing,' she said slowly, 'but I just can't imagine what it will be like not to be a nun, not to be here. It's outside anything I can conceive. But you understand that, don't you?'

'Yes.' I knew exactly how she felt. There was the cold, hard knowledge that leaving was the inevitable and painful uprooting from everything that was familiar and valuable. And there was no easy comfort I could give her. I couldn't jollily say that she'd soon find her feet or that leaving the Order must be a great relief. It wasn't that simple. 'What finally decided you?' I asked. 'Or wasn't it any one thing?'

She stood up and looked out of the window at the garden outside. I noticed how stick-like her legs still were, and how her skirt hung limply over her hips. 'There's no place for me here any more,' she said at last. 'After the *anorexia*. They can't forgive me for it, you see.'

I looked round the room. It used to be one of the students' bedsitter rooms when the Convent hostel was full. Now it was for one of the nuns and Rebecca was using it during her brief visit to Oxford. There was a pretty open fireplace, an electric kettle, a delicate collection of cups and saucers from which we were drinking tea. It was all so far removed from what Convent life was four years ago; the very idea of a nun entertaining a secular in her room was revolutionary enough, let alone the softening touches of a poster on the wall and a pretty bedspread.

'Everything's changed so much,' I said. 'Surely that doesn't just mean a change in external things, like bedrooms and no Rule of Silence. Surely there's a more humane spirit here now.'

Rebecca shrugged gently. 'They want to be humane. And they wanted to be kind; they really did. When I came out of hospital they were falling over themselves, trying to be helpful and attentive. But ultimately they're still the same. Feelings don't count, remember?'

'And your feelings were so strong that they nearly killed you.'

'So did yours.'

'Ah, but you really did knock that theory on the head,' I said. 'I can see that. My breakdown was so overt and obvious that they could only feel pity for my complete collapse and loss of self-control. But you went on, dying on your feet, but still being dutiful, calm, unemotional. Still being the perfect young nun with iron self-control.'

'And they can't change overnight. How can they? Some of the older nuns have been in religion for thirty, forty, fifty years.'

'I've found it hard enough to change after only seven years in religion,' I agreed.

'How do you think I'll get on after only twelve?' Rebecca

turned to face me and in her face I could see her fear of what lay ahead.

'I wonder if I'll feel as detached as you do from all this.' She gestured round the hall at the crucifix and the large portrait of the Foundress over the stairs as we walked down to the front door.

'I don't know about detached,' I said, startled. 'After all, it's my past, you know. I don't want to sever myself from my whole past – that can't be healthy.'

But even as I said this I saw how my attitude to the Order had changed. Rebecca was right. I was no longer homesick for it; no longer angry, as I was immediately after my suicide attempt. 'One day,' I said to her, 'I'm going to have to find out what these years here meant to me. After all, they were the most important years of my life. They can't have been all bad.'

'No.' But she spoke uncertainly and I could see that for her it was too early to begin to think like that.

We exchanged the nun-like kiss; I wished I could have hugged her more closely, but she wasn't ready for that yet. Over her shoulder I saw again the large crucifix and suddenly saw it in a new way. It wasn't just a proclamation of suffering: it was meant to be a shock. This is what God was said to mean by victory and by love. An overturning of all human expectations. And, I suddenly felt, all preconceptions. Perhaps God hadn't, after all, quite finished with me yet.

'Good-bye. I'll see you. *Soon.*' It was wonderful that Rebecca was well enough to take such a huge step towards a fuller life, when only a year ago we were both at death's door. She was to have her own hard road back into the world, a struggle quite different from mine. But it has had a happy ending. She has just got married.

'A baby!' Guy said, and I could see all my original horror reflected on his face. 'You must be bloody mad!'

'Of course. That goes without saying. But I've told you what the doctor said and I want to know what you think.'

'I've told you what I think.' Guy wrenched a handful of grass out of the ground violently. 'I think it's the most stupid idea I've ever heard.'

We were sitting by the river in Port Meadow watching the

boats flit erratically up and down the water in constant danger of collision. I lay back on the tussocky grass and closed my eyes.

'I know what you mean! Look, I'm not completely sold on the idea at all. There are loads of problems.'

'Your immediate problem,' Guy said, tickling my nose with a feathery blade of grass, 'is going to be finding someone to get you pregnant. Because I,' he said emphatically, slapping my leg as he pronounced each word distinctly, 'am not doing it. Here!' He pulled me up into a sitting position and forced me to look at him. 'You haven't been messing about with the Pill or anything, have you? Not taking it, I mean!'

'Of course not!' I retorted, deeply shocked. 'Of course I wouldn't do that without telling you. And, as I say, I'm not at all sure that this is the answer. I'm not sure that I want a baby! I'm really not! I just wanted to know what you think!'

'Right,' Guy relaxed visibly. 'I'll tell you, then. For a start, suppose you have a child like Simon for instance. I know he's a great bloke. I know you're used to him. You're used to his epileptic fits, the lot. But supposing, just supposing, you had a handicapped child. It could happen, especially with your propensity to disaster!'

'If everyone thought that, no one would have babies.'

'On your own!' Guy overrode me. 'Stuck in some cheap and horrible bedsit, living on social security. It'd finish you off. And anyway, same applies even if the kid's normal for Christ's sake! Use your head, darling! You've only just started to live. Enjoy your bloody freedom. You don't want to saddle yourself with a kid now!'

'But I might love it when it came.'

'You won't love it when it cries at night and you're both in some tiny box of a room with a horrible landlady bashing on the ceiling and calling you a bloody whore and telling you to keep your bleeding bastard quiet. Because that's what it'll be like, Karen. I think that Dr Webster's fucking irresponsible. She wants to think before she starts handing out these instant recipes for disaster!'

'Oh, Guy!' I sighed and leaned against him. 'I know all that really. It's just that it would be so marvellous to get better.'

'I know, love. I think Charlotte's idea's a better one. Go to London. Change of scene. I'm in London half my time with this job. I'll still see you. A bit of new life, the big city away from all this academic crap. You know what I think of your thesis.'

'I know! I know! But I can't afford to live in London without a grant.'

'Then you can't afford a baby!'

'Anyway, there's one person we haven't considered in all this,' I said slowly. 'The baby. The real reason I've had against all this, the more I've thought about it, is that I've got no right to use a baby to cure my own neurosis. It's not fair!'

'Too right! And I'm not going to be the father!' Guy capped. 'So tell your Dr Webster to put that in her pipe and smoke it.'

When I saw the envelope Judith had pushed under my door I felt cold and apprehensive. Clumsily I tore it open and forced myself to read. Then I read the letter again. I'd got a job as a tutorial research fellow at Bedford College, London. I was to teach undergraduates nineteenth- and twentieth-century literature.

It was like a reward for making the right decision about the baby. It was odd how often, when things seemed to have reached a stalemate, the world offered me a prize to show that I could cope. Despite everything. I stared hard at the letter. I felt a rising excitement; it was a new chance, a fresh start. I would no longer be a graduate student living on the periphery of University life, as I now saw I was at Oxford. I needn't be just an ex-nun any more, either. I'd be a teacher; it was a whole new image.

London. I thought of the vast untidy city. For a moment Oxford seemed so safe – and irretrievably lost to me. I'd applied for the job in the spirit of fantasy. There didn't seem a hope that I'd get it. They'd be getting hundreds of applications from indigent graduate students throughout the country. But I had. I had pushed myself outside the cosy confines of the elegant, civilized city. I waited for the terror to grow as I felt the cold breath of a new freedom.

But it didn't. My concerns would still be the same and the world of scholarship would be a capsule of security inside the teeming metropolis. The glow of anticipation returned. I'd be all right. Even though London would certainly be a tough proposition.

★

'Miss Armstrong? Dr Webster will see you now.'

Absently I thrust my paperback into my handbag and smiled at the receptionist. 'Thank you.' As I walked down the corridor to the familiar office I wondered whether Dr Webster wanted to transfer me to another psychiatrist in London. I rather hoped she would; it would be frightening to have to manage on my own.

'Come in, Karen! Take a seat.'

She was standing at the window, bending over her filing cabinet, and something in her stance caused my mind to prickle with attention. Dr Webster straightened herself slowly, putting one hand on the small of her back; I watched her settle her weight on her heels and lean slightly backwards. As she swung round to smile at me I registered the crisp yellow smock. Her stomach.

'You're pregnant.'

There was a brief pause while I could see her adjusting to this unusually bald statement of her condition. Then she smiled, her face taking on a glow of satisfaction. 'Ah!' she laughed and lowered herself carefully into her chair, with an amusing wry little glance down at her stomach. 'Yes, indeed. Again. But still we are delighted. Quite delighted.'

'That's not quite what I meant.' I could feel the last remnants of my habitual deference towards authorities crumbling away.

'I don't quite understand, Karen.'

'What I meant was – *you're* pregnant.'

Dr Webster's bland face crumpled in bewilderment at the hostility in my voice. She leant forwards, her head on one side, her eyes searching mine for the answer that now erupted from me.

'What the Hell did you think you were doing telling me to have a baby? Do you realize I could be pregnant myself by now – I was desperate enough to think about it very seriously!'

'But Karen – ' She was shaken momentarily out of her superior psychiatrist's pose, looking hard at her blotter. 'A baby *would* be good for you. I really think that. It's not just because I myself – ' She gestured lamely at her stomach and looked at me pleadingly.

'Yes, it *is*! You must be able to see that! You're supposed to be the psychiatrist, for God's sake!' My voice rang round the little room, trembling with anger and with the sense of huge peril accidentally averted. 'You were speaking to me directly from your own preoccupations at the moment. You're obsessed with maternity just now, understandably enough! All your hormones are shoving you more deeply into it every day. But that doesn't mean that I have to have a baby too to get rid of my problems!'

She was making little stabs at the blotting paper with her fountain pen. Concentric little pools of dark blue ink welled up round the nib. She looked suddenly vulnerable.

'Oh, what's the use?' I got up and was struck by the absurdity of it all. 'It's not just you,' I said slowly, looking round the room for the last time. 'We're all like this. Shut into ourselves by our own experience. None of us should legislate for one another.'

I smiled cheerfully at Dr Webster, feeling slightly winded by the freedom that I'd just acquired and certain that it was the only possible decision. 'I'm not coming back. I don't want any more psychiatry.'

'That's your decision, of course.' She stood up to face me, safely back in a role she knew how to discharge. 'But in London – at first – you may find it difficult to cope. If you want help, let me know.'

I nodded vaguely and we solemnly shook hands. From now on I would find my own answers.

CHAPTER NINE

No Abiding City (1973–5)

'OH MY GOD!' said my father gloomily as we pushed open the door of my new London flat.

'Oh, I don't know,' said my mother, bravely and brightly. 'It's quite nice really, John. A hundred times better than some of the places Lindsey lived in. No,' she looked round the living room at the drab pink wallpaper, the limp brocade curtains that didn't quite go with the chintz-covered armchairs and the dark, cheap table and sideboard, 'I think it's got definite possibilities.'

'I think it's great,' I said firmly. 'Look, I've got my own telephone which is a huge advantage – no queuing in the corridor with everyone listening in to your conversations, and it's a lovely big room. I can get some rugs and things to cover the lino, buy some prints for the walls.'

'Where's the bedroom?' asked my mother, still, I could see, trying to hide her real dismay.

'Through here.' I opened the door that led into the adjoining room. 'It looks directly on to Highgate Wood and it's quite a nice bed, with a good mattress.'

'Rather odd having the kitchen in the bedroom, isn't it?' commented my mother, dubiously peering into the tiny little cubby hole. 'Still, I suppose you've got everything you need here. Not much working space, though.'

'None at all,' said my father, 'unless you count the top of the fridge. And look over here. The walls are running with water. It will be freezing in here during the winter.'

'Oh, come on! It's not as bad as all that!' I said bracingly. 'I'm pleased with it; it will be fun doing it up and it will be wonderful to have all this space. My room at the Stanleys' was nice, but it was getting a bit cramped.'

Footsteps sounded on the lino in the living room next door.

'Have you got everything you want?' A plump woman with a

face that might once have been pretty but was coarse with age surveyed us with her head on one side. Black hair, obviously dyed, framed her head and matched her darting, curious eyes.

'Oh, this is my landlady, Mrs Christopher.' I hastened to introduce her to my parents. She came up and patted both my cheeks as though I were a child.

'Doesn't she look bonny!' she said to my parents. 'Oh, we're going to love having you, dear. Do you know,' her voice fell into the room like dollops of sickly syrup, 'I could have let this flat one hundred times over. Yes!' she glanced sharply at my father, whose expression was extremely caustic, 'it's been in such demand. But you see, I'm fussy. I knew I was waiting for somebody special. And when I met your daughter with her pretty little face and wise little heart I knew it was meant that she should come here.'

There was a short, embarrassed silence. My father cleared his throat and examined the pattern on the wallpaper while my mother rushed to the rescue.

'Have you been letting rooms long, Mrs Christopher?'

'Ever since my husband died. Oh, we had some happy years in this house. This used to be our bedroom.' Mrs Christopher settled herself comfortably in one of the chairs and fixed us with a sadly spiritual smile. My father sighed restlessly. 'And I couldn't sleep here any more, you know. No, I still cry for him at night. And sometimes the only way I can get through the day, can even contemplate another moment without him,' her voice rose to histrionic heights, 'is by taking out all his letters – I've kept them all, you know – and reading them through with bitter, bitter tears.'

'Oh dear,' my mother tried valiantly, 'was it very recent? His death, I mean.'

'Seventeen years ago, dear,' she smiled, enjoying her sorrow. 'And ever since I've lived here with my daughter. I've only got one child – I'm not strong, you know, I couldn't have another child. The anguish I endured! I said to my husband afterwards that I could never have another child, I'm too sensitive, too delicate to face it again. And he agreed, of course. "Marcia," he said, "I wouldn't risk your health for anything in the world!" But I've been lucky in my Patricia. She's never married, you know – oh, she's had heaps of offers, she's as pretty as a picture, you'd

202

never know she was 38 – but she turns them down. "I want to stay with you, Mummy!" she says.'

'Poor bitch!' snorted my father under his breath.

'And are there any other tenants in the house?' my mother went on determinedly.

'A young couple, Frank and Lucy. They're very sweet – a couple of mice! You won't know they're there.'

'And they're the people I share the bathroom with?' I asked.

'Your dear mother will want to see the bathroom her little girl will use.' She got up and led the way down the landing while we collapsed into helpless giggles behind her. 'Mad as a bloody hatter,' my father groaned.

To say that the bathroom was antiquated was an understatement. A huge geyser that had to be fed with five-penny pieces filled the room, which was obviously going to be very cold.

'The water will be freezing by the time it's fallen all that way into the bath,' said my father in horror. 'It's like the Niagara Falls.'

'Just a moment, dear.' Mrs Christopher shot my father a venomous look and disappeared, returning a few minutes later with a long brown length of rubber tubing.

'You'll find Frank's always in the bath.' She lowered her voice secretively, summoning us with her eyes to bend forward and listen. 'He's got a very peculiar body odour.' Her voice was thick with prurience. 'I've said to Lucy time and again that I can smell him. He leaves his smell in the air, you know, and she says she knows exactly what I mean. There's nothing he can do about it apparently, poor boy. You know, Mrs Armstrong, I've been a mother to those two young things and you can rest assured I'll look after Karen too.'

We studiously avoided one another's eyes. Ludicrous as the situation was I was feeling more and more uneasy. Mrs Christopher was not just a harmless old eccentric. There was something wrong. Her eyes were too sharp, too pointed in their gaze. I made up my mind to avoid her as much as possible.

'Here, dear.' She showed me how to fit the tubing on to the spout of the geyser so that the water flowed through it in its long drop into the bath and didn't get cold *en route*. 'You keep that.' Her eyes widened as she thrust the limp brown snake into my hands. 'But hide it, will you, from Frank and Lucy. I lent it to them but had to confiscate it.' She lowered her voice dramatically. 'I don't trust them. I think they were getting up to something very nasty with that tube. Something very nasty indeed.'

The telephone rang and I groped my way towards it. I only had three candles left and was trying to survive the evening by the light of my gas fire. Thank goodness I had gas. It would be terrible to be cold as well without electricity.

'Karen? It's Lindsey!'

'Lindsey!' How strange to speak to someone three thousand miles away. 'How are you? How's Canada?'

There was a disconcerting transatlantic hiccup before her answer.

'Tell me. What do you feel about the political situation?'

My jaw dropped in astonishment. Lindsey had never shown the remotest interest in politics, and I couldn't believe she'd make a hideously extravagant call to enquire about events that must seem so remote. I decided I'd misheard.

'Sorry, I didn't quite catch what you said. It takes a bit of time to get used to this tiny pause while the sound catches up, don't you think? How *are* you? How's your job?' She had a job on one of the Winnipeg radio stations.

'Fine. Look, can you give me your impressions of the political situation in Britain at the moment? I'd love to hear your views about Mr Heath's position. Will he resign, do you think? And what's morale like in London at the moment with all these shortages and electricity cuts? Do you think you're on the verge of some kind of revolution back there? I'd be fascinated to know what you think, as a Londoner.'

Whatever had happened to her? Canada must have effected some kind of personality change. I tried again.

'Lindsey, I can't believe you're really interested in all this. I'd really much rather hear your news. Did you find that man you went out to look for? And – '

There was a clicking noise on the other end and she spoke again with a giggle in her voice.

'Shut up, you dumbo. I'm recording this conversation for the news show. It's a big scoop for me. A real live voice from beleaguered London. The station is thrilled.'

'Oh, I must say I'm relieved. I thought you must be having some sort of breakdown! You interested in politics!'

She giggled again. 'Sorry, I should have warned you. Okay, can we go now? Let's try again . . . Karen, as a Londoner perhaps you can tell us all how people are feeling at the moment.'

What could I say? The hours sitting in freezing, dark rooms during the power cuts, waiting for a chance to heat a tin of soup, peering owl-like at goods in a shop lit only by a guttering candle.

'Oh, it's not too bad.' I heard my voice hearty with forced cheer and tried again. 'But you do feel that the whole complex edifice of technology is about to tumble down. Nothing in London can work any more without electricity and oil. Perhaps we're being punished for an overwhelming pride in building cities and structures that can so easily be made useless.'

'Are people very depressed?' I smiled at her caring, interviewer's tone.

'Well, there's a chirpy, war-time spirit building up. People are going into work and trying to carry on as usual. But underneath I think people are frightened. Frightened about what could happen if this strain and these shortages go on for much longer. And frightened of its implications for the future.'

'Fine! That's great. We're off the air now.' Lindsey sounded much more normal now. 'It's great to hear you. I had to grasp the opportunity of telling you the big news *and* getting the station to pay for the call.'

'Big news?'

'I'm getting married.' Her voice wobbled with joy.

'Lindsey! How exciting! Is it to the man you went out to look for?'

'No. He proved to be a dead loss once I saw him on his home territory. No. Stephen is someone completely new. And guess what! He's an Englishman. From Golders Green. I have to come half way round the world to find him. Isn't it strange how things work out?' She sounded bubbling over with an excited and nervous joy.

'How long have you known him?' I was trying to make some calculations. She'd only been gone about four months.

'Six weeks! But it's right. I just know it's right. For the first time in my life I've been loved before I've been bedded. He's marvellous. Handsome, kind, attractive, sexy, a great sense of humour. We're getting married over here next month.'

'So soon!'

'What's the point of waiting?' Lindsey sounded surprised. 'It's what we both want. And we're both so happy. We really can't believe it. It seems almost indecent to be so happy and lucky.'

'I'm so glad for you.' So it had paid off, her quest for love. Perhaps you just had to be bold enough to make crazy gestures in the pursuit of happiness, throwing aside all obstacles of sense and reason.

'Oh – and Karen! We're moving to California. I can't stand the climate here. The snow's shoulder high, you know, and I've already had an attack of what they call cabin fever. This weather goes on till March at least. So, we're driving right through America down to Los Angeles. Maybe I'll get into films in Hollywood. Who knows – my luck certainly seems to have changed. Anyway in the meantime I'm going to do the real-estate exams. Apparently you can make a mint that way. I can't wait to get there – endless summer, vines and lemon trees.'

'It all sounds like paradise.' My head was reeling. So she was setting off again, changing her career, pulling up all roots. Of course. This was the only sensible way to be, given the precarious state of the world. She was using the world. Making it hers, in a way that took my breath away.

'I've got to go. The producer will go berserk.'

'Lindsey, I'm so glad. You really deserve it.'

'Thanks. It's fantastic to talk to you. Bye . . . Say, Karen.'

'What?'

'Why don't you come out here? England's finished. Join us in LA. You'll find work, college teaching.'

'Thanks, but I don't really. . .'

'Think about it anyway. Okay?'

Again the very thought of such an uprooting appalled me. Lindsey made it sound so simple. 'All right,' I lied, 'I will think about it. And Lindsey – I'm so glad for you. Be happy now.'

When, a few weeks later, Lindsey's wedding photographs arrived, I was strongly reminded of Jane's wedding earlier in the year. Lindsey's face wore the same shaken expression, slightly foolish with happiness, that I had seen lighting up the faces of Jane and Mark as they'd left Wadham Chapel. I remembered being shaken myself by the awesome solemnity of the Vows: 'For better for worse, for richer for poorer, in sickness and in health.' To love another frail and fallible being 'until Death us do part'. We want so much, I'd thought, as Jane glanced up at Mark as if to assure herself that he was still there beside her. I studied the photograph of my new brother-in-law – eyes slightly hidden by his misted glasses, floppy velvet bow tie, checked shirt. Could he possibly fulfil Lindsey's every changing need until one of them died? It seemed an impossibly brave venture. And yet bride and groom stared confidently out of the photograph seeing a vista of happiness stretching securely ahead.

A few years later, in 1978, I went out to visit Lindsey and Stephen in Los Angeles. They seemed extravagantly happy together, anxious to display their happiness, their marriage, their house, dog and seven cats and their apparent delight in one another's company. After a wary start Stephen and I took quickly to one another: he had been a little alarmed at the prospect of entertaining an ex-nun, but when he discovered that my enthusiasm for Californian vintages and good food was equal to his own, his early reserve crumbled away. I liked his superb sense of humour and his tenderness with Lindsey when she got tired or threw one of her panics – panics that bear a familial relationship to my flurries of rhetoric at the trivial accidents of life. I came away happy for both of them. Yet only a few months later their marriage was over. A couple of years ago Jane and Mark separated and have both since found new partners. On my Profession day, it would have been inconceivable to me that only three years later I'd be writing to Rome for a dispensation from my Vows.

'Don't you *want* to get married?' People ask me that very often with a hint of exasperation in their voices. Some people, I know, however hard they politely try to conceal the fact, see my lack of eagerness in this direction as proof that ultimately I have been badly damaged by my convent experience. It would certainly provide a very neat *finale* to this book as it has to so many novels; a wedding giving a cast-iron guarantee that happiness is possible and can be nailed down and made to last for ever.

Other friends of mine, including some of the married couples, take a different view. 'A wedding at the end of your book might well provide an ironic end,' one of them said recently. 'Yet again the reader could picture you walking up the aisle in a white bridal dress as you did on your clothing day, to begin once more a new life of drudgery and frustration!' It was, I hasten to add, a joke – not a heavy feminist comment.

I am sure it is true, indeed I know it is, that neither Lindsey nor Jane regrets her marriage any more than I regret having spent my youth in a convent. They were important times for us all. Some people seem to remarry very happily indeed and many nuns and priests who have abandoned the religious life go on to make excellent marriages like Rebecca. An earlier 'mistake' need not preclude another lunge after eternal happiness. It just happens not to be my way, although my life has changed so radically so continually that perhaps it is absurd to say that I'll never marry; it will be clear already that I've done many things that I never expected. At present, however, it would seem most unlikely.

'Karen! I heard such chilling news about you yesterday.'

Mrs Christopher was standing at the foot of the stairs in the darkened hall. The heavy stained glass in the front door shed lurid, ecclesiastical light, her eyes glimmered up to me moist and eager. I groaned inwardly. Mrs Christopher and I were always colliding in the hall and the encounter never failed to make me uncomfortable. It was not like being at the Stanleys' – and oh, how I missed the casual cheer and warmth of my former home. Whereas I'd frequently met Edwin or Judith about the house and stopped to chat, this had always been accidental. These meetings with Mrs Christopher were contrived. I felt she lurked, ready to pounce as I came in and out of the house. I listened to endless monologues, about her health, about the iniquity of Patricia's wanting to get married, about the boorishness of her future son-in-law. I often tried to be sympathetic – poor old lady, terrified at the prospect of living on her own, nothing to take her mind off things. But each time I came away repelled. My feeling earlier that year that she was evil in some way intensified. There was nothing spectacular or dramatic about any of it – but, then, evil isn't spectacular, it was dreary – even her hysterical rows with Patricia, her storms of tears and highflown rhetoric were dreary. Dreary and mechanical. But perhaps this was all too fanciful. I shook myself impatiently.

'Something very chilling indeed!'

I tried to quell the flicker of fascination that her words kindled. Don't get involved, just walk straight past.

'Oh, really? What can that have been, I wonder? Sorry, I'm afraid I can't stop. I have a class a 10.00.'

Mrs Christopher leaned against the front door, barring my way. Oh Lord. Why couldn't I be really rude to her? That would probably shut her up. Jane – even Charlotte – wouldn't put up with this. But it was no good. In some odd way Mrs Christopher had made me afraid of her: I was afraid of being thrown out – dismal as it was the flat was cheap by London standards, definitely all I could afford. I was on her territory; by some devious method she made me feel that she owned me, that she had rights.

'Patricia and I went out yesterday.' She was speaking slowly now that she knew she'd got me, her eyes ran over my face restlessly. 'To Southend. It's nice, you know, out of season. And on the pier we saw a fortune teller. Patricia said: "Oh, Mummy, let's try it!" And so we did, just for a bit of fun. Well.' She lowered her voice dramatically and, cursing myself, I felt my attention engage with hers. 'She turned out to be remarkably accurate. I mean, I don't usually believe in that sort of stuff. Not at all. Do you?'

'No. I'm sure it's all rubbish,' I said, feeling suddenly, for some inexplicable reason, no longer sure at all.

'I'm sure you're right.' Mrs Christopher beamed at me and patted my cheek. 'You're such a sensible, clever little girl,' she crooned. I flinched and smiled tensely.

'But I must say, dear, that the things she told me about myself were spot on. Things no one could have known. But then,' she moved closer, seeing me glancing at my watch, 'she said that she could see a girl. A fairly young girl. Who was talented and eccentric. And who lived in *our house*!' She delivered the last sentence triumphantly and smiled. 'I mean, it can't be Lucy, can it? She's a dear little thing but absolutely conventional and you couldn't call her talented. Not really. I mean she – '

'Look. What did she *say*,' I demanded, cursing myself for my interest.

'This is the awful part, dear.' She put a hand on my arm and spoke softly. 'She said that the girl would die before the year was out of an overdose of sleeping pills!'

I froze.

'I mean, I don't believe it for one moment. But you never know, do you? So I just thought I'd warn you, lovey. Just in case.'

I swallowed, feeling a shaft of ice slither down to my stomach and settle there.

'Well, I mustn't keep you, must I?' she laughed gaily. 'I wouldn't want to make you late for your students.'

It wasn't really that I believed any of it, I told myself firmly as I walked through Highgate Wood. A grubby little fortune teller on a pier. And yet there was an uncanny accuracy in her picking on that form of suicide. I didn't want to do it again, did I? All that was over and in the past. My body was plumper and I weighed eight whole stone; the cuts on my arms and on my breast had healed. It could never happen again. Yet last time I didn't intend to kill myself. There was something nasty here that I didn't want to look at. A crazy logic and weird insight.

It was a wet, cold spring day. The cars swept past angrily, slashing water onto the pavements, and the trees dripped steadily from every one of their newly-minted leaves, their trunks stained and dark with rain. I pulled the collar of my mac up round my face as a protection.

Why had Mrs Christopher wanted to tell me?

I patted the three bulky parcels, pleased and excited. Three copies of my thesis, duly typed and bound in important black covers with gilt lettering. I had the soaring sense of a task completed. Against all odds I'd persevered, shaped an idea; during the last months its different facets dropped perfectly and effortlessly into place. It was something I had done. Something creative and something that expressed me. Dear Tennyson.

My supervisor was pleased; two professors who had read it were impressed. And I was pleased. Here was one part of my life that did escape disaster. Part of my brain might be out of control but this was a guarantee of its ultimate integrity and health. It was my passport to a future job, my assurance of ultimate survival, at least on an economic plane.

I watched the girl behind the grille slap on the stamps and stickers cheerfully; the stamp of approval. Then she put them in a pile beside her from which they would be carried to Oxford.

The Lady of Shalott, in what was obviously a supreme final effort, raised herself into a sitting position in the elaborate little boat. Her tapestry, the fruit of all her years locked up in her prison, floated away downstream, becoming waterlogged. Ruined and wasted. The lady's face had already taken on the pallor of death and was as grey and stone-coloured as the sky and her expression was one of wild despair. Quite different from that other lady over there who was also floating towards a watery death. There Ophelia lay supine on the water surrounded by a lush, brilliantly green foliage. The water was pulling down her garments but her hands were lifted slightly from the river as though welcoming death, and her face was caught in a surrender that was almost sexual. Not so the Lady of Shalott. She'd smashed out of her prison and now, when there was no turning back, she saw the folly of her rebellion. . .

With a start I suddenly became aware of the world outside the large Pre-Raphaelite canvases. An Art student was copying Dyce's *Pegwell Bay* and one or two other people had wandered into the Tate Gallery that Saturday afternoon. Like me. Except – and something jolted into place in my mind – I had no business to be in an art gallery this Saturday. I should be – oh, no – at Greenwich theatre with two of my colleagues and a party of students from the College. I looked at my watch. Four-thirty. The matinée performance of Genet's *The Maids* would be half over by now. There was no point at all in trying to get to Greenwich. Suddenly feeling weak with fright I sank on to a bench still staring absently at Waterhouse's famous painting of *The Lady of Shalott*, but now no longer seeing it. What had happened?

I did some quick calculations. For the last three hours I hadn't really been conscious at all. Something had taken me over and brought me to the Tate, miles away from where I intended to go. The last thing I could remember clearly was getting on the tube at Highgate. I was going to meet the party at Charing Cross station at two-fifteen and I allowed myself lots of time because the Northern Line tubes tended to be unreliable and I was afraid of missing the train to Greenwich. I must, I realized now, have got out of the tube at Charing Cross underground station, and instead of walking up to the Main Line station, I must have walked along the embankment – a long walk, really – to the Tate. Why? I'd often come here to look at the Pre-Raphaelites in connection with my thesis. My mind had forced me to come here instead of getting on to the Greenwich train. I tried desperately to think hard about the last three hours. Tried to remember deciding to come to the Tate. No. There was nothing. Where the responsible decision should have been there was nothing but a blankness. Yes, now that I thought hard I could recall the steely grey Thames, the wet, cloudy sky, umbrellas and mackintoshed figures. But nothing else.

How was I going to explain my failure to turn up to my colleagues? I'd have to say that I'd missed the train or something. I couldn't possibly tell them the truth. They'd think I was as mad as poor Ophelia there. In fact it was a wonder, really, that I hadn't jumped into the Thames. I could count myself lucky that I'd been impelled to come to the Tate. I could easily have ended up in a brothel in Soho. I must, I told myself grimly, as I got up to leave, have a deeply cultural subconscious.

Dazed, my head aching, I stumbled up the stairs and wandered through the galleries, blindly searching for a way out. I felt sick and had a strong desire to lie down on one of those long leather seats and sleep for hours. The cold autumn rain cut into my face and seemed to penetrate my already damp mackintosh. My hair, I noticed, was soaking wet. Obviously I hadn't been conscious enough earlier to put up my umbrella. As I walked towards Pimlico station the white, peeling houses, decayed relics of a once splendid past, looked shuttered and blank.

'You bleeding Irish pig!' There was a smash of glasses breaking, a grunt, a high-pitched scream. 'Go back to the bogs where you belong.'

'Oh, no!' I buried my head in my hands. Guy lunged across the bar and aimed a heavy blow at the barman. There was now a seething rugger scrum. Guy's curses filled the air together with a cacophony of squeals and moans and a confusion of flailing limbs. I got up unsteadily to my feet. How could I break in on all of that? My mouth was dry and I felt slightly sick. It was months since anything like this had happened in public. I'd hoped it was getting better.

'My God! Karen, what happened?' I turned around to see Charlotte, white-faced, gazing in horror at the fray.

'Right, mate. I've just about had enough of you!' someone was yelling self-importantly. A woman was laughing hysterically at the other side of the pub and the other drinkers were lapping up the scene avidly, hardly daring to believe their luck at this excellent, free entertainment.

'I'm sorry, Charlotte,' I murmured tiredly. 'What a ghastly evening for you.'

'Well, it was fine up till now. He seemed perfectly okay.'

'Yes, this is one of Guy's famous freak-outs. I expect the barman refused to serve him or something. Anything can spark it off.' My voice was weary. With a sigh I started to walk towards the seething mob. Why didn't they just let him go and have done with it? He was struggling in the grip of two rather weedy-looking men who contrived to look dishevelled and terribly pleased with themselves at the same time. The trouble was I might start the whole thing off again. He could strike out at me as he had that first time in Oxford. Now at least he seemed to be giving up. His struggles were slowing. I felt weary of it all. It couldn't go on.

'Don't go any closer,' Charlotte warned me, putting her hand on my shoulder. 'It's awful, isn't it? I'd always assumed you were exaggerating.'

'Here's the fuzz!' someone shouted, and to my horror, through the open door walked four, five, six policemen. Guy gave a yell and began struggling frenziedly again, the whites of his eyes rings of panic. I stood paralysed with horror as the policemen between them picked him up as though he were a rag doll, pinning his arms behind him. How absurdly young they look, I thought abstractedly, and then suddenly snapped awake and started pushing my way through the cluster of ghouls standing gawping at the pub door.

'Dear God! There's no need for that!' Charlotte's voice was shrill with disgust. The policemen were pinning Guy to the ground with their bodies. He was still shouting and suddenly there was silence and a sick sound of expelled air.

I leant back against the pub door feeling faint as I watched him being bundled into the Black Maria. The sight of that callous, legalized violence filled me with a sudden sharp nausea and I felt something inside me breaking away. This had nothing to do with me any more.

Inside the police station a cheerful red-faced policeman in his shirt sleeves grinned at us companionably.

'Oh, him? D and D. Just a moment, dear, and I'll see.'

'D and D?'

'Drunk and Disorderly,' muttered Charlotte *sotto voce* at my side.

'That's right. You obviously know your way around the terminology. Now what are two nice young ladies like you doing getting mixed up in a mess like this?'

What indeed? I wondered with a renewed clarity as I smirked feebly back. For two years now I'd taken these scenes of violence absolutely in my stride; they were just a part of my life with Guy to be accepted without question, just as I accepted and loved him without reservations. I still loved him, yes. Even now I was straining anxiously for a sound of him, feeling in my own mouth the panic and fear that I knew he'd be feeling. But the violence, no. That I suddenly knew was long dead in me, largely due to Guy himself.

The policeman, leafing through the file on his desk, yawned widely and noisily with a mixture of boredom and detachment, and smiled apologetically. 'Sorry, ladies. No offence meant. No, he's all right, luv. Don't you worry. Can you hear him?' He opened a door behind his desk and a volley of curses greeted us from a distance. 'In good voice, you could say. Limp as a baby he was when they brought him in, asked for a drink of water and when Sarge took it in, he chucked it all over him and started hollering. *Not* very friendly, was it?'

'I'm so sorry,' I said lamely, feeling sharply the absurdity of my conventional drawing-room apology in this setting. Inappropriately I felt the corners of my mouth twitching and a sense of enormous relief at this young officer's unimaginative but safe normality.

'No, don't worry, luv,' he went on. 'Nothing you can do for the mo. Just give him a while to quieten down and we'll let him go. He'll have to appear at the Magistrates' tomorrow. Get him to plead guilty, there's a good girl. Save everyone a lot of time and bother.'

'I'm sure he will. Thank you so much,' I said, mirth arising yet again. I sounded like someone thanking a hostess for a cocktail party.

He stretched himself and got to his feet 'Tell you what. Why don't you go and sit in the waiting room? I've no idea how long he'll be and I've got a murder on my hands tonight and I'm up to my eyes. I've really not got time for a D and D, if you see what I mean.'

'Oh, absolutely,' I agreed, following him down a short, tiled passage.

'Here you are.' He swung the door open and winked. 'Join the happy crew in here.'

One look at the glum depression on the faces lining the wall of the waiting room finished me off. Charlotte too I could feel shaking at my side. With one accord we hurried outside and leaned against the railings, laughter shaking through us in healing, painful convulsions.

'It's not even remotely funny,' I gasped at last. 'Oh, Charlotte, I'm so glad you were here with me.'

'No, it's dreadful. Dreadful. A murder. What are we doing laughing like this? They could have been friends of the victim. A tragedy.'

' "I've got a murder on my hands".'

' "Up to my eyes".'

' "Join the happy crew in here".' We clutched one another, moaning, our insides straining. The laughter had worked; the hard knot of tension had melted and I'd accepted the implications of what I'd seen tonight. Of course it wasn't funny. Violence was tragic and ugly. And the laughter was just my way of letting it go away from me, once and for all.

'That murder certainly put our little drama firmly in its place, didn't it? As well as seeing where all this could lead to.' We looked hard at one another and Charlotte took my hand. I squeezed it gratefully, thinking back to that time years ago when I'd pulled my hand away from her comfort. 'All in a day's work,' I said quietly, 'for him.'

But not for me. I knew that now. Yet when Guy appeared at the station door a little later, looking dazed, as though he wasn't seeing us but was lost inside a drama in his own head, I found myself moving forward instantly to take his arm and kiss him reassuringly on the cheek. Arm in arm we walked off in the direction of Highgate.

My thesis failed.

It was not an absolute failure. I did get a Higher degree, the Degree of Bachelor of Letters, but the thesis was not considered by my two examiners to be worthy of a Doctorate, the highest of the Oxford degrees. It wasn't even an ordinary failure. To my miserable bewilderment I found myself the centre of an Oxford scandal. The details really don't matter any more. Suffice it to say that my examiners failed the thesis; when their report was presented to the Board there was some kind of spontaneous outcry about the report's validity and a row began which lasted five months. Finally it was decided, for internal university reasons, that the thesis could not be re-examined and, with many apologies from people in high places, I was offerd the B. Litt.

If it was an embarrassment for the University, for me it was a catastrophe, not just because now all my hopes of an academic career had folded. The thesis had sustained me during the last four years. I had lost my God, seemed in danger of losing my life and my reason, but in the midst of this carnage the thesis went on growing and developing. Slowly, gradually, the argument had formed. However dry and abstruse it was, for me writing that thesis had been an act of creation. It became an amulet, a promise that I had some worth, some hope. Now that hope was dead. For months, for years afterwards I skirted round the pain of this catastrophe gingerly, wincing when anything jarred the sore spot. The numb despair I felt when I first heard the news gave way to grief, bitterness and a sense of futility. Why go on? Whatever I tried to do seemed doomed. I'd failed as a religious, failed as an academic, was failing as a balanced, sane human being. There seemed little point in making any further effort.

I couldn't have known that this failure was the best thing that could have happened to me. And that is not a cynical statement. It gave me one of the biggest shoves I've had in my life to throw me into something different.

I was not meant to be an academic. The disciplines involved

are too confining for my particular mind and personality. It was a seductive idea. Safe; another cloister; it would shield me from so much. From so much that I'd now be poorer without. I didn't wake up with this realization all at once. But slowly, one by one, I noticed things about myself. For one thing I found that I had started to read again with pleasure. Of course I had been reading hard during my university years, but there was something rather dutiful and joyless about the exercise. I'd read a novel and find myself desperately casting around for a clever thing to say about it at a dinner party with colleagues. And not surprisingly the clever things refused to come to order. Now I suddenly discovered myself devouring books with a wholly new relish – for themselves. I no longer cared whether my ideas were clever or not. Similarly in discussions I'd find myself inundated with ideas and the words to express them, instead of sitting, paralysed with academic self-consciousness. My mind was given back to me in a fuller way than ever before. At last I felt I owned it. I became aware too how much my academic aspirations had, without my knowing it, put a strain on me and refused to allow this freer self to find expression.

There were other benefits. I found that, unconsciously, I'd adopted the post of the academic woman – a *virago intacta*, as Jane used to say. I was a blue stocking to whom clothes, my appearance and lesser pleasures like cooking and gardening were inferior. Gradually I found myself becoming more frivolous. I experimented more with my clothes; I had a new haircut; I learned to cook. And, more importantly, I found I was loosening up. I was less pathetically anxious to display my knowledge as a guarantee of my academic worth, less anxious to cut other people down to size with a witty Parthian shot. One day I realized that I no longer winced when anyone mentioned Tennyson or Doctorates. I really didn't mind any more. The door of the academic cloister had finally closed behind me and I was free of it.

But there was no remarkable and dramatic moment when all was made clear to me. Just a slow, snail-like series of private discoveries, each so tiny that I scarcely noticed them when they happened. I had no idea at first that my failure would have such a positive outcome. But even on the day after the news first came through I knew that the despair I felt was not the same as I'd have felt a couple of years ago. I'd been out for a walk, wandering restlessly round Highgate, trying to wear myself out and stop my mind from churning. Eventually I went home, pushed open Mrs Christopher's front door and stole up the hall to the stairs. The house was dark and silent.

'Karen!'

I jumped. Mrs Christopher, in a pale dressing gown, emerged from her room. She put her hand on my arm and clutched it and I felt a mild thrill of disgust. Her lips were trembling, her eyes watching me greedily. 'Don't do it!'

'Don't do what, Mrs Christopher?' It was a rhetorical question. I knew quite well what she was talking about. And she knew that I knew. Weary antagonists, we took up our accustomed positions.

'Don't kill yourself! It's a horrible way to die, an overdose.'

We stared at each other. I looked at her eager face, covered in pale grease to shield the skin from wrinkles that had long since arrived. This wasn't the first time she'd made this plea. It was quite a regular event for her to jump out of her bedroom and tell me some horrible story about a suicide and implore me to be careful. Either that or she told me that she was so lonely and unhappy that she wanted to kill herself. Yet somehow tonight her plea seemed especially eerie. Was that what I had to settle? There didn't seem much to go on for, really.

'Your stomach bleeds, you see.' Her blackcurrant eyes were pointed and darting. 'And you haemorrhage internally. It's not a peaceful death, my dear. You start vomiting too, and then you can choke on your own vomit – '

I listened, fascinated. She's quite mad, I thought with a faint shock of surprise. I thought I was mad, but I know I'm saner than that. I've got to get out of here. As soon as I can. I'll get a job – any job – buy my own flat. Get away from this.

'And you're such a dear little thing. So talented, too. With your doctorate all finished and your excellent university job. It would be a tragedy – '

'Good night, Mrs Christopher.' I smiled firmly at her and started walking away upstairs. Away from the mad sickness up to the sanity of my own flat. How odd that at this moment I should be making plans for the future. At the turning of the stairs, I looked down and saw her staring up at me, baffled. Her mouth hanging open comically. I nodded to her. 'It's very late,' I called conversationally. 'I'd get some sleep if I were you.' Then I went on up, leaving her alone.

The light was on in the bedroom, I noticed. I must have left it on by mistake. Wearily I flung my coat over a chair. I felt tearful now, as though something hard inside me had melted. I walked over to the bed and jumped with shock. Guy was stretched out on the bed, asleep. A half-finished glass of Guinness was on the bedside table. On a scrap of paper were some mapped-out stanzas.

I made a move to wake him, cautiously, but he suddenly sprang into a sitting position. He rubbed his eyes, shook his head and then grinned foolishly at me. 'Sorry. Meant to be awake when you got in. Must have nodded off.' He looked up at me inquiringly.

'I failed, Guy.'

He nodded. 'I reckoned something was wrong. You were going to phone me yesterday in Oxford after the Viva, remember? When you didn't, I guessed. Do you mind my being here?' he added, almost shyly. 'I thought you might like some company.' I felt the tears run down my cheeks, saw Guy open his arms and clung to him. Feeling his comforting solidity.

CHAPTER TEN

Cloud of Unknowing (1975–6)

'I'VE SOMETHING TO tell you,' Guy said worriedly, swirling his rum nervously in his glass. 'I'm getting out.'

The noises in the bar suddenly faded, closing the two of us in a cocoon of tension. He was avoiding my eye, gazing at the amber liquid that was going round and round in the glass. Then suddenly he picked it up, knocked it back in one gulp and looked straight at me, his eyes frightened but determined.

'Getting out?' I repeated stupidly. 'Getting out of where?'

'Out of London, out of Oxford, out of the job.' He was speaking quickly, his words tumbling over one another. 'It's no good, Karen, it'll finish me if I stay here. I'm getting worse. That time last year when I finished up in a police cell really made me think. What's going to happen to me? I'll end up in Broadmoor with a life sentence if I'm not careful.'

'Where will you go?' I asked, saying the words carefully, concentrating hard on getting them out clearly one by one, studying intently the small puddle of beer on the table, watching the light catch it, examining the pattern it made. Anything to shield me from the implications of what he was saying.

'Back home,' Guy was speaking eagerly now. He leaned forward and took my hand, pressing it so that I was forced to look up. 'Back to Lincolnshire, to the farm. That's where I belong. I was mad to leave it. I'll work on the farm with my uncles, get my body really physically tired every day so that my mind just won't have the energy to freak out. My writing'll be better too, once I've stopped drinking myself into the ground.'

'But why is it London that's ruining you?' I asked, hearing the pain in my voice. 'Surely it's something inside you that you'll have to learn to come to cope with wherever you are. Do you really think that you can change just by changing your environment? You can't, Guy! I've tried that – you don't leave yourself behind just by a change of scene.'

'Of course you don't.' Guy shook his head, sadly. 'I'm not that stupid, darling. It's just that all this – ' he gestured round the crowded city pub; the door was open and outside in the sunlight the road was jammed with traffic, horns were honking querulously – 'just isn't *my* place. I'm a fish out of water here. What use do I make of London, for Christ's sake? Do I ever go to a film or a gallery? Never. I just spend my time off in places like this. When I'm working I'm stuck in a van in a bloody queue of traffic. It's no life. I like working with my hands – always have done. It's great up there on the farm, when I go back every year and help my uncles for a couple of weeks. Working hard like that with my body makes my mind quiet.'

I nodded. Already the sense of loss was growing.

'This violence of mine,' he said, a worried line creasing his brow. 'It's beginning to scare me. That night I was in the police cell – I never told you this – I was like a madman. Kicking and squealing like a lunatic. Then suddenly I snapped out of it and everything went sullen and dead inside. It was strange. I can't explain it. It was almost as though that blast of fury belting through my brain destroyed part of it. I was scared. And then the police let me out. You remember there was a murder that night? Well, they took me through the room where the bloke was being interrogated – I think they wanted to frighten me. They succeeded.'

'Are you afraid of ending up like that man?' I asked. He pulled his chair over to mine and put his arm round me. I could feel his grip on my left shoulder, as though he were pulling me to him to fight off the possibility. 'No brain, a destroyed brain and just brute strength.'

He nodded. I relaxed against him while for a moment our private nightmares merged. 'When I got outside,' he said at last, 'and saw you and Charlotte there I couldn't believe it! It was like another world. Innocent and harmless. Supposing I hit you so hard one day I killed you?' The grip on my arm tightened and I could feel his blunt fingers bruising my flesh. 'It could happen, Karen. It's no good pretending. I've just got to get out before it's too late.'

I tried to imagine it. Soon he'd be gone. For good. And

welcomed the pressure of his fingers as a sign that he was still there.

'Come with me,' he said suddenly.

I jumped and he released me. We sat staring at one another and for a moment I felt a rush of joy.

'To the farm?' I asked, conjuring up the world he'd so often told me about. His uncles. And then the images of violence – the little fox hanging from a beam in the barn, which had stamped itself on his brain and somehow marked him for life. Yet in one sense I knew he was right. In a city he was a caged animal, his emotional energy cabined and confined. Lincolnshire was a flat empty county.

'There'd be space,' I thought aloud.

'It's Tennyson country,' he agreed, coaxing me gently. Flat, wheat-covered acres on either side as far as the eye could see.

'On either side the river lie
Long fields of barley and of rye
That clothe the wold and meet the sky'

I quoted. It was Lady of Shalott country. And then, sadly, I knew.

'I can't go with you, Guy,' I said, paradoxically reaching out to hold his hand, as though to deny the words of separation. 'I'd just be running away.'

'From what?' he flashed back, gripping my hand painfully. 'There's nothing here for you any more.'

'Yes, I know that.' I leant against him, feeling my body respond to his automatically. 'I know that I've got no academic future, but – '

'All right!' he argued, 'you can get a job in a school. Big deal! But how long do you think you can hold down a regular job? With your hallucinations and blackouts. Come with me, darling.' His voice dropped, suddenly, and he leaned his head against mine. 'I don't want to lose you. You're the best thing I've got. Please. Come.' The emptiness of those vast wheatfields had suddenly scared him too and already I felt the emptiness of my body without him and the first pangs of physical bereavement. 'I love you, for Christ's sake!' The admission was made angrily and I felt my heart tighten.

'I love you, too.' I spoke flatly. 'But I can't come with you. The farm isn't my place.' I heard my voice wobble and swallowed hard. Dear, lovely Guy. He'd given me so much. The least I could give him was the gift of his future. I must let him go forward, unimpeded and free. 'You know that we seem to spark off violence and distress in one another. We're too close, too alike.'

There was a silence. 'It's over, isn't it?' he said at last. We turned to face one another, tears standing unashamedly in our eyes.

'You know that; that's why you're going. We mustn't cling to something that's finished or it'll get distorted and ugly.'

'There'll never be anyone else like you.' He smiled crookedly and rumpled my hair, just as he had the first time we met.

I smiled back, sadly. 'No. Not for me, either. Who else will beat me up, throttle me in the middle of the night?'

'Who else can I reduce to tearing at herself with razors?' We laughed, trying to make it easier for one another.

'Coming back to the flat?' he asked diffidently. 'Or don't you want to?' Our hands reached blindly together and held on fast.

Quickly we got up and started walking up Muswell Hill Broadway, arms round each other, fitting together easily yet sadly for the last time.

'It's raining. Blast!' I said, trying for nonchalance. 'My hair will get curly.'

'Here! Take my hat.' He whipped off the old-fashioned trilby hat he often wore and settled it on my own head. Then he laughed, his hands on my shoulders, his eyes fond and amused. 'You look really good in that. Look!'

He pushed me round to face a shop window. Our reflections were clear. I was leaning against Guy, he was behind me, his hands on my shoulders, pressing me close. I peered at the glass. And smiled into his eyes. He was right. It did suit me. With my new, short hairstyle my face was free. It no longer hid behind a veil of hair. And the hat made me look rather wicked. I looked – I suddenly realized – worldly. It was a description which would once have horrified me. Now I was pleased. I belonged to the world now. And Guy, for all his feelings, had helped that to happen. Perhaps more than anybody else.

'Keep it. It's yours,' he smiled into our reflection. 'My father gave it to me, and now I'll give it to you. It'll help you remember me. Not that we'll never see each other again,' he added. 'I'll be up to see you, you know. I don't want you to forget me.'

'Oh, Guy.' I put my hands over his, closing my eyes to hide the pain that I knew was there. 'Do you think I could possibly do that?'

My students looked up expectantly as I walked into the seminar. Smiles played round their faces, eyebrows were raised archly. Something was afoot.

The room looks different, I said, puzzled, looking round. They were sitting in a circle as usual, notebooks and texts on their laps, but – and here was the difference – the large armchair reserved for the tutor was pushed into a corner and the place where it usually was was filled with two or three students who were grinning perkily at me. There was one empty chair halfway round the circle.

'I see,' I said nervously, 'a democratic seminar.'

There was a gust of laughter followed swiftly by an expectant silence.

'Explanations?' I asked, feeling a smile hovering behind my face; I looked round the circle. 'Are you trying to tell me that I'm a tyrannical tutor?'

'Well, yes, in a way,' Lotte, one of the mature students, said. She had been a social worker before coming to University and she gave me a quick professional smile to temper what she was saying. 'You see, you terrify us.'

'What!' I sank into a chair and stared at them incredulously. 'Sorry. What did you say?'

'You terrify us,' Lotte repeated patiently. 'You're so ferocious-ly academic that you make our little ideas seem puny and we get scared of opening our mouths.'

I stared round the circle of students. There was no hostility. One or two of the younger ones were giggling out of nervousness but most of them were trying to reassure me by smiling encouragingly and with studied nonchalance.

'Let me get this straight.' I swallowed hard, shook myself and tried again. 'You mean *I* actually scare *you*?'

I looked at them again, all so apparently at ease with their surroundings, so sure of themselves. Lotte was not the only mature student in this group; there were at least eight others out of the twenty here to study Henry James. Eight people who, like me, had put aside one life to start another, but who, unlike me, seemed to be effecting this change with the minimum of stress. Scilla, for instance, had been a nurse, Julia an actress, Marcus, who reminded me disconcertingly of Guy, a teacher, Wendy a legal secretary. Beside their easy self-assurance I felt flimsy and ill-defined.

'You mean,' I said slowly, 'I *frighten* you?'

'Terribly!' Scilla beamed at me. 'You've no idea how terrifying you are. You're so absolutely secure in your grasp of the subject and so decisive in your manner that you just can't imagine what it's like to be us – not understanding half of what you're saying.'

'Me. Decisive?' I repeated in the hollow tone of advanced shock.

They nodded.

'But *I'm* scared of everybody else.' The words burst from me and I knew suddenly that it was true. I'd been frightened of my Superiors, scared rigid of God. In the world nearly everything and everybody conspired to frighten me. I'd seemed shut out from some basic knowledge about how to cope, how to be at ease, how to enjoy myself. 'I'm frightened of *you!*'

There was a general explosion of mirth and instantly I could feel waves of friendliness reaching across the circle to embrace me. It was as Dr Piet had said once. To show one's vulnerability produced not disgust in other people but warmth. A form of love.

'You're frightened of us!' Wendy exclaimed through the laughter. 'You can't be!'

'Of course she is!' Lotte protested calmly. 'All frightening people are frightened themselves. They've learned at first hand how other people terrorized them in the past and they just reproduce those methods in their own behaviour.'

'Oh, stop talking like a bloody textbook, Lotte,' Marcus exclaimed in disgust, patting my knee protectively. 'Karen doesn't mean to terrorize us, for Christ's sake.'

'No, of course she doesn't. It's just that fear is the mode in which a frightened person operates and – '

Marcus snorted with disgust.

'Actually,' I smiled across at Lotte, 'you're probably right.' I thought of the way I'd been taught myself in the religious life. 'I'm really sorry,' I said contritely, 'but how can I change?'

225

'Oh, no, Karen!' Scilla interjected quickly. 'This isn't meant to be a put-down at all. We *like* your teaching. We really do. It's just that we crawl out of here feeling pretty thick. And futile, if you see what I mean.'

I knew. Only too well. 'Well, if it's any consolation I feel pretty formless myself sometimes.' I wondered what they would think if they knew how near to ultimate disaster this had brought me.

'So we thought,' Lotte went on, 'that today somebody else could take the seminar and you could be here, putting us right and telling us things we should know.'

'But on your terms, not mine.' I nodded. It was odd how relaxed I felt suddenly. I'd come into the room, my head bursting with the things every student should know about *The Bostonians*. Yet at the same time, I suddenly realized, I'd intended to stun them with an intellectual firework display, so that there would be no chink which would reveal my basic inadequacy. 'Right!' I planted myself in my chair. 'Over to you.' I nodded happily to them. 'I'm entirely relinquishing all control.' Loss of control no longer seemed to guarantee annihilation. 'Who's going to take over?'

'You choose,' someone said.

'Oh, no!' I protested. 'That isn't in the spirit of the thing at all. Someone must either volunteer or else you've got to choose one of your number.'

'All right. I suggest Lotte,' Wendy urged.

'Oh, no!' Lotte's face expressed pure dismay. Then she smiled, defeated. 'Talk about being hoist with your own petard. Still, I suppose I'll learn something as well about the horrors of being a teacher!'

As the seminar progressed I realized that over the last three years I'd been stuffing these poor students with enough knowledge to acquire a Doctorate on the author under discussion. That wasn't what teaching was about. Friendliness was seeping into the room. They were calling me by my Christian name. Until today nobody had called me anything but Miss Armstrong.

After another quarter of an hour I found I was enjoying myself. It was fun tossing an idea lightheartedly into the room and watching the students turn it over and play with it until, gradually, you could transform it into something important.

The door opened and Charlie, one of the younger students, wandered in. He crept carefully across the room, his pretty girlish complexion flushing apologetically.

'Sorry I'm late,' he said. 'I had an interview with the Careers Advisor.'

I nodded and watched his slight, elegant figure pull out an extra chair. Charlie's effeminate manner and long curling hair were, I'd learned, deceptive. He was thoroughly heterosexual and had a robust sense of humour. Now, I noticed, he was shaking with laughter and was whispering rapidly to his neighbours who were suddenly convulsed themselves.

'What is it, Charlie?' I asked curiously, noting that this was again something I should never have done before. Up till now Literature was a sacred study not to be profaned by mere human frivolity and irrelevance.

He leant back in his chair, laughing helplessly. 'I told the Careers Advisor that I wanted a job to do with people,' he said, tossing his blond-streaked fringe out of his eyes. 'I also said it would be nice to be out of doors.' He paused and braced himself, crossing one leg daintily over the other.

'Well?' I prompted.

'She suggested that I should be a traffic warden!' Charlie confessed, shaken, as the rest of us were, by a gale of laughter.

Eventually I wiped the tears of laughter out of my eyes.

'Come on,' I said firmly. 'Back to James.'

At the end of the seminar, I got up to go, dazed by the implications of the last hour.

'Karen,' Wendy said as I got to the door. She'd been speaking in an undertone to Mark and Marcus who'd nodded enthusiastically. 'We're having a party next week. One or two of the other tutors are coming. Will you? Please?'

I started, blushing at my pleasure in the warmth that filled the room. How nice they all were, and how unexpectedly good life could be.

'Do come!' Scilla urged.

'Thanks,' I replied, 'I'd love to.'

Not long after this I applied for and got a teaching job in an excellent academic girls' school and spent there six very happy years. My hunch during that seminar that teaching could be creative and exciting proved right. Quite often, of course, I made mistakes, but gradually I learned to relax from the strained stance of a fierce, all-powerful and infallible authority figure, the guardian of the secrets of academe.

I'd wondered whether it wasn't a mistake, whether I wasn't entering an institution too like the convent. But Prayers on my first day reassured me. The girls didn't look as I'd looked at their age, strained by a vision of perfection. They looked confident, relaxed and happy. Of course they would have their problems, but they would be different problems. As the piano crashed out the opening chords of 'Lord, behold us for Thy blessing', a hymn I'd never heard in my life, the difference became clear to me. At my old school we'd have had three rousing verses of 'Within the panting heart of Rome' or several wailing stanzas to the Sacred Heart. This was not a Catholic school and for me that difference was significant. Some of the girls in the Sixth Form were older than I was when I had entered my convent. What a baby I'd been, I thought suddenly with renewed insight. But then at 17 you think you're so grown up and mature. None of these sixth formers looked as though they'd be entering a convent, I thought, looking at the zanily dyed hair and the eccentric clothes. And if they got there they probably wouldn't accept the intolerable as meekly as I had. Already they seemed to have some sense of themselves and their own dignity. Of course, they were trying out rôles; the clothes showed that. They were searching for an identity that it would take them years to discover. And already I could sense that in this school they would have a chance to do this freely and creatively. I wanted to help them to do it.

I can remember very clearly the occasion when I suddenly realized how far I'd moved. It was during my production of *A Midsummer Night's Dream* in my second year at the school.

'It's a play about sex, of course,' I heard myself remarking casually to the cast. 'About sex and the absolutely arbitrary nature of passion; any partner will do, that's why they all swap round so frequently. It's not just a pretty fairy play.'

How odd, I thought fleetingly, as the girls scuttled into position on the stage, that I should have chosen this play at all. I, choose an erotic play, when only a few short years ago the thought of sex had made me physically sick! And the knowledge that, whatever might be thought of my production, no one would criticize the right I had as producer to have my own ideas. It was strange too that I was able to discuss topics like this with school students when I thought back to my own highly-censored childhood.

'Now, look!' I said to Demetrius and Helena. 'This is a very nasty, very violent scene. It's desire gone bad and become cruel.' I looked at the two girls, feeling a sudden empathy with their adolescent awkwardness on the stage, their arms folded tightly round their breasts, legs plaited nervously round one another, hips stuck out at agonizingly awkward angles. 'Demetrius, I want you to throw Helena across the stage.' I had a quick mental picture of myself being slung across the floor by Guy in one of his rages. The girls giggled and brightened. 'Miss Armstrong, how can we?'

'Loosen up a bit,' I said briskly, aware again of the extraordinary irony that it should be I saying this to them. 'Try and feel more relaxed physically. Loosen up a bit.'

'Loosen up!' I said week after week to Bottom and Titania. 'I want this to be a beautiful scene, funny and beautiful. That's why we've given Bottom this beautiful white ass's head.'

'Loosen up' became the watchword for the period of rehearsal. And gradually, incredibly, they did. Demetrius and Helena fought with a lack of restraint that would have put Guy to shame, Hermia shrieked with surrealist abandon when she woke from her dream, the fairies combined freedom with a really creeping feeling of menace.

For me the production worked and, I think, for the cast too. This became clear to me on the first night. Titania had gone sick with glandular fever and at the eleventh hour I'd imported Rowena, who had acted for me the previous year but had since left the school and was having a year off before going up to university. She was superb. On the night of the first perform-ance when we came to the end of Act IV and Bottom was waking up to the loss of Titania in his extraordinary speech 'I have had a most rare vision', I felt suddenly enormously moved by the quality of attention in the wings. Beside me, my colleague and indefatigable stage manager, Sally, pointed silently to the cast who, crammed up in the tiny space available, were staring intently at Amanda, who was playing Bottom. They must have heard the speech scores of times during the last weeks and we had carefully discussed its importance, but now I saw that its poignancy had moved them in a new way. It celebrated a moment of vision that could transform a life, rather like the vision I had had when I had gone to seek God in my convent. Like Bottom's, my vision seemed to have vanished and yet it was present in every moment of my life in its effects. 'The eye of man hath not heard, the ear hath not seen... what my dream was.' Bottom stumblingly quoted the words of St Paul about the Beatific vision which would ultimately make sense of our smaller splintered revelations of significance in life. Together the cast, Sally and I had shared one such vision during the production, I suddenly realized. Even the fairies, most of them only eleven years old, who had borne admirably with my endless bullying – 'Fairies, where the Hell *are* you?' – were sitting in absolute silence. One of them, a tiny child, who was playing Moth, even had tears in her eyes. At the end of the speech, the curtain went down for the interval and Amanda was left staring at the empty cushion where Titania had been. She looked absolutely lost for a moment, dazed by her performance. Suddenly Rowena, 19-year-old school-leaver and sophisticate, erupted on to the stage and threw her arms round 14-year-old Amanda, all her studied cool gone. 'You were fantastic!' she crowed, beside herself with excitement, the immense gap between her and Amanda momentarily forgotten. 'Miss Armstrong, wasn't she brilliant!'

I should have realized that intensity of personal vision is often incommunicable to others, and this production was the only one I did at the school which was greeted with bewilderment., though I thought and still think it my best. Criticism officially centred round the fact that the fairies had bare legs, which was found to be offensive. Word from the Powers That Be told me that the next night those legs had to be encased in thick tights. Helena was also a little too plump; couldn't I put her into a corset? 'A corset!' I spat with such venom that the suggestion was hastily withdrawn. (What had happened to my former abject obeisance to authority?) The only corset shop in the vicinity was, oddly enough, in the Post Office which sold an extraordinary medley of old-fashioned garments: I'd had a quick picture of poor Helena being jacked into a corset in a back room by the Post Mistress. Was this to be the end of our 'loosening up' during the last weeks? Ah, well. No quarter was given on the matter of the tights and the poor fairies were thrown into a strange selection that clashed badly with their bright psychedelic costumes but which were all that could be found at the last moment. On Moth's bird-like legs they hung in folds, like leggings. The cast and I looked wryly at one another. 'It doesn't matter at all what you're wearing,' I told them with professional loyalty to the authorities and Governors. 'The tights look great. Just concentrate on giving as good a performance as you gave last night. Now, where am I going to sit tonight? Yesterday someone said she had been able to see my foot sticking out under the curtain.'

'Never mind, Miss Armstrong,' said Oberon grimly. 'You had your tights on.'

In the end, of course, other people's incomprehension matters little to the integrity of one's own vision. The play was important to me not only because it was a landmark of my progress and change during the past years, but because it showed me for the first time the teacher's role in shaping her pupils' attitudes by means of vision. And it made me realize that the great vision of my own religious life, which seemed, like Titania, to be lost irrevocably, needed to be celebrated. Even Bottom, at the end of his great speech, decides to incarnate his rare vision in a ballad, which he would call 'Bottom's dream, because it hath no bottom'. That way the transient vision would be preserved from oblivion. Perhaps, I thought that evening, watching Amanda, I'll write about my religious life one day. Not in a ballad, of course! But perhaps writing it down will make me look at it anew, redeem the beauty of the experience from the mists of bitterness and pain that are obscuring it. Not yet, I thought. I'm not quite ready yet. But in a year or two, maybe I will write it all down.

'Karen!' the Professor leaned back and whispered quietly so as not to disturb the discussion. 'Will you propose the vote of thanks?'

I nodded, smiled and turned back to the discussion. Susan Hill, the novelist, had come to the College to give a lecture to the students. It was one of those brilliant days in late February when spring seems to have come by mistake. The sunlight was pouring in through the french windows of the long lecture room and the dark red walls were splashed with light. It had been a good lecture and the question time afterwards gave me the opportunity to ask Susan Hill many things which intrigued me about her work and the ideas were bouncing back and forth, cheerfully and briskly. At last it seemed to be petering out and I looked towards the Professor and raised my eyebrows inquiringly. She nodded.

As I got to my feet it hit me. The stench, the lights flashing frantically, the terror. But this time it was worse than ever – the smell overpowering, the panic unbearable. I had to get out, get away. But how? There was only one exit, through the long double doors directly behind the lecturer's rostrum. How could I barge past Susan Hill? Perhaps it would go away. I leaned forward and gripped the desk hard and started to speak. Then my thought processes started to splinter. I could see faces turned up towards me in alarm. I could dimly hear a voice that sounded familiar saying over and over again, like a record stuck in a groove, 'Thank you – thank you very much.' Was it my voice? I felt a touch on my arm and looked down at a colleague but could no longer recognize him. The terror grew and the flashing of the light became blinding. I had to escape.

Lurching blindly against desks I crashed my way out of the room. And then it happened: there was a sudden explosion of happiness and significance. Suddenly – at last – all the conflicting pieces of the pattern seemed to fuse for a dazzling second. It was an unimaginable world of pure joy, complete fulfilment; peace and a vision of perfection that shot the world through with a final significance. It was God. It lasted for a second – for less than a second – before I heard myself screaming with the pain of its loss and blackness blotted everything out.

Inside the lecture room they heard my appalling scream and rushed to the door. The Professor and the English department, Susan Hill and as many students who could saw me hurling myself to the ground, rolling along the length of the elegant entrance hall, foaming at the mouth, and heard the drumming of my heels against the parquet floor as I thrashed about.

When, some two hours later, the casualty department of the

hospital to which I had been taken, told me that I'd had a *grand mal* epileptic fit, I simply threw back my head and laughed. What other possible response was left but laughter at the absurd cruelty of life?

'The EEG shows that there is an abnormality in the brain rhythms,' the neurologist explained to me some weeks later. He was a lean, elegant man with a sharply intelligent face and kind, brown eyes which were holding mine steadily. Since the fit in the lecture room I'd had several more while waiting to see Dr Wolfe – once on Baker Street station, once alone in my flat and once in my bed in the middle of the night. I'd been to the hospital for a preliminary test, the EEG – Electro-encephalograph – where numerous small electrodes had been inserted into my scalp to measure the brain rhythms to confirm the diagnosis.

'So it is epilepsy then?' I asked wearily. In one sense I was not too alarmed. I'd dealt so frequently with Simon's fits that I had no real fear or prejudice about the condition. The fits were unpleasant and frightening but after the beginning stages – the smell, the terror, the lights – I knew nothing about it. But was I always going to have to go through life with people being sorry for me? Meet Karen Armstrong, the mad, epileptic ex-nun. The list of my claims to abnormality was growing longer every year.

'Yes, it does look like it,' the neurologist, Dr Wolfe, said briskly, 'but it's really not the end of the world, you know. We can do quite a lot for you with drugs and you can learn how to help yourself avoid unnecessary attacks.' He picked up his pen and smiled briskly. 'There are one or two questions I'd like to ask you, just to give me a clearer idea of whereabouts in the brain the trouble is. Tell me, I know you'd not had a *grand mal* fit before but have you ever had any fainting attacks – blackouts – anything of that kind?'

I remembered my fainting all those years ago in the convent. The same symptoms, muted, but definitely the same.

'Yes. I started having blackouts when I was about eighteen.' I explained to him about the convent and my attacks there.

'And the good nuns didn't have them checked medically?'

'No, we thought it was emotional. Doctor, is epilepsy caused by emotional disturbance?' This was worrying me a lot. If, yet again, I was having psychosomatic illness, I wasn't sure that I could bear it. Yet again, to be told that my feelings were out of control and needed to be quelled by will power!

He shook his head. 'It's entirely physical,' he said firmly. 'People think that because it's a disease of the brain it's psychosomatic in some way, brought on by strain and emotional disturbance. That's not so. It's entirely due to abnormality of the brain rhythms. It may have emotional *effects*, because your brain, where the feelings come from, is disturbed. But they're not the cause of the illness. You feel terror, don't you, before an attack?'

I nodded.

'When you had these fainting spells, were you distressed after them?'

'Yes. I was often weeping when I came to. Was that really epilepsy? Even though I wasn't foaming at the mouth or thrashing about?'

Dr Wolfe nodded. 'I should think so. And the fact that you came out of these attacks weeping is an important clue about the kind of epilepsy you have. That and the fact that you have this warning of panic and flashing lights and odd smells beforehand. We call that an *aura*, by the way. Look,' he smiled at me and paused. 'Can you tell me – honestly – I won't accuse you of lunacy if you say "yes", don't worry – ' He paused again.

'What?' I asked, alerted by the tentative note in his voice.

'Have you ever had any hallucinatory experience – have you seen visions, horrid things that aren't there? Anything like that?'

For a few seconds the world stood still. Then I took a deep breath, afraid to speak in case the sudden stirrings of hope were going to be crushed. I looked at him for a long moment.

'Yes,' I said. My voice was trembling with incipient relief. 'Yes, I have.'

Hesitantly at first, then as he nodded, jotted things down and smiled in recognition my words started tumbling over one another.

Dr Wolfe nodded. And nodded. 'Yes. These are all very common symptoms of a certain kind of epilepsy. Temporal lobe epilepsy.'

Joy flowered inside me and I could feel a constriction round my chest. I wasn't mad. I never had been mad. My mind was not tainted or doomed. I couldn't really take it in, I'd lived so long with the fear of insanity gnawing away, corrupting my confidence and my view of the future. But relief was beginning to flood through me in blissful tidal waves. So I had epilepsy? Anything was better than the horrible uncertainties of madness.

Dr Wolfe was unaware of the happiness he had caused. He was explaining that there was probably a discharge from the part of the brain that controlled the memory – the temporal lobe which is also the seat of many of the emotions – and that images I had seen or experienced in the past – like my drooling old man, for instance – were not able to be controlled, as they should be, while I was having an attack. Those visions of mine were simply epileptic attacks, 'and we should be able to control them with the drugs,' he added.

I stared at him dewily. The thought of swallowing a pill and getting rid of these horrors that lapped always at the edges of my world was the final drop in my already brimming cup.

'Have you ever had any lapses of memory?' he went on. 'Times when you've blanked out, done things without knowing you were doing them, perhaps started to go somewhere and gone somewhere else? Anything like that?'

I nodded. 'Yes,' I said faintly, and answered his questions in a daze of relief. Eventually Dr Wolfe pushed his notes away and looked up at me, puzzled.

'Look,' he said, 'this must all have been most alarming for you. Haven't you seen a doctor about it?'

'Oh, yes,' I nodded. 'I saw my GP who referred me to a psychiatrist.'

'How long did you see him?'

'Nearly three years.'

Dr Wolfe covered his eyes with his hand. 'Do you mean to tell me,' he asked with devastating quiet, 'that you saw a psychiatrist for three years, describing these attacks, and he never once, in all that time, suggested that you had an EEG?'

'Well, no,' I said awkwardly, suddenly feeling rather sorry for Dr Piet, 'you see, I'd just come out of my convent and I was pretty mixed up. I –' I faltered slightly, 'I thought I was going mad, you see. He did help me a lot.'

Dr Wolfe sighed and flung himself back in his chair. 'I dare say he did,' he said grimly, 'but he'd have helped you far more if he'd recognized these classic symptoms of temporal lobe epilepsy and treated it properly. Look.' He leaned forward again, tensely, speaking gently and clearly. 'There is no cure for these attacks of yours except through drugs. No amount of counselling can touch them.' He smiled rather sadly. 'You're a classic case in more ways than one, you know. I always tell my students that patients will very rarely tell them about their hallucinations, in case it's thought that they're mad. Till relatively recently, of course, the medical profession didn't know about this manifestation of epilepsy. It makes you wonder, doesn't it?' he said, 'how many people there probably are mouldering away in institutions for the insane, who simply need a few of these pills.' He sighed impatiently.

I stared at him, lost in my own memories. I remembered Dr Webster. I might have had a baby to get rid of these hallucinations. 'I suppose,' I said tentatively, wanting to get Dr Piet off the hook, 'it's the compartmentalization of medicine.'

'You can say that again!' Dr Wolfe sighed. 'But it's not as if you had a very abstruse neurological disease. You're not seeing a psychiatrist now, are you?' he asked suddenly.

'No, no. I gave it up as it didn't seem to be doing any good.'

'Well,' he spoke gently but firmly, 'will you promise me that you won't again. Really, if you can survive three years of psychotherapy with this kind of temporal lobe activity and depression, you must be exceptionally sane. Quite exceptionally sane. Do you understand?'

I smiled back at him and nodded slightly, feeling again that bubble of joy. I had to get away quickly; before it burst and overwhelmed me in a happiness I couldn't control.

'These pills,' I said, as I picked up the prescription. 'They won't make me dozy or sleepy, will they? I mean, I'll take them! I'll do anything to get rid of those attacks, but are they likely to do anything funny to my brain?'

Dr Wolfe shook his head and caught my eyes in his. He spoke slowly and there was a smile in his voice. 'I promise you,' he said, 'they won't make you anything but better.'

Outside in the street I closed my eyes and felt joy break all over me. Then I opened them again and looked at the world. For the first time for years I could trust what I saw, could rely on the integrity of my brain to interpret it. I looked up at the grimy

236

London buildings, the bedraggled pigeons flapping untidily round the gables, the littered streets. Not an inspiring scene. But I felt a smile cracking my face, a clutch of acute happiness in my throat. The world, with its imperfections, had been given back to me. Because for the first time in my life I felt I owned myself.

I didn't give much thought to the illness. I was fortunate that in looking after Simon during his fits I had conquered any revulsion or fear epilepsy might otherwise have had for me. It was almost enough to believe that a friendly Providence – dared I say God? Perhaps not, I decided, uneasily, not yet, anyway – had been watching over me. I felt free and intensely happy. After years of dreading insanity epilepsy seemed a laughable triviality.

I had been liberated from the last of my prisons. I suddenly saw the medical world as divided into tightly sealed cloisters, each branch of knowledge excluding the others. An exaggeration, of course. But still there was no doubt that yet again I'd been trapped by one set of ideas in interpreting everything exclusively through the wavering insights of psychiatry, when all that was needed – bemused, I looked down at the prescription slip in my hand – were a few pills.

Of course my epilepsy has been a nuisance to me, but a manageable one. I have had excellent medical help and met with nothing but an intelligent sympathy from other people. I have to be careful sometimes, careful to take my pills, careful to get enough sleep, make sure I eat regularly so that the blood sugar doesn't get too low – no wonder I had so many temporal lobe attacks during my anorexic phase. Having fits is far from pleasant and there are times when I feel very sorry for myself, but all I need is the chance to have a bit of a moan to regain my equilibrium. It seems a small price to pay for the immense privilege of sanity.

My neurologist once told me that people with temporal lobe epilepsy are very often intensely religious. Certainly just before I have a *grand mal* fit I have a 'vision' of such peace, joy and significance that I can only call it God. What does this say about the whole nature of religious vision? Certain episodes in the lives of the saints have acquired a new meaning for me. When Theresa of Avila had her three-day vision of hell, was she simply having a temporal lobe attack? The horrors she saw are similar to those I have experienced, but in her case informed by the religious imagery of her time. Like other saints who have 'seen' hell she describes an appalling stench, which is part of an epileptic *aura*. Is it possible that the feeling I have had all my life that something – God, perhaps? – is just over the horizon, something absolutely unimaginable but almost tangibly present, is simply the result of an electrical irregularity in my brain? It is a question that can't yet be answered, unless it be that God, if He exists, could have created us with that capacity for Him, glimpsed at only when the brain is convulsed. What I can say, however, is that if my 'visions' have sometimes let me into 'Hell' they have also given me possible intimations of a Heaven which I would not have been without.

As I walked into Blackfriars on that summer afternoon I was struck anew by the astounding nature of Judith Stanley's request. She wanted to have Simon baptized.

'But *why*, Judith!' I'd asked, amazed.

She deflected my questions. 'I want him to have the whole thing. To do it properly. Of course I don't think there's anything in it for a moment! But Simon needs it. He needs religion, I think.'

It was a muddle. Probably Judith didn't fully understand her own motives. I thought she'd forget about the idea. But she hadn't. The ceremony was to take place this afternoon. I was to be his Godmother.

I sat down in one of the chairs in the back row, ready to meet Judith and Simon. It was peaceful here, and I found myself enjoying the large stone emptiness. No statues with bleeding hearts, just the crucifix on the high altar.

A door opened and Father Paul, who was to perform the ceremony, walked up the aisle. He smiled at me shyly and lowered his heavy frame carefully on to the chair beside me.

'Good to see you, Karen.'

'And you too, Paul. All ready for this afternoon?'

He nodded, smiling. 'Yes. I thought we'd have it in the private chapel upstairs. I'd imagine Mrs Stanley would prefer that.'

'I'm sure she would. Paul, what do you think about this? I know you believe that the sacraments work automatically, but

apart from that how valid is a ceremony like this? Simon doesn't
know the first thing about the faith.'

He smiled to himself, looking away from me up the Church.
'Does any of us, Karen? Does any of us really? Most of our thinking about God isn't very much to the point anyway.'

I followed his eyes to the Crucifix and remembered what I'd
said to Rebecca. 'You mean because He confounds all human
expectations?'

'Yes. Oh, we go on and on talking away about the faith,
making up dogmas, constructing a theology. But do you remember what St Thomas Aquinas did when he'd finished writing the
Summa Theologica?'

I smiled. I liked that story. 'Yes. He put down his pen and said
that all he'd written was straw compared to what he'd seen.'

'That's right.' Paul shifted his weight a little on the chair. 'You
see, I firmly believe Simon "sees" something of God, experiences
Him in some way when he comes here. None of us could say
what or how, least of all Simon himself. And it may very well be
that his lack of analytical thought is an advantage.' He put
quotation marks into his voice. ' "Because God may well be
loved, but not thought. By love He can be caught and held, but by
thinking never." Do you recognize that?'

I nodded. 'It's *The Cloud of Unknowing*, isn't it?' I'd studied
this fourteenth-century text when I was an undergraduate and
before that it had been one of the books Mother Walter had given
me to read while I was a novice. I'd forgotten all about it. Slowly
I started to quote from it:

> "When you first begin to pray, you find only dark-
> ness, and as it were a cloud of unknowing. Do what
> you will this darkness and this cloud remain between
> you and God, and stop you from seeing him in the
> clear light of rational understanding . . . For if you are
> to see Him in this life, it must always be in this cloud,
> in this darkness."

'There you are, you see?' Paul smiled. 'Simon's just like the
rest of us. We're all in the same cloud of unknowing. Karen,
Karen,' he patted my knee affectionately. 'Forget about institutional religion. After your experience it may never be for you

239

again. Throw away all the theology you've ever learned. Do what the *Cloud* says – cast it all under a cloud of forgetting. And then there's just you and God. No man-made thought, no man-made institutions. Just you and a totally mysterious but loving God.'

I smiled ruefully. 'It's all very well for you to say that. But look at my life. How worldly I've become! That's what the Church would say.'

'So what! What's wrong with being worldly? You live in the world, don't you? No. Remember what the *Cloud* says at the end. "It is not what you are or what you have been that God looks at with his merciful eyes, but what you would be." ' The words and the love they implied made me shiver with a sharp longing. 'Think about it. Or rather,' he added, '*don't* think about it.'

There was a clatter of footsteps. 'Here they are, I think,' Paul got up. 'You go and let them in and bring them upstairs.'

'Karen! You're here first.' Simon had to stoop down to speak to me now. His eyes bulged slightly with excitement, his lips struggled to express the thoughts in his wounded brain. 'This is a very special occasion, isn't it?' he asked slowly.

'It certainly is!' I reached up and patted his shoulder.

'It's a special occasion, a special occasion!' he beamed at Judith who was standing on the Church threshold, rigid with years of prejudice and embarrassment. 'Mummy! you haven't been to Blackfriars before, have you?'

'No, I haven't.' She bared her teeth in a strained smile. 'Hello, Karen. It's lovely to see you. You look very well, you really do! Quite transformed, in fact.'

'Mummy! This is *my* place. Not your place, not Daddy's place. But my place and Karen's. But you can come this after-noon, just this once, because it's such a special occasion!'

'Thank you, Simon. Thank you very much,' she said gravely, swallowing hard as we set off down the Church, obviously profoundly grateful that if this was her first visit it was also her last.

Paul was waiting for us in the small chapel and he and Judith bowed gravely to one another. She sank into the chair that he held out for her, trembling slightly, her hands clenched tensely in her lap. As soon as we entered the chapel, Simon quietened and stood, his head to one side in that listening posture, his face thoughtful and serene. I smiled reassuringly at Judith, suddenly full of admiration for her generosity in not only allowing this but for coming herself to see it through. She wanted the best for Simon, even if that conflicted with her strongest views and convictions.

'Simon,' Paul said quietly. 'Would you like some incense for your baptism?'

His eyes lit up. 'Oh, Paul!' he breathed softly. 'Can I make it?'

'Certainly, you can. Come over here.' With his hands on his knees Simon bent down low over the thurible, his blond head close to Paul's tow-coloured one. 'Snap, crackle and pop!' he whispered as the charcoal spluttered. 'Karen!' he hissed in a loud stage whisper. 'Watch this! Just watch me now!' He spooned the incense on to the glowing charcoal and the cloud of fragrance rose. I glanced worriedly at Judith. Incense must really be the last straw – archetypal Catholicism.

But Judith was watching Simon as he swung the thurible to and fro with a rather sad smile, acknowledging this new life of his that she had no part in. His face was transfigured, his head was flung back as he sniffed luxuriously and the cloud filled the room, hanging mistily in the air.

'Right,' Paul nodded at Simon, who instantly replaced the thurible.

'Did you see me, Karen? Mummy, did you see me make the incense?' He was like a child and the pathos of his broken child's mind in his man's body struck me anew.

Paul cut the ceremony down to a minimum. There was no complicated creed for me to recite as a proclamation of Simon's faith. Under the circumstances it would be meaningless. For both of us. He omitted the exorcisms; wisely, in case the idea of a devil lodging inside him seized Simon's imagination and provided him with another trauma. Instead there were just the bare essentials. I stood behind him and made the responses on his behalf. Simon knelt on a prie-dieu, bolt upright, his hands joined and his eyes fixed sternly ahead of him.

'What do you ask of the Church of God,' Paul asked.

'Faith,' I replied. Paul smiled slightly at me. Was he right? Did I believe, really? I thought of all the times I found myself arguing with God, having to remind myself forcibly that He didn't exist for me any more. Yes, he was there for me somewhere. I couldn't seem to let Him go.

'What does faith bring to you?' Paul continued.

'Life everlasting.' Life. Not the endless death I'd sought for so long. I listened hard to the next words.

'If, then, you desire to enter into life, keep the commandments: You shall love the Lord your God with your whole heart, and with your whole soul, and with your whole mind, and your neighbour as yourself.'

I looked down at Simon, whose face was intent and solemn. At each phrase he nodded to himself. There was a terrible poignancy in the phrase 'your whole mind'. Simon's mind could never be whole but he did know how to love. I thought of his tender gaiety. To be baptized all you had to do was undertake to love God as best you could. That was all.

Now he approached Paul slowly, and stood stock still while he made the sign of the cross on his forehead and his breast. With a sudden clutch at the heart I noticed Paul laying salt on Simon's tongue. At any other time he would have spat it out with scant ceremony, but now he swallowed it gravely.

Grant, we pray you, Lord, that Your servant who tastes this savour of salt, may no longer hunger but be filled by heavenly nourishment.

Paul was right. Simon did hunger for something. When he came here he seemed to find it. His face now was clear and peaceful as though he knew quite well what was happening. And I too. I also hungered for God. At one time I'd starved myself, so that my body wasted away. I'd learnt to cope with my physical hunger. But my spiritual hunger was still there. A nagging, inconvenient craving. And as I watched Paul place in Simon's hand a lighted candle to signify his new life in God, I knew that my basic belief in God was still alive. It could never be the same as it was. I'd had to leave behind the comforts of certainty and dogma. But a belief in the mysterious God Paul had spoken of persisted stubbornly, underneath all the pain and rubble of things I'd had to forget. At least, I thought it did. As I acknowledged that, I felt a sudden lift of joy and excitement. I had no idea where this new 'faith' was going to lead me, nor what it was exactly. I'd never be able to define it clearly, because God defied definition. But I knew that I'd spend the rest of my life trying to penetrate that thick cloud of unknowing.

'Now, bend your head forward, Simon,' Paul said gently. I glanced nervously at Judith. Simon hated getting his head wet. But once again his fear seemed to have gone. Paul sprinkled a few drops of water over his head, raised his voice, and the words filled the little chapel triumphantly: 'Simon, I baptize you in the name of the Father and of the Son and of the Holy Ghost.'

'Ah!' Simon breathed out a long sigh of satisfaction. He shut his eyes and stood sternly to attention while Paul rubbed the water from his hair. His face was puckered with concentration and a tiny, secret smile played round his mouth. 'Ah!' The sigh this time was one of release and he shook himself gently, opened his eyes and smiled broadly at Paul.

'Go in peace, Simon, and the Lord be with you.'

Paul accompanied the conventional greeting with a gentle touch on his shoulder. I thought of the turbulence of Simon's life, the terrors that gripped him of which I too had a glimpse. For just a moment his face told us that he'd found a peace. It wouldn't last, but that wasn't the point. The point was in the last five words. I knew that in some wholly indefinable way the Lord, whoever He was, was with him. And perhaps even with me.

With exaggerated precision, Simon blew out his candle, laid it on the prie-dieu and turned round to face us. Slowly a huge smile broke over his face. Then he turned back to Paul. Carefully he put his arms round his neck and laid his head against Paul's.

'Thank you, Paul.'

I looked across at Judith, who was watching the scene closely. She returned my glance and I saw there were very uncharacteristic tears in her eyes. She blinked impatiently and made them disappear. But she held my gaze. And we smiled slightly.